Bondage of Self

Kaitlin Sine Riordan

ISBN: 978-0-9888178-4-5

Cover by Barbara Gottlieb
www.gottgraphix.com

Published by Kaitlin Sine Riordan

Purple Distinctions Independent Publishing
www.purpledistinctions.com
Palm Springs, CA

Printed in the United States of America

2

Dedication

This book is dedicated to all those who have lost or taken their lives because of the tremendous social stigma and pressure for being transgendered, which comes from a lack of understanding. Those like, Mike Penner, the famous LA Times sports writer, who died at the age of 52, two years after announcing publically in his column that he was transsexual. His death inspired me to write my book because I, too, was at the point of "to be or not to be."

Zebedee, my 11 year old Black Labrador Retriever, saved my life one dark night in which I was full of despair. He has been by my side through it all and has been at my feet the entire time this book was being written, edited and re-written. He listened with great interest when I read it out loud to him and raised his head when his name was mentioned to give his approval. We love each other unconditionally and he is my very best friend. I love you so much Zeb!

To all those who are transgendered that each person my find their strength and courage in the face of adversity to be true to themselves. For the family and friends of those transgendered that they may show compassion, educate themselves, help, love, and be grateful for this wonderful person. To the alcoholic and drug addict who is masking the pain because they do not feel comfortable in their own skin, you must know there is a solution.

To my children, that we restore our relationships and be together for those special moments. John, Mark, and Rebecca, I love you so much and wish to finally show you. My parents and siblings, I love you all so much.

Acknowledgments

It is not I who wrote the book; it was the *Spirit* that dwells within me!

I would like to thank all of the men and women who work a 12 step program with me in Palm Springs, California and around the world. Your encouragement was so important in helping me stay on my writing path. I am forever grateful for the lessons and support that you have given me.

Nye Wilden for spending a great deal of time with me. You shared your inspiration, words, lessons, and wisdom and I am grateful. You picked me up when I was down and pushed me when I needed to write more. Thank you so much for reading and editing this book. You are a true and trusted friend and I hope to follow your example of being of service to others. "You have helped me to keep my light on and bright". I hope to pass the torch one day.

The people who are close to me and who I would call when I was in despair, Beverly Maggio, Marcie Gilman, Luke Watson and Diane Reardon. My sister Ann and my brother David, you are among the elite. Thank you for your open and honest feedback. My three children, John, Mark, and Rebecca for being willing to keep an open mind and work through the issues a little by slow and giving me hope. John you have literally stood beside me, especially the past 13 years and I am very grateful.

I am grateful to Michael's House for the great experience while I was in Rehab. You started me on the "tools for living" and pointed me in the right direction. I enjoyed my 83 days there. To George Thalwitzer who provided me a place to stay after rehab in a sober living in Palm Springs called the New Step Sober Living House. I wrote the first draft of the book in a little studio apartment at the sober living.

Dr. Christine McGinn, I am forever grateful for believing in me and for masterfully performing gender reassignment surgery. I have no problems whatsoever after all of my surgeries. You are a miracle. Teresa and Bethany thank you for being with me and supporting me through these surgeries.

Sister, your retreats saved my life, as I no longer believe I am predestined to hell. I thank you for the three retreats and the spiritual guidance. I think of you each day with a tremendous amount of gratitude.

My Mother and Father, I love you unconditionally. Dad, I learned how to be strong and courageous from you. Although, you do not understand, the strength to be myself was taught to me by you. Your lesson to face adversity head on and never to back down from the truth is well engrained. To my siblings, I hope that one day we can all sit down face to face and enjoy each other's company.

Dr. Ronni Sanlo, thank you for the encouragement and the means by which this book is published.

All the girls at James River Transgendered Society (JRTS) keep it going; make sure it's a group effort.

Zebedee, you are so special, always being there for me. You waited by the front door every day and on the floor beside the bed each night. Our time together is great since the very first moment in March of 2002. We played with the tennis ball endlessly throwing it down an incline and you catching it while running away from me over your head as a puppy. You stayed on the property and ran through under the oak and pine trees in the country of Virginia. Then into the inner city we walked and you would growl every now and then to warn me of a character you did not approve. Zeb always stayed close watching every move I would make and followed me throughout the house or yard. He protected me like a security guard.

I would practice my presentations for work with him and he would sit or lay down and was very attentive. His moods and demeanor were a true reflection of how I was feeling. He understands and we laughed and cried together. We routed for the same teams and walked each day to pick up the newspaper. He waited for me to come home from work, from going out half the night, and while I was in rehab. He waited and waited and when the magic moment arrived he would bust through the door from where he was staying and jump into the back seat of the car. He loved to travel and ride in the car of truck. I would take him to the grocery store in my truck and when I came out he would be sitting behind the wheel as if he was the driver. He has a wonderful sense of humor and makes me laugh all the time.

Zeb swam in the James River, the ponds around Courthouse Creek, and has seen the Pacific and Atlantic Oceans. He has chased tennis balls, baseballs, golf balls, sticks, birds, deer, turkey, cats, snakes, dogs, raccoons, groundhogs, coyotes, and people. He has traveled across the United States five times and has peed in 16 states; he has one more time left in him. We were together to see the diversity and beauty of our great country. He is a joy, pleasure, warm, loving, and fun to have in my life. His example taught me how to stay in the moment.

Zebedee was at my feet during the entire writing of this book. We would take reflective walks in the desert sun and return to the computer. I read aloud this book to him and he understood, smiling at the parts where he was named. A beautiful Black Labrador Retriever with big brown eyes that always with abandon showing unconditional love. He taught me this lesson too. He is the alpha male from a litter of seven. Today, he is over 11 years old and weighs 138 pounds, just like his father and his hips are bothering him and sometimes creaking when he squats. I must do all that I can to help him remain comfortable. He saved my life and I want to do whatever it takes to help him. Zebedee, I love you unconditionally forever! We will be together forever. If he passes on before me, I know that he will be waiting next to the puerile gates watching and waiting for our reunion. If I go before him, I most certainly will be standing there waiting for him.

Chapter 1 – The Confusion

Born breached and squalling, the first steps out of my mother's womb were the beginning of a world filled with chaos, confusion, guilt, shame, anxiety, anger, but most importantly, fear and pride. Most of these obstacles would have to be overcome for me to live a "normal" life, a life of serenity, which I believe is what we all want. For me it would take fifty-three years of facing each challenge, each step being even more painful than the one before.

Conquering each level of pain has brought a little more peace, and eventually real happiness. My quest has been a never-ending process but each step has brought greater fulfillment. Although the trauma that was my life later led to alcoholism and drug abuse. I suppose I could have chosen the easy way out and continued that addicted lifestyle, hiding the root cause of my self-abusive behavior, never disclosing my dark secret. Instead I have chosen the painstaking steps which have allowed the misery that was once my life to slowly release, as I became willing to divulge the truths buried so deeply within.

To begin to understand who I am, it is important to start with my roots beginning with my father. Dad is the second child of seven. He was the seed of an Irish Catholic father who reared his children to staunchly practice the Catholic faith. And subsequently, he sent them all to parochial school. His father, an alcoholic, was also a nationally syndicated cartoonist who, although brilliant and successful. Roamed the streets of Richmond, VA often drunk, setting the stage for his progeny to follow. With a very gregarious personality, he was well liked and a practical joker. However, the drinking and joking played an enormous toll on his family which often left his children and my grandmother to fend for themselves.

As a child, my father delivered the Richmond Times Dispatch each morning and worked at the local drug store in Highland Park every afternoon. The money my father earned went to support not only him but to help his family as well. He attended Benedictine High School in Richmond, VA., an all-male Catholic military high school. The High School was run by the Benedictine monks who received financial and operational assistance from the US Army. Upon graduation he worked for the telephone company, where he would remain for forty-two years. During those years he took a four- year leave of absence at 19 and enlisted in the United States Marine Corp. It was during his time with the Corps that he became obsessed with working on body building. At only 5'9" he was broad-shouldered and extremely muscular with a classic weight-lifters physique.

After leaving the military, he joined the local YMCA and continued his work-out regime, to keep his body chiseled to perfection. In 1953, he was named "Mr. Virginia". He continued competing in body-building competitions until 1967. Once at the age of 8, I traveled with him to Roanoke, VA, because he wanted me to watch his competition and see "real men". After that he continued lifting in the basement of our home and maintained a perfect physique. And continues to do so at the age of 80!

He was 23 years old when he returned to Richmond, met and married mother, who was the same age, and a year later I was born. His philosophy toward himself and his family was hardly ambiguous. His Catholic upbringing and years in the military had molded him into a highly disciplined man. He was well respected in the church, community, and his job. He was overjoyed in 1955 when he was blessed with a son, who was named after him. "John, Jr." seemed to be a child full of happiness and joy and the father was committed to making a man out of this fine boy, a man molded in his own image.

I was a very sensitive and intelligent child and soon learned that the rules of the house were not to be broken and that father was a strict disciplinarian. I have a very lucid memory when I was six years old of accompanying my mother downtown to shop for my two little sisters who were four and two years old. I was excited because I had always enjoyed playing in the dress racks. On this particular shopping trip, mother told me several times to "stop playing with the dresses"! She became so agitated that she snapped and said, "Wait until I tell your father when he gets home!" That put an end to my fun. I immediately became sullen and withdrawn for the rest of the day and fearful of what awaited me when my father arrived home.

Later, in my room, my terror grew. I awaited father's arrival with great trepidation. I lay on my bed shaking and fearful. Suddenly, I decided I would not sit in fear. I would take action on my own! I looked around in my tiny bedroom for a suitable "weapon" for the self-inflicted punishment I had in mind. I saw and picked up my heavy metal toy pistol. With the butt of the gun I began beating myself on the legs. I kept doing this until my legs were purple with large welts protruding from my tender skin. After this painful self-flagellation, I stared at my handiwork, in terrible pain but satisfied with the punishment I had inflicted on myself for the terrible crime of being attracted to girl's dresses. I never shed a tear or made a sound as I beat myself.

When my father arrived home, I made my way painfully out of my bedroom and went to him. I told him I had been bad today and I puffed out my chest and told him that he "did not have to beat me because I had already done it for him". With tears suddenly streaming down my face, I showed him the purple and blue welts covering my legs. My father glared at me with a look of stoic, cold indifference. He simply rolled his eyes and walked away and did not take the opportunity to beat me, as I expected.

I stood there, chest out, fists clenched, and watched his back as he left the room. I knew this particular altercation was finished and I walked back to my room with the full knowledge that the fight was over and somehow, in my mind, I felt that I had won the first battle of wills with my father.

It was during this period in my life I became aware that I was somehow different from other boys. I thoroughly enjoyed being in the company of my mother. We would talk, go shopping, and go to church together every Sunday. I also played with my imaginary friends named Dick, Lurk, and Zarkin. With these friends, I could be anything or anyone I wanted and they would never laugh at me or make fun of me. My sense of feeling was of not belonging and then to isolate with them which only added to the confusion. I did not know why I had this confusion only that I did. I remember going shopping again with my mother and I would sneak and look under the manikins' dresses to see if they had the same type of equipment that I had only to find nothing. I played outside in a small yard and kicked a ball or swung on the set. My two younger sisters were lots of fun and I always enjoyed playing with them as well. Even at my young age I knew full well that I was more like them, meaning that maybe I was a girl but that somehow something was horribly wrong. But I did not dare act like them, play like them, or even tell anyone my "secret" because I was fearful of the outcome. Somehow I understood that these feeling should never be discussed, should never be uttered aloud, and must be suppressed.

So, when I was about 8 years old, at 8:30pm on a school night where it was chilly outside but cool enough to wear a light sweater during the day, I was dressed in my pajamas. The pajamas were full-length pants, red, made of cotton with train designs going every which way and I had on a white undershirt. After I finished using the bathroom, which was across the hall from my bedroom, I turned right and looked in my sister's room. My sister was getting into the bed and got up to come to the door and I asked her if she had one of these. I showed her my penis. She immediately ran downstairs into the basement and told my father. I said out loud, "Oh No"! I jumped in bed; wide awake, and prepared for the unpleasantness that I knew was coming very soon.

My sister came to my bedroom and told me that Dad wanted to see me downstairs now. So, I got up and walked slowly down the hardwood floor hallway, onto the tile in the foyer, down the wooden steps holding onto the handrail to the concrete tiled floor in the basement and through the door that separated the finished to the unfinished cement floor where my father was lifting weights. The floor was cold to my bare feet as I thought

10

about should I pick out the brown or the black belt because I was always given a choice.

My father stopped lifting weights and asked me, "Did you show your thing to your sister"? I answered, "Yes, sir" and I knew that I was wrong. He told me that "boys do not go around showing off their thing to your sister". "I want you to go stand in the doorway with your pants down and stay there until you learn not to do that anymore". I walked around the corner to the doorway that separates the two basement areas and pulled down my pajama pants and underwear to my knees and stood there with my penis exposed to the world. He checked to see if I had followed the instruction before going back to his workout. I can visually see myself standing there from a right back shoulder view, looking down on my crewcut dark brown hair with my pajama pants and underwear down to my ankles and standing there in utter humiliation. This feeling of degradation was imbedded in the core of my heart as I had this indescribable fear. I thought that I would rather take a beating than this type of punishement.

My father finished lifting weights and went out the basement door to run and left me standing there with my butt exposed. In this part of the basement the walls were cinder block and the windows were 2 feet by 2 feet and they did not have any window coverings over them. I dare not move because he could check on me through the window at any time. Not only that, I stood there fearful than anyone could come by and look at me. My father finished his jog 45 minutes later and as he came in, asked me, "Have you learned your lesson"? I said, "Yes, sir" which is the way I had to always address him. "Pull your pants back up and go to bed". "Yes, sir!" This experience is permanently bound deeply within my brain that I can still feel and see it clearly even now.

I became a person who followed instructions based solely on fear. Creativity and self-expression were not an option in my home; because I was a boy the requirement was to act as such. The only time I had for being creative or for expressing my true self was in my mind or when I was alone, sure that no one would walk in and find me. Like my father, I attended parochial schools. Their Catholic rules taught me that there was absolutely no place in heaven for sinners. This meant respect for your family, being kind, minding your manners, and reading your Bible. You must respect, priest, nuns, and the church and attend Mass every Sunday, obeying every one of the Ten Commandments, and heaven forbid masturbation! According to Catholicism, if you practiced the deviant lifestyle of the gay, lesbian, or bisexual, you just did not have a chance for eternal salvation, as the story of Sodom and Gomorrah was used out of context. Since transsexuals in those days were considered gay, I spent many years hiding my secret and over emphasizing my masculinity in order to give a totally male appearance to the outside world. I often went to the library in search of some information on what I was, and where I may fit in this confusing world, all the while living in fear that I would be "caught" researching a strange and forbidden subject matter. The only information I ever found was one single word, transvestite, and that was in the dictionary. There were no card files or reference materials on the subject. Obviously I felt as though I was the only person in the world who was male who believed he was female and liked dressing up in mother's clothes! Instinctively I believed if I were the only male with in the world with this "problem" then surely, there must be something horribly wrong with me. I must be a huge sinner of grand proportions! My life was in bondage, a girl trapped in boy's body. How could this be? I was born in a box and had to operate within these walls in order to survive. The feeling of being trapped in a box confused me and at the same time, filled me with anxiety and guilt. I felt that I must have done something to cause this mistake and wondered, why couldn't I be like other children? I decided if I were to survive my internal turmoil, I would have to mask my emotional issues by acting externally as if I was male. My thoughts were that by doing so these feeling would subside and never return ... I was so wrong!

In my adolescent years I was very athletic. My father coached me in baseball for 8 years in little league. He would practice with me on a regular basis during the season by playing catch, hitting fly balls, coaching the team, and taking me to the diamond when we did not have a game to pitch batting practice. He was dedicated to this endeavor and I did enjoy his training as he threw the ball to me with his left hand. He attended all my High School, American Legion, and college games. This was my connection to my father's love that I so desperately needed from him and it made it seem that all was well with me internally and that I was a real boy, but the confusion always came back. For instance, one night sitting with the family for diner I asked my father for some help with taking the four packed full trash cans from the back yard to the street. I told him "that they were too heavy" for me to carry. His response was "then we will need to take you to Thalhimers and buy you some pink panties". Those words excited me and I felt my face turn red because he had pushed a button in me and I thought that he was right and wanted to go right then. I wanted him to take me to Thalhimers and buy me those pink panties. Fearful as not to lead on, I did not say a word and fell back to a position of embarrassment. After diner I dragged the cans, by tearing the grass out of its roots, to the street for the men to pick up in the morning.

I excelled in football, baseball, and basketball. When not in school or playing sports, I did odd jobs around the neighborhood, all of which demonstrated my "manliness". I such mowed grass, raked leaves, shoveled snow, even did some basic auto mechanic work. Like my father before me, I delivered the Richmond Times Dispatch. I woke daily at 5:30 am to deliver the morning newspapers. I would secretly dress in panties, stockings, and a slip under my clothes during the fall and winter months. It was an exciting time and always eased my anxiety to be able to spend the one and a half hours physically dressed <u>right</u>, or at least near-ly right. While my mind experienced a feeling of well-being, I also experienced an intense fear of getting caught being dressed that way due to some type of accident or some other way of being found out. The thought of being caught brought the fear of being beaten to death by my father or being sent to Central State Hospital, or being sent to a live-in Military School. This caused intense anxiety issues, as a teenager if I did not adhere to the rules of the family I was constantly threatened with being sent away to a military school or worse, to being locked away in a mental facility. Oddly enough, I could not stop this behavior, nor did I want to stop. This is who I was and I was willing to risk anything to be who I really was even if it was just for a short time daily. It was who I really was.

This point in my life was the perfect time to learn the art of manipulation. I manipulated by going to the local swimming pool a full <u>two</u> hours before my family and returned home just as they were leaving for "family swim time". It was like clockwork every Saturday during the heart of the summer the family would be gone from 3-5pm. I did this so I could use this precious alone time to dress in my mother's clothes, and being the oldest of six children, getting this alone time was not always an easy feat. I loved every secret second though and took full advantage of the opportunity it provided me! It enable me time to dress fully as a lady and show my femininity around the house. I sashayed around and even opened the front door and looked out, almost as if I wanted to be seen by someone. Although the exhilaration was both awesome and intense knowing the consequences of being caught, but I was powerless to stop. This was inherently me and I <u>needed</u> to express myself, I <u>needed</u> this time to be me.

One Saturday, at the age of 12, I was dressed in my mother's panties, bra, full slip, girdle, stockings, and blue dress with matching high heels. I pranced through the house and down the halls for an hour and decided I better change before they came home. As I walked into their bedroom to change I heard the back door open and it was them. I reacted by running into the master bathroom and locked the door. My mother talked through the bathroom door and asked me "what are you doing" and I told her "taking a shower". With the water running, I quickly undressed and got into the shower. Afterwards, I hung

14

my mother's clothes on the inside of the shower stall behind the curtain and prayed that my parents would not find them. When I finally emerged from the bathroom, my mother was in the kitchen preparing dinner and my father was outside in the garden. Swiftly but cautiously, I went to the shower and placed everything carefully back in the drawers and closet just as I had found them. It was reactionary, fearful, and then exciting as I remained hopeful that I had placed everything back just right.

I knew every crack in the floor of our house, and some nights I would go down into our basement where my mother kept bags of clothes she had prepared for the Goodwill. I would go through the bags and take the nice nylons and wear them to bed so I could enjoy the feminine feeling against my body. It was such a glorious feeling that it always sent me off to sleep in no time at all. However, when I awoke, in the morning I often felt guilty and full of anxiety, as if I had done something dirty and wrong. I felt as though I had wronged someone and I was never able to figure these feelings out and just lived with this inner turmoil for many years. As I went through my day those feelings would eventually dissipate only to return the next morning, but return stronger and last longer as the years progressed. When I was 18 years old and coming home from a date at 1am, I went down to the basement and picked out of the bag a pair of panties and a slip and put them on. My mother appeared at the basement door and walk up to within four feet of me as I crouched down in her underwear and she said, "What are you doing". I said, "Nothing" and she turned around and went back to bed. I was really scared and felt guilty and shameful but she has never said anything about this night, ever.

At the ripe old age of 14 I found a new friend: alcohol. My new friend had a name and its name was Budweiser. Budweiser made me feel better about myself. I would walk the neighborhood at night drinking a couple Budweiser's and I had no worries in life. Bud for short, took away my fear and anxiety and I would live in the moment and be whoever I wanted to be, nothing could stop me. Bud proved to be very significant in my life especially in my adult years because it gave me the courage to go out into public as a female; it was truly my liquid courage.

Despite my seemingly rigorous rearing, I filled myself up with my own joy even though I was very much confused. The feeling of being different and having to suppress my feelings led to increased anxiety and guilt. I was only an average student, but the inner angst I was experiencing led me down a slippery slope academically. In grade school I often became a below average student. My parents had me tested at the University and the results were that I had above average intelligence as indicated by the IQ test. I spent a lot of time agonizing over the mysterious things going on inside my head. I tried not only to understand, but tried desperately to find answers as well. My mind was very disruptive, almost akin to a war zone! I did not have a clue what action to take to resolve my issues and resume a normal lifestyle. All I knew was that I had a horrible secret and no one could ever know lest I be sent straight to hell. I did know for certain that I did have to continue living in my male role because it was my physical form.

I always experienced a great deal of excitement when I furtively tried to educate myself concerning my "condition", only to become frustrated finding no real useful information. The first real compelling information came to me in the form of a television broadcast when Dr. Renee Richards had undergone a sex change operation. There was a huge controversy concerning her desire to continue playing tennis as a woman and the ruling by the women's tennis association to allowing her to play made national news. This inconceivable news opened my eyes to the fact that I was in fact not the only person in the world with these feelings. I was not the only person who was a woman on the inside and male on the outside. I was not the only woman imprisoned in a male body! If possible, I rather than feel relieved, I felt even more confusion and anxiety. How this could happen and why didn't more people talk about it and worse, why didn't someone try to help us who were suffering in silence?

16

I caught another glimpse into my "world" when I read the book "The Catcher in the Rye". In this book, a gentleman went into his hotel room at night and dressed as a female. I clearly remember the excitement I felt upon reading this section of the book. I read that chapter of the book over and over many times. At the time, it was inconceivable seeing something like this in print.

Chapter 9 of "The Catcher in the Rye", published in 1951, talks about how Holden Caulfield gets a room at the Edmont Hotel in New York City and he looks out of his hotel window: *"You'd be surprised what was going on on the other side of the hotel. I saw one guy, a gray-haired, very distinguished-looking guy with only his shorts on, do something you wouldn't believe me if I told you. First he put his suitcase on the bed. Then he took out all these women's clothes, and put them on. Real women's clothes- silk stockings, high-heeled shoes, brassiere, and one of those corsets with the straps hanging down and all. Then he put on this very tight black evening dress. I swear to God. Then he started walking up and down the room, taking these very small steps, the way a women does, and smoking a cigarette and looking at himself in the mirror...... I'm not kidding; the hotel was lousy with perverts."*

"Lord, am I a pervert"? The feelings I felt only intensified with age. Conversely, the need to suppress my inner feelings became more urgent. As I reached puberty and entered high school, I was elated to have facial hair growing nicely on my face. This facial hair I now had gave the appearance that I was all-male and further hid the deep rooted feeling of my gender identity confusion that loomed deep within me.

I attended a private military high school and was selected president of our senior class. I participated in very masculine activities and even made the varsity baseball team in my sophomore year. Also my military competence did not go unnoticed as I was promoted to Major of the Corp of Cadets! I was quite the stud alright and no one had a clue as to my deepest thoughts; God, what would they if they had even the faintest of ideas that this man's man likes to wear women's clothes ... oh perish the thought! Believe it or not, I did date and had a steady girlfriend for two years in High School. Liz was wonderful and we were together all the time until we went separate ways to attend different colleges.

One winter night, in 1972, when I was a senior in high school, I was driving around Richmond with three of my friends just looking for something to do. One of the three presented an idea that we go find some beer and then ride downtown to "harass the queers". He stated that on 2nd St and on Adams St is where there are a "bunch of queers that walk around in women's clothes." The other two guys started laughing and said, "hell yeah". I thought that it would be in my best interest to participate so I laughed and said 'great idea". I drove over to the U-totem on Main Street in my bluish green 1965 Oldsmobile Dynamic 88 with a 424 engine. The oldest looking of the four went in and bought a 12 pack of Schlitz and we drank and drove a few blocks over to Adams Street near downtown. I circled the block around 2nd and Main a couple of time and we spotted three guys dressed a girls and drove up beside them and yelled "faggot"," queer" with expletives and threw half full and empty beer cans at them before taking off. So, I thought, I am still one of the guys and my secret is safe. Internally, it just felt wrong and I did not like taking that action but only did so for my own survival.

I played baseball from little league through college, and participated in the American Legion. I received a letter from both the New York Mets and the Cincinnati Reds to join them at a tryout camp in Highland Springs in my senior year in high school. I remember hiding the letter from my parents and skipping the camp because I thought if I really made it to the major leagues what an embarrassment it would be for me and my family if I were caught wearing women's clothes and even worse yet, if it were ever learned that I really was a female trapped in a man's body. I would be a laughing stock in front of the entire world and my family would be humiliated. The media would have a field day!

18

In college my desire was to major in Anthropology, however my mother had other ideas. Mom is a petite woman about 5 feet tall and she weighs 110 pounds soaking wet. She wore a dress or skirts every day down about knee length and always an apron in the kitchen. She had very dark brown short hair and beautiful green eyes and was very beautiful. In the summer the dresses or tops were short sleeved and she wore the same with a sweater in the winter with nylon stockings in her slippers. Mom stayed at home with the children and kept the house clean, washed clothes, prepared the meals, and shopped for the family. Breakfast was at 7am, lunch at 12 Noon, and dinner at 6pm. If you missed those times you had to wait until the next meal. No snack between meals was the rule of the house. Normally when I came home from school she was sitting at the sewing machine making clothes for one of the kids. The television would be on across the 30 by 15 foot finished basement room and I would lay on the steps and watch "Queen for a Day" which aroused me physically and emotionally at the age of 8 years old. She made me a plaid shirt and I loved it, the buttons were on the left side. My mother was very smart and had a degree in English and she worked very hard around the house as it was expected.

Mom would often ask me to help her move furniture around in the house or to hand scrub with a brush the linoleum brick pattern kitchen floor which was 18 by 10 feet and she would follow me with a mop and get up the wet. We did not have a dishwasher so all the dishes had to be washed and dried by hand. I would take turns with my two sisters in the evening when it came to the drying. Just after finishing my freshman year at the University and being at home, after dinner, I helped my mother pick up the dishes from the table and lined them up on the left side of the counter from the double stainless steel sinks. I took my place by standing in front of the counter and cupboard to the right of the sink and set myself up to dry the dishes.

Mother asked with her yellow rubber gloved hands in the dish water, "How is school going"?

"It has been a bit of a struggle this first year working to pay for my education, playing baseball, and being in a fraternity".

"Well, you do not need to devote time to a fraternity".

"No, it has been helpful to me to get to know so many people and have some fun".

I quickly changed the subject. "My English course is really tough this year and Dr. Ball is a real stickler and demands perfect writing".

"Dr. Ball was my English professor when I was at Westhampton about 25 years ago. I majored in English and love to read. Have you thought about what you would like to major"?

"I am leaning toward Sociology and Anthropology".

"Why on earth would you do that"?

"It's the study of society and the study of man and I would like to understand the evolution of man".

"You should be more like your father and go into some type of business. There is no real future in Sociology, besides business will allow you to make something of yourself. It would be best for your future".

Thinking for a few moments, while stacking the eighth dried dinner plate on the counter and picking up the stack to place them in the cupboard.

"I do want to make something of myself and this is my real interest".

"I think that you are wrong and if you want to have something for yourself you should be like your father and go into business". In a very soft voice, "Maybe you are right".

I picked up the broom and swept the kitchen floor and got it up and placed the dust and crumbs in the trash. I pulled the trash bag out of the can and walked out the back door onto the screened in porch, stepping down the three steps into the backyard and put the trash in the metal trash container at the back of the lot. Thinking that I really need to understand what is going on with me and I need to know why I feel as if I am a female. This weighed heavily on my mind as I walked back into the house and went down stairs to my make-shift temporary basement room. I guess I can do business and figure this out along the way.

I returned to UR my sophomore year and elected to take Sociology and made an A in the course. I took and advance course my second semester and was given a project to do something unusual in the world and report back the reaction of others in doing this unusual thing. It was my plans to put on a skirt and a pair of stockings and go into a shoe store and have the clerk help me try on a pair of high heeled shoes and write my report on that event. However, as I was getting ready to do this, a great fear came over me and I never carried out this project. My fear was reflected in my grade as I never told the professor the idea.

So rather than select the field that I had a keen interest in, I majored in Economics. The reason I wanted to major in Anthropology is because it was the study of man in his natural habitat and I felt I could research the transgendered world in this field. Although, I enjoyed Economics and later continued my education and earned my MBA, I was resentful that I never followed my dreams and studied my area of interest. My own fear so great that someone would figure out my truth.

My evenings were filled with working for The Dairy, the Richmond Newspaper, and the United States Post Office. Every Monday I would hand over my paycheck to the University bursar for my tuition, books, and room and board. My fourth check however, I was thankfully able to keep for myself. This money went to keep me cigarettes, booze, and my two newest college friends: speed used a couple of times to study all night and recreational marijuana with my fraternity brothers. Although quite busy, I still managed to date, attend football and basketball games, and play on the baseball team my first two years, all the while hiding my feminine attire and internal identity.

My junior year at UR, I lived in Freeman Hall on the same floor as my friends and Jay lived in the room next door by design as he was a close friend and fraternity brother. He would often help me by taking me to work and we played music and backgammon on a regular basis. During one of the sessions he told me that a girl friend of his was coming from Roanoke to see him later that afternoon. This girl friend he had met at a dance the previous year and she attended Hollins College. Later, Jay stated that he really did not feel like going out that night and I took note of it as we continued our backgammon game. Two hours had past and we were still playing our game when there was a knock on the door and outside stood two girls both had traveled from Hollins.

One was the sister of a person that I went to high school and the other was Kathleen the girl that had come to see Jay. Kathleen was petite and stood just a touch over 5 feet tall wearing beige bell bottom pants and a lovely pink top. A gold necklace, earrings, and a puzzle ring glistened from her neck, ears, and hands. The shining brilliance in her green eyes was stunning, olive tone skin, and the naturally curly golden blond hair about a quarter of the way down her back makes her absolutely beautiful. She smiled pretty and seemed very happy.

I struck up a conversation with Kathleen and learned that she was born in Saudi Arabia, went to high school in Greece and Richmond, and was now a sophomore at Hollins. She had a sister that lived in Highland Springs, VA and that she was in town for the weekend. Knowing that Jay was not up for a date that night, I assertively right in front of Jay, asked her out and she responded with a "sure". So we went to dinner and over to the Continental Lounge on Cary Street which is across the street from her High School , and back over to the fraternity house and had a wonderful evening talking with other couples and playing spades.

It was the beginning of a great relationship as we saw each other just about every weekend. Kathleen transferred to the University for her junior year as she lived with her sister and we continued to date, meeting on campus, going to fraternity parties, the football games at City Stadium, and basketball games at the Robbins Center. We would go downtown in Richmond and take trips to Washington DC to see our favorite band, Bruce Springsteen and sat on the front row in the auditorium at Georgetown

University in December 1975 and we were like two "Sprits in the Night".

Kathleen and I married during our senior year. We graduated together in 1978 and moved to a garage apartment owned by Kathleen's father, in New Kent County. A year later her parents purchased a home for us in Highland Springs. We had our first child, a son, in 1980 who we named John III. After graduation I was hired, and then laid off, by a supply company before ever really getting my feet wet. Shortly afterwards I found a position with The Paper Company as a credit manager. On occasions, during lunch hour, I would discreetly go over to Willow Lawn and purchase items for my growing feminine alter ego collection. After work, I would pick up Kathleen from her banking job, with my purchase hidden in the small trunk of our 1975 Red Camaro and drive home. Upon returning home, at the next available opportunity without being caught, I would go straight up to the attic and hide my treasures away, lest someone find out my well-kept secret and my life be left in ruins. During the second year of my employment at Wilson Paper, I resigned and immediately found a job with Phillip Morris USA, which started my 25-year career with this company.

It must be understood, despite my internal feelings of being a woman trapped in a man's body, I truly loved Kathleen and my son John III and wanted to be the best husband and father possible. I spent as much time with them as humanly possible, only to have my internal conflict continuously flare up. I even spent a great deal of time with Kathleen's father, so much so that he and I became drinking buddies but I did not utter a word. I never had anyone to talk to about the issues that constantly troubled me. There was no psychiatry, no psychology, no social worker, no EAP, no one. I lived as if these feeling never existed! In 1982 Kathleen and I welcomed our second child. We were blessed with another son whom we named Mark. My two sons were wonderful. I loved and adored them both very much. I did my very best not to allow my secret to be seen and was quite successful living a lie ...

I began work for Philip Morris USA as an hourly "miscellaneous" employee on the cigarette manufacturing floor. I worked the graveyard shift for the first three years. After 18 months, I was promoted to Production Supervisor in the Leaf Processing Facility known as Primary. I received excellent reviews and was selected for a temporary project in Lexington, KY, which was scheduled to last for three months. I was elated to be selected for this project as it afforded me the opportunity to dress as a female privately in my hotel room when not working, dining, or associating with any colleagues. At the end of the three month project, I threw away all my female attire before I returned home to Richmond. Obviously it would have been far too risky to return with a suitcase full of female attire; how on earth would I have explained that?!

Philip Morris, USA was building a new manufacturing center in North Carolina, so in 1983 I called the moving company and had my home packed up for the big move to Concord. However, it would be a full eight weeks before my family would finally arrive. In the North Carolina plant, I worked as a supervisor in tobacco processing and assisted with supervision of the equipment installation, tuned and tested, and trained the employees in their production roles. It was a wonderful and fulfilling experience to be instrumental in the start-up of a highly technical operations facility. During the eight weeks without my family, I had the opportunity to dress in my hotel room and took full advantage of my opportunity. Just like the gray-haired guy in "The Catcher in The Rye," I was too afraid to venture out of my room dressed as a female. Being in the South, I had real fear concerning what might happen to me physically if I were caught dressed this way. Also, I drank a six-pack after work to mask the pain of my continued internal turmoil.

As time progressed I moved up in levels of management. I understood the tobacco manufacturing business and possessed wonderful interpersonal relationship skills. I always saw a person not for what they looked like or believed, but as a person. My employment with Philip Morris, USA was one of my "saving graces" in that it kept me very busy, paid well, and helped my family. I thoroughly enjoyed my job and felt as though we were a family.

After my family arrived in Concord, we found a beautiful three bedroom brick ranch-style home with a garage on two acres of land that was once grazed by cattle. We fell in love with it immediately and knew it was the perfect place to call home and raise a family. It was situated between Philip Morris, USA and the Charlotte Motor Speedway, just off of Highway 29. Not long after settling into our new home, we welcomed our third child into our family: a daughter we named Rebecca. She was the most precious girl I had ever seen and with this child, I was actually permitted into the labor room as my wife gave birth! It was an experience that filled my heart with peace, one that I shall never forget. She loved her father and grew up always wanting my attention and love.

The sons grew to be typical boys and enjoyed common "male" identified activities. They played in the creek and in our fields. They also played on baseball and soccer teams and naturally, I assisted with coaching duties. Rebecca was athletic in her own right participated in gymnastics, softball and later became a cheerleader in High School and at the University of North Carolina- Chapel Hill. I kept the yard neat and grew a beautiful vegetable garden every year. Additionally, I planted trees and flowers and was always very friendly towards the neighbors. I loved my family so very much and tried my best to make them feel that way, with my actions and words. We would take vacations to the beach and Disney World in Orlando and have a great deal of fun as a family. I still had my secret and guarded it very closely. I stored my feminine attire in a very safe place in the attic and also locked them up in the garage of our house. Stolen moments to be alone and dress were not as difficult as it once was as a child, although I had to be a lot more patient because timing was everything. Being caught now meant that I would lose my marriage, children, home, employment ... my entire life! I would literally be the laughing stock of the

25

community. It was a very lonely, guilty, anxious feeling. Often I felt as though I just did not want to live anymore. There was a time when my suicidal ideations became more than just thoughts. I actually devised a scheme where I could hit the bridge abutment on Highway 29 at Little Buffalo Creek just right while driving to work, and my misery would be over. I would die instantly and my family would get my life insurance money and live happily ever after. Every day for a very long time I would look at that spot to figure the exact angle to maneuver my car to hit just right so I would not miss killing myself. Several times I practiced by jerking the car right and then back, but instead went to work thinking that I should have just done it. My alcohol consumption became increasingly worse over the years and it worked really well to dull my pain. It also gave me courage to take risks of dressing as a woman when I knew my future would be at stake. I drowned myself in my work and attended Pfeiffer University where I earned my MBA. I stayed busy, learned everything I could, worked hard and just didn't think about my life as a female. I buried who I was deep inside … it was my bondage of self.

My confusion was immense; I took any criticism from Kathleen as a personal attack on me not understanding that she was trying to be helpful but how could she since I never revealed to her my secret. The most notable was the philosophy on the raising of our children. The influence from my father to be tough with the kids, to raise them Catholic, and basically not allow them to be creative was in conflict with Kathleen who had a degree in Early Childhood Education. I had my family on a pedestal and I had all the pride that came with my traditional Irish Catholic background, not understanding the dysfunction that I was carrying forward with my actions. Being raised to appear that everything was great with the family, church, and the world came first and I was doing the same to my family and children. I had it backwards because I thought the outside world was greater than the inside world.

Kathleen recognized this dysfunction but I did not until about 16 years after our divorce. This made me angry inside and I grew resentment toward her to the point that I convinced myself that maybe I should leave. I with my confusion as the feeling to express being female was very strong. My fear and self-centeredness destroyed this marriage. I do not know who I am and so I leave a trail of malady that affected the lives of my wife and children that will take the rest of my life to make amends and even then that may not be enough. I moved forward in a faction of not looking back and today it is sad that my actions were such irresponsible. I was embarrassed and feeling unworthy of having my own children and that hurt the kids more than anyone.

So in not dealing with my gender identity issues I only created another huge issue for myself and the entire family in the community, both in Concord and Richmond, which brought about additional guilt, shame, and anxiety. So internally there was an issue hidden behind the issue behind that issue which was alcohol, divorce, gender identity. This was pushing my true issue deeper from the surface.

Perhaps because of my determination to hide who I truly was, I became a workaholic and the quantity of drinking increased as well. Naturally this led to the demise of my marriage and consequently, Kathleen and I divorced. The drive to just be alone in my confusion was severely heightened during this time in my life. I wanted to be free of the manipulation and live where I could at least be dressed properly in my own place. The pain was excruciating to explain to my three children that I was not going to live with them anymore. As I saw their crying hearts and faces, it felt like a knife ripping though my soul. I convinced myself that maybe I could have the best of both worlds. They could come visit me regularly. This did not work out very well as the separation and divorce took on a painful ugliness for all involved. The separation actually caused the desire to show my feminine side to intensify. Instead however, I purged all my women's clothes after moving out of our home. I threw every single item identified as female into a dumpster outside of my new apartment in Concord, all the while wondering what was wrong with me. This was my second major purge where I got rid of everything, only to start all over again in less than a week.

A year before my separation with Kathleen, I was promoted from a Production Supervisor to a Group Supervisor. This meant that Philip Morris was entrusting me with the responsibility of 9 production departments making up all the tobacco processing areas, 9 Production Supervisors, and 125 hourly employees on third shift, 11pm – 7am. This was the beginning of a new shift and new employees had to be hired, trained, and run Production. The shift did very well with the start-up of a new process and getting all the new employees on board. It was very tiring as I worked hard 5-6 days a week and slept the days away while working all night. Kathleen worked very hard to keep the children from waking me up and I was elected PTO President at the Elementary School and coached my children in little league baseball. It was quite a busy time. This kept me out of myself but somehow I think it contributed to the divorce. My real issue did not have much of an opportunity to surface so it lay dormant for some period of time which continued to antagonize me from within. I was backing myself into a corner without the realization as to what was taking place in me.

As the year passed, one such person hired on to third shift was a lady by the name of Diane. She was assigned to the Burley Tobacco Department and during my rounds of the shift I would stop and talk with her concerning the job. She always had a lot of questions about the process and company rules. However after several months the conversation turned a little more personal as we shared some experiences that we were going through outside of work and talked about our children especially since they went to the same school.

Diane was petite, long hair, deep dark brown which almost looked black, half way down her back, green eyes, and very pretty. She had a small percentage of Indian blood in her as one of her ancestors was Cherokee. She stood 5'2", slim and trim, hard worker, and all the guys wanted to take her out. She was mechanically inclined and focused on her work and did not let the guys bother her. If someone said anything out of the way she would run them off in a heartbeat, as she spoke her mind and did not want to be bothered. She was a single mother with two children, both girls, Stephanie who was 16 years old and Alisha a child, 8 years old.

After my separation, I started to talk more with Diane and we eventually started to see each other outside of work. I would visit her and invited her to my newfound apartment in the middle of Concord and she would only stay a few minutes. We would go to yard sales on Saturday morning. Eventually and quickly, this turned a little more serious as we started to date. This did not set well with Kathleen, my children, friends, or my fellow peers at work.

After she and I had been dating for six months, I told Diane that I enjoyed dressing in women's clothes and she was the first person that I had ever revealed this secret. She was an opened minded person who did not see anything wrong with that as long as it did not hurt other people. Once we discussed the issue I was totally relieved and then after she left my apartment a sense of anguish came over me, completely worried that would get out. Now there was someone who knew a little about my dark secret that I have kept hidden all my life. I became very worried, horrified really. It took months of agonizing over it and wondering if I should take the risk and tell her the truth. This is something I had never discussed with Kathleen or my children out of great fear and now this fear had intensified. I felt as though I could trust Diane and I had to express it. I let the women's clothes conversation go away for a while. Diane was a wonderful person and it was even more wonderful that I did not have to hide my feminine apparel from her. However, I still did not share with her everything because there was still a great deal of confusion going on with me. I would see her practically every day, and when she asked me to move in her home with her and the children, I readily accepted. We were soon married and I suppressed my feelings once again. Again I wanted to prove to myself that my feelings of being a woman trapped in a man's body were not true. It was merely a sickness that I could eventually overcome.

I began to receive a lot of pressure from my fellow employees at Philip Morris, USA concerning my relationship with Diane because the families of the employees who moved from Richmond to start up the facility were very close. This particular group constantly watched me and reported my activities back to Kathleen. My passive aggressive nature took over as I often fed one member of this particular group information just to see if it would get back to me. Naturally it got back in record time! I realized if I could lose friends over something as every day and "heterosexual" as dating, then I knew it would be much worse with my deepest secret of all. This backstabbing within the company by individuals made for very ugly times, so when the company offered an early retirement package to downsize, I accepted it.

In 1992, after the buyout from Phillip Morris, USA, I started my own business. It was a solid wood furniture business; I sold, finished, refinished, and even built wood furniture. Diane continued to work for Philip Morris but was heavily scrutinized for many years by the same people who harassed me. Philip Morris was a company that did not tolerate harassment of any kind, however; individuals could privately harass an individual in a way that left no solid proof of harassment. My mindset was if an employee complained, it only made their situation worse. I personally, sought legal advice concerning my issue, only to learn it would have involved many people in the plant and it would be my word against theirs. At the time it didn't seem worth it to me to go through such an argument. I was ashamed because I loved my work and I allowed the pressure of the situation to run me off and accept the early retirement.

Diane and I moved a mile away to Harrisburg, NC, into a brand new home of our own. Diane continued to work for

Philip Morris and I had started my furniture company, O'Riordan Furniture Company. I had accumulated a fair amount of profit sharing stock and my severance package continued my salary for one year. So, I had the time, education, and money to take on this new and exciting endeavor. I worked on the development of my business but also found myself wandering to the lingerie shop to purchase sexy feminine underwear and lycra dresses for myself. I went to an adult book store in an attempt to find information on transsexuals. Unfortunately, all I found were pornography books involving "chicks with dicks" and "she-male" nude photos, and lewd sexual stories. Even though this was not the information I was seeking, it was an education in the fact that again I realized I was not the only person in the world with gender issues. I realized a big issue for transgendered individuals was that most people think it solely concerns sex, when in fact it has to do with gender. Sexual orientation is a totally separate issue.

During the early 1990's the Internet had become increasingly available to anyone with a computer or computer access. Chat rooms of all sorts had cropped up all over a new Internet provider named America On Line (AOL) which allowed several that concerned transsexual issues. There were people online that I would chat with about feelings of being a female trapped in a male body. However, I had to struggle with many men who weren't transsexual at all; they just wanted to play games with "trannies". I was able to find a few online friends who seemed genuine and discussed dressing up and going out as a female. One such person was named Laura who lived in South Dakota. After some time, we developed enough trust with each other and exchanged telephone numbers. We spoke on the phone sometimes and discussed how our wives were dealing with the issue. Both wives were fine as long as we kept it at bay. Privately, we discussed having gender reassignment surgery. The Internet at that time was prevalent with sexual connotations about transsexuals; however there still was not much information about gender identity issues. It left me feeling like a freak in need of a cure for my insidious disease. Obviously this did not help my self-esteem, nor did it help my continued downward spiral into my beer bottle either. At the time however, I continued to consider myself a very functional drinker. I never missed work or appointments of any kind. My work ethic was always beyond reproach.

I began to venture out in public by dressing and going to the local grocery store across town to buy groceries for my family. Diane gave me a list; I would go shop in my full feminine attire. This would entail make up, wig nails, dress, stockings and heels! The first time I did this other shoppers in the store looked at me oddly, and two Asian women walked up to me and laughed not once but twice. I looked like a man in a ankle length black dress, stockings, with a white scarf hiding my neck in the middle of the summer. It has been funny to look back on myself, I was scared out of my mind but simply felt compelled to finally go out into the world as myself, a real woman. I remember the cashier checking me out and then leaving to run to the office. I left quickly, packed my groceries in the car and hurried out of the parking lot, both excited and relieved to have had the experience.

Once, Diane needed to have her check cashed and I offered to do it for her. She gave me her driver's license and a check endorsed to her and I dressed up to go to the bank to cash it. I was exhilarated at the challenge yet fearful at the same time. However I was never one to back down from a challenge so I dressed as closely as Diane as possible and went to the Wachovia Bank branch in Charlotte. I pulled into the furthest drive-through lane which was three wide, and presented Diane's license and check to the cashier. I was trembling with excitement and fear, and very politely in my softest voice explained that I needed to cash my check. I was shaking but managed to pull it off without a hitch. I was elated when the teller said, "Have a great day mama!" It was truly music to my ears. I drove off on cloud nine; playing the music on the radio really loud and may have even sung the whole way home.

Once in a blue moon, in the evenings when Diane worked and the children were asleep, I dressed in my feminine clothes and drove down the interstate and waved at all the truck drivers. They tooted their horns and motioned for me to pull over. I turned on my signal but never stopped. This was normally done after several rounds of drinks because it gave me the courage to "drive as a lady". I drove into the downtown area of Charlotte to a bar that stayed open until 2 am that catered to cross dressers and drag queens. One night I performed there, lip syncing: "I'm Your Private Dancer." My Performance earned me five dollars in tips. I was such a mess back then, I risked everything...

I learned from watching a talk show that there was an organization in the United States called Tri-Ess for cross dressers. This was an international group and had chapters across the country. I went online and found the Kappa Beta Chapter that met in Charlotte, NC. I was scared to death but I wrote to the contact person and explained that I was male and enjoyed dressing as a female, and wanted to attend a meeting. I waited with bated breath for the mail until finally one day it arrived. The letter explained that I needed to call for a screening. When the house was empty and I was absolutely sure I would not be interrupted, I made the call. I shared that I had been dressing as a female since I was a child. The contact person gave me the meeting location and time. The meetings were held one weekend per month near the downtown area in Charlotte. I told Diane about this group and she had no problem with it whatsoever. On that particular Saturday I put on my best dress and make-up, with the assistance from Stephanie, and drove to the meeting in Diane's car. I had a truck back then and felt that it would not have been appropriate for a lady to show up in a truck. I was very cautious hiding behind sunglasses driving with the visor down so that the neighbors would not see me, and I never looked anyone in the eyes.

Upon arrival at the hotel, I felt very apprehensive when I approached the designated room. I was so driven however; I just got out of the car and put one foot in front of the other and marched right in the front door. As I walked in, I was welcomed by, Linda, Janice, and Rachael, three men dressed as females. My nervousness immediately subsided as we sat down and we excitedly began talking about dressing and going out as females. There was a lunch planned at a restaurant about ten blocks away and I fell back into my old state of mind, which was panic and fear. I willed myself to join the group and prayed that no one would recognize me.

Traveling in three cars, seven members of the Kappa Beta group got out the cars and walked through the side entrance of a prestigious Italian Restaurant in uptown Charlotte. This was my first activity with the group after meeting Linda in the designated hotel room where those attending were instructed to meet. Linda was the elected leader of the group and she and Janice took me under their wing. Linda was about 40 years old and wore an ash colored wig, solid blue dress, big bold jewelry, and a pair of flats. Janice was a big "girl" about 6 feet 7 inches tall and the four inch heels made her almost 7 feet. She had been a football player in her earlier years. Her shoe size was a 17 in women's and she discussed on the trip over of a specialty shop in town where she had to purchase her shoes. She wore a big floral print dress with stockings and heels. Her wig was shoulder length and dark brown with long dangly gold earrings and rings on 6 of her 10 fingers. These two girls had been meeting here in Charlotte every month for quite a while. She spoke in a very deep voice with a Southern accent.

We approached the long table which was made up of three tables put together in a row in a private area of the restaurant. The table cloth white made of linen and each place set to perfection looking out onto the main thruway in Charlotte's uptown. It was a narrow area of the restaurant with a wall open on both ends to the main part of the restaurant and I felt as if we were on display sitting in front of the glass front window. I chose a seat with my back to the street as having the fear of being recognized by someone.

Linda was sitting next to me and was telling everyone about her adventures of going out dressed as a female. Cary was sitting next to Linda and this was her first meeting. She drove over to Greensboro from the Raleigh area to meet Linda the night before and they followed each other into Charlotte.

Linda opened up the conversation, "I bought the Mercury that I drive because it looks like a female car and I use it only when I am dressed. I putt around town and it fits my personality and I only use it for that reason". "I meet Cary in Greensboro over at the Wal-Mart parking lot last night and took her into the store dressed as a female".

Cary said, "I was so scared to go inside and asked, suppose somebody says something to me"?

"I told her to not look anyone in the eye and just mind her own business and if anyone said anything just keep shopping as if you did not hear them". "It has happened to me before and I just ignore them and everything was fine".

Cary explained, "It was really exciting for me to have gone in and shopped and back out again. It was exhilarating. When I left I was so excited that I got stopped on I-85 by the North Carolina Highway Patrol for speeding but I was lucky that the policeman was very kind, as he wrote me a ticket".

I chimed in with my story about taking Diane's check to the bank and cashing it and told the group "that the moment and the feeling afterwards was that I felt right with myself, especially after having so much fear".

When we finished our lunch, the restaurant owner came over and gave Janice and Rachael cigars and had a few words with them which I did not hear but they laughed. At the time I found this terribly odd, but apparently it was his way of expressing his feelings of acceptance with the group and his happiness that we chose his establishment to patronize for our public dining.

That same evening everyone except myself, changed into a gown or suit for dinner. I already was wearing a very nice small floral print, dark blue, Ann Taylor dress, with stockings and heels. This formal dinner was attended by approximately twenty cross dressers and one even was there with his wife. We had dinner and shared experiences of going out in public as the opposite gender. It was an awesome experience for me. I felt great apprehension and anxiety, while being relieved all at the same time.

That night at the banquet Rachel told a story about the time her car broke down about 5 miles from her house near Hickory, NC. *"My car stopped and there was water leaking all over the road and I was not far from a friend of mines house. So, I undressed in the car and put on my male clothes and walked to his house. I wiped off the makeup from my face and walked up and rang the doorbell. My friend answered the door and I noticed at that time I still had on my fake fingernails. I was embarrassed and hid them until I could get them off by pretending to have to go to the bathroom"*.

When I returned home Diane was upstairs in the room overtop our garage. She was on the computer and watching television about 11pm. I told her about the entire experience and that I appreciated her willingness to listen and understanding of me attending. She stated, "I can remain very supportive, provided it does not get out of hand". This sudden appendum worried me a great deal. Nevertheless, I attended the meeting the following month and with the same "girls" we visited a dress and make up shop. The women in the shops were not fazed by us at all and rather looked forward to seeing the group, as they expressed. This gave me a sense of belonging and even hope that maybe there was understood in the world. To cap off the night, we all had dinner and shared our experience surrounding the days' events.

The greatest lesson for me in the two meetings that I attended was it reinforced the notion that I was not the only one like this in the world. I still could not explain why this was true but I knew in my heart that it was the truth. I learned of the wig, dress, and makeup shops that I could go to that were accepting and it gave me an inkling of relief for a short time. It was helpful because I was going alone to lingerie shops on my own and still continued to do so when I found one that was accepting or nice to me. My favorite was in Midway which is between Concord and Kannapolis. I would often think on the drive over if I was sick and why was I born this way.

My fear of being caught remained extremely great. After my second meeting, as well as going alone in the city from time to time, my neighbor took a good look at me as I pulled into the driveway which frightened me. I considered inventing the story of a "visiting twin sister" if ever asked about that particular event. I was back to that old feeling of losing everything that I worked so hard for: family, home, work, and friends. I decided not to attend anymore Tri-Ess meetings however, I continued to go out alone.

I participated in this type of activity for years. Kappa Beta provided me with valuable information, like where to go to be fitted for a nice wig for example. They also showed me that I really was not the only person in this world who felt the way I did. However, it still did not make it easy. Society still looked down on this type of behavior. Although we went out, the places we frequented were safe places and kept our secret. So was my secret was not really out? I shared the same secret with a group of about 20 people. In reality Tri-Ess groups were for cross dressers only and did not support the activities of gender reassignment surgery. At the time, there was no real information about how one could go about changing one's gender. Tri-Ess was primarily a group of people wearing the clothes and behaving as their opposite gender. It was merely a starting point for many transsexuals. There were many phases I went through to reach the point where I am today. Having been with a group such as Kappa Beta was very instrumental in my development as a transgendered woman.

After four relatively successful years, I closed down my furniture store and went to work in a Greensboro Tobacco Company for 26 months. I did very well during my employment there. I worked the second shift and traveled from my home in

Concord, NC to Greensboro, NC five days a week. I supervised production in the tobacco processing facility and became very close friends with a gentleman named Riley. Riley and I worked together in management and eventually, I shared my secret with him. When I revealed all, naturally he asked for pictures of me dressed as a female. After work on the night of his request, once I made it home, I emailed the pictures to him. One night, several weeks later, while at work, he pulled out an 8.5" by 11" photo and showed it to me. Much to my surprise and shock, it was a blown up photo of the one I had emailed to him previously. He seemed very proud of his handiwork and offered no real explanation for having it there, hidden away in the office. He also seemed to harbor no ill will either, so we both just laughed and went on with our business.

A month passed after the "photograph incident" and we were scheduled for a meeting the next morning in Greensboro. Riley invited me to stay at his house that night because his wife was out of town. He said it was fine if I wanted to dress. He made steaks on the grill, and drinks as well. We sat around and ate and drank and talked. He seemed to be very accepting of me as we talked about his issues, our wives, and situations going on at work. Over-all we had a very nice evening. Later we went off to our separate bedrooms and went to sleep.

About a month after that dinner, my previous "tobacco employer" Philip Morris asked me to come back to work because of a great need for experienced personnel in tobacco processing where experience was required. I jumped at the opportunity to return to the place I wished I never left! On my last night with the Greensboro Tobacco Company, my so-called friend Riley showed all the employees on the second shift in my department the picture of me dressed as a female. I did not know this until the next day when a fellow supervisor called me. I was shocked, embarrassed, and humiliated beyond anything in my life. I was hurt to the core and in disbelief beyond my worst nightmare.

I called him and asked him why he had done such a horrible thing. He said that I was doing so well with the company that he was saving the picture in case I ever received a promotion before he did he planned to use it against me. He provided me with no further explanation and I told him he was not my friend and he was an extremely mean person. This experience took away my trust in human beings and proved to me that my gender identity issues were to be kept very private. So I drank away the anger, fear, and loneliness.

My boss at the Greensboro Tobacco Company retired during the following year and he invited me to his party in Greensboro. He called me several times and I eventually told him that I was simply too embarrassed to face my co-workers again. He tried to convince me that he wanted me there but I just could not place myself in that negative environment. I felt betrayed and ashamed that these people had knowledge of this information. I felt it was a step backwards in my progress in becoming the woman I am today.

Chapter 2 – The Crossroads

In March 1999, I went back to work for Philip Morris at the Concord, NC site as a Production Supervisor and was then promoted to my old job of Group Supervisor within three months. I was there about 16 months before being promoted again and transferred to their facility in Richmond, VA. I accepted the transfer thinking that if I could just be back home it would enable me to face my fears of possibly transitioning. I knew in all actuality, it would be tantamount to living in the lion's den and looking straight into the mouth of the beast! I was still very confused, but Diane and I sold our home in Harrisburg and purchased a beautiful four story house near the James River in Maidens, VA. The house was down a gravel road, nestled in the woods with only one neighbor on the road. (I later learned my new neighbor worked from home, so at first I had to be discreet with my dressing since this neighbor would always be around.) Diane stayed on with Philip Morris in Concord and lived with her mother near the factory. For the next several years, I drove from Richmond to Concord every other weekend to visit with her. Occasionally I would wear women's undergarments and sometimes even my feminine blouses on my drive, but always had a cover just in case. I would then change before going in the house to see Diane.

One of the employees that I supervised in NC had a dog kennel and raised Black Labrador Retrievers. She gave me an alpha male from one of the litters as a thank you for helping her while I was at the plant in Concord. I named him Zebedee, and he became very important in my life as soon as I got him back to Richmond. Zebedee was a fast learner and began sleeping on the floor next to my bed after the first week. He was house trained within three weeks and soon we were inseparable. He retrieved thrown tennis balls making "circus" catches by leaping into the air and catching the ball, and he always brought it back to me immediately. He guarded the house and always kept a close eye on me. Zeb was like having a friend who I could talk to about my feelings. He always seemed to listen and understand; he'd tilt his head to the side and furrow his brow just at the right moments. I often wished he could talk, because he seemed to know me better than I knew myself. He was truly the best friend I had at the time when I needed a best and loyal friend.

The second year I was in Maidens, VA, my son John came to live with me and I soon realized his mental health diagnosis of schizophrenia had become worse. He had begun hearing voices and described it as "seeing a black cloud off to the right filled with people he knew speaking to him and telling him what to do". I worked with John for months, often until the wee hours of the morning, answering the same questions over and over again. The primary question was "why does my face change in the mirror?" He talked about the voices telling him to do things and about how his face looked as though it were constantly changing. Then my son showed me a speeding ticket for driving 105 mph in a 65 mph zone, telling me that the voices made him do it and he later declared that he was going to kill himself as he descended the staircase with a knife saying he was going to slit his wrists. I immediately took him to Tucker Pavilion, a psychiatric hospital at Chippenham Memorial Hospital in South Richmond. This proved to be a very difficult time. We made five trips to the hospital over the next year for similar incidents and, each time he was kept for about a week. Finally I was forced to have him placed in a group home, only to have him leave there after two days. He did not like this group home which was located on Chamberlayne Avenue on the outskirts of the hood in the middle of the North side of the city. He dialed 911 and had an ambulance pick him up and take him back to the hospital to treat his anxiety. John told me he just could not stay there and that it was horrible. So, with the help of the Doctors, we located another group home in the country where he was admitted and where he lived for the next 18 months. I picked him up most weekends to bring him home for visits. During that time, my parents told me a story about one of their friends who had a child with similar problems. I knew the family but never knew about the child until my mother told me about him. This family obliviously kept it quiet. Back then, mental illness was very much "taboo" and still remains a very sensitive area of discussion in most social circles today. My family "advised" me that John needed to stay in a group home for the remainder of his life. This distressed me greatly and I refused to believe them. I felt with love, patience, and the appropriate psych medicines he would one day be able to function in mainstream society. After 18 months of the group home, I brought him home and helped him get a job at our local grocery store where he worked for seven months. He was on his psych medicines and doing well until he met a girl and they started using alcohol, marijuana, and cocaine. Because of this, I had no choice but to place John back into the group home. I still had faith that he could become a productive member of society by showing him love, patience, and understanding. He remained there for another 18 months.

My life had become very hectic with work, travel, and my son's illness. After work, I used what little free time I had to shop online for clothes. My shopping started to become an obsession; as I would purchase at least two Ann Taylor outfits a week. Ann Taylor is a high quality, professional, up to date, in-fashion, and sexy clothing line for women. My closet had more women's than men's clothes. I found a nice set of silicone breasts on the internet and I felt as though I had struck gold when they arrived. A beautiful pair of 38 DD's, so naturally I bought bras from the best places like "Vickies Secret" and "Vanity Carnival" that would support my "girls". Shopping on the Internet made life easier because I was still too embarrassed and apprehensive to shop in stores. Although at times, provided I had a few drinks to raise my courage level, I would dress and venture out.

The Internet became a great help for me when I discovered chat rooms. I was able to find rooms where other people were experiencing many of my same or similar feelings. Also, I used this avenue to search for local or nearby places that were accepting to people like me. On a website which listed bars and clubs in Richmond, VA, I found just such a place. After I looked at the site for about a month, I finally had enough courage to call this place, (a bar). When I called, I inquired if it would be alright if a "male to female" person was acceptable in the bar. They assured me it was perfectly fine in this place. I'll simply refer to the place as "Doll's." I waited another couple of weeks and called them again, just to double check and assure myself. A week later I drove into the Carytown section of Richmond on my way to work to check out the place. Carytown was known for its liberal attitude where they, actually catered to the gay and lesbian community. Today, it is an area that is welcoming and accepting of everyone in the Gay Lesbian Bisexual and Transgendered (GLBT) community.

A week later, I went to Doll's for the first time. Doll's was located on a street corner in the middle of Carytown. As I walked in, I immediately saw a bar with a mirrored background with bottles of liquor lined up on the four glass shelves running the length of the 20 foot wood bar with about 10 round stools. Glasses slid into a wooden rack hung above the young bartender who had very short brown hair and a lovely smile. She was quick about making drinks. One "lady" swiveled around on her stool to look at me as I came through the door. To the left side were booths along the side of the wall. The bar, floor, and booths had many years of wear. Through the opening on the Cary Street side of the bar was a large room with another bar, two pool tables, bar tables and chairs. The floor area was used for dancing and at the opposite end of the dance floor was a disc jockey stand. A hallway led to the backdoor where there was a porch and volleyball net sitting in a sand box.

I was alone as I sat in a booth, drank and had dinner. I was dressed in a pretty Ann Taylor short plaid skirt, matching top and four inch heels. I was afraid to look anyone in the eye and made sure I minded my own business. I saw no other transgender persons there. Although I felt very uncomfortable, I stayed for nearly two hours watching others from a distance. Every other week, after that I would go to Doll's. My home was 28 miles from Carytown. After I returned home from work and played with Zeb, I dressed, waited until dark and drove to Doll's. I continued my search on the Internet for friends and finally found a person named Matthew who dressed as Shelby. We talked about dressing and going out in public. I finally got up enough nerve to ask her to meet me at Doll's. I followed my normal routine, went to Doll's, sat in my booth, had dinner and drank. Shelby never showed up. As it turned out, she was just as frightened as I had been to walk into Doll's. I spoke with her later and she explained that she drove around for quite a while but could not muster up enough courage to come in. About two weeks later she finally made it through the front door and we talked and exchanged stories. We really had a good time too. This was the first time, in Richmond; I had actually talked with another person on a one-on-one basis. It was nerve wracking for me because I was not sure how she would react towards me and quite frankly, I really did not know her true motives. She actually turned out to be really nice but interested in dressing primarily for sexual reasons. A person who dresses as a female to have sex with other men is called a "fetch". She was definitely not a female in a male body.

Shelby and I met a few more times afterwards at Doll's and we'd talk about our dressing. She would discuss her sexual orientation and I discussed my gender identity issues. One Tuesday night in Doll's we were having drinks and dinner and I thought the girls at the next booth behind us were dressers. I was not sure but I kept looking over at them. By this time and having been to Doll's alone or with Shelby I had enough courage to roam around to the bar where others could see me. There were two girls and a guy at a booth adjacent to the bar and as we walked by one of the girls, she then introduced herself as Marti and asked Shelby if we would like to join them. Marti was short, had long curly dirty blonde hair down to her waist. She had a round face, body, and was very quiet but down- to- earth and did not drink alcohol. We joined them at their table and learned they were male to female and used to be part of a group known as the "Virginia Secrets". This was the first time I met Marti, Teresa, and Ivan. Teresa was a pleasant person, about 60 years old. She had short curly light brown hair and wore glasses. She had a definitive and soft voice as she sat eating and drinking very slowly. Ivan was a tiny gay male who later surprised us all by getting married and joining the Republican Party- "seriously". They told us about a former group that they used to hang out with every Tuesday and Saturday night at Dolls and they have continued this tradition even after the group disbanded.

Shelby and I were scheduled to meet again at Doll's but she did not show up. I learned about two weeks later that her father had come over to visit with her that night and caught her dressed as a female. She later told me she was leaving to visit me when her father pulled up in his car when she was getting in her car while being dressed in female attire. He freaked out, forbidding her to ever dress like that again. Shelby who lived in North Richmond, went back to being Matthew for the next year because of the shame, guilt and humiliation his father made him feel.

Finally, there was a place to go all dressed up! It met my needs for a while because I was able to eat, drink, and be myself. On week nights I would leave around 10:00 p.m., on the weekends it was well after midnight. As I had one DUI back in North Carolina in 1999, I was fearful of the 28 mile drive home especially being dressed as a female. This did not stop me from driving after I had had a few, although I did try to take a few precautions with my driving. For example, I stayed on the Interstate and consistently used my cruise control. The last five miles of my drive were winding country roads. Even if I had not been drinking, these roads scared me because they were just dangerous at night with roaming deer and other animals! I was also afraid I would get stopped by the County Sheriff Deputy and be either treated terribly or even beaten to death. This was my fear but it still did not stop me from going into town on Tuesday and

Saturday nights. I considered it was my escape into my world which I desperately needed.

I continued to drive to Charlotte/ Concord at the end of the work week to see Diane and my children while John stayed in the group home and although these visits were becoming less frequent. I would stay with Diane, her Mom and my step-daughter Alisha who was taking college courses at the local Community College and working as a Cosmologist. She was confused as to which direction to take in her career path, so we would talk about it. She was very petite and had a happy go lucky attitude. Alisha was not a good driver so Diane would show me the dings and bumps that she had made on her car while telling me she was not having them fixed anymore. Diane's mother loved me a great deal and she treated me as one of her children. She would tell me that I should return to Concord and be near her. Diane's mother, who I called Grandma, had a heart condition which required her to have a pacemaker. She was short with white wavy hair, wore glasses and lived in a double-wide pre-fabricated home on an acre of land. She had been a nurse in her younger years and was retired with a small income. She was very pleasant and very supportive of her 6 daughters and son. She was very kind and tender hearted.

On an occasional Saturday, I would venture down to Columbia, SC to see my son Mark at the University of South Carolina. Mark was 5'8" tall with light brown short hair and broad shoulders, polite, and a very fine young man. When he was 8 years old, I bought him a set of golf clubs and took him for lessons at the Cabarrus County recreational center and he loved the sport. He played golf on the team in High School and was a scratch golfer and was also in the band and played the base drum. He was very well liked in High School. He enjoyed sports and I would join him in Columbia to watch the South Carolina football games when they played Alabama and LSU. We would tail-gate, throw football, eat, and drink beer and he never knew that I had a deep dark secret. I was his father and I loved my son although I do understand that I did not show it. Mark earned a BS and MS Degree in Sports Management and then went to NC State and earned his MBA.

My daughter Rebecca was in Chapel Hill but I would see her on occasion. You can tell that Rebecca is my daughter because her features are similar to mine. Rebecca has long blonde hair, tall, slim and trim from gymnastics, and studying for her Bachelor of Science degree in Mathematics at the University of North Carolina. She only once came by Diane's mother's house to see me but on several occasions we would meet for lunch.

Diane made the trip to Richmond on her vacations, July 4th, Thanksgiving, and Christmas and normally Alisha, my step-daughter, would accompany her. We would have her children and the dogs stay over at the house in Maidens, VA, for Christmas and have a wonderful time. I enjoyed Diane's company and we were really best friends. She would see my outfits in the closet and often made comments like "you have more women's clothes than I do". Brandon, my son-in law who was married to Stephanie, my step-daughter and who looked like her Mother, would help build a fire in the fire place or the barbeque pit, or find a spot outside, and play with the dogs which she loved. There were 4 of them – Oddie an alpha boxer female with Sheppard and chow mix, MJ a hyper Gordon Setter, Scooby a half bred Collie with legs like a Dalmatian, Koda a Tibetan terrier, and of course Zeb. The dogs would run around and as we made up our own songs while burning brush and tree stumps and trash off the three acre tract of land. One such song was, "Burning stumps and drinking beer, while sitting here and watching deer, not caring about any fear"... I would drink and coax the others to join me. We would drink and play backgammon until 2:00 a.m. We would get up the next morning and do it all over again. It was a wonderful time!

I took John to the Catholic Church and convent in Rockville for Mass and also to visit with my mother and father. I felt less guilty when I went to church because I was raised that you did not miss Mass on Sunday, to do so would brand one a sinner! I did this for about six months and then stopped going to Mass for a while. Attending church pleased my parents more than it did me. Although, I had faith in God, I feared His wrath because I was transgendered. Usually we would go to my parents' home for an afternoon lunch that my mother had prepared from the time she got up, until time for church, and then after. She had a very rigid routine probably because of my father's demand for discipline. As a child, breakfast, lunch, and dinner were exactly the same time every day. If you were late, you had to wait until the next meal. In my home, you ate what you put on your plate or you were made to sit there until you cleaned your plate. My father was especially strict and controlling when it came to eating our butterbeans because he grew, picked, and shucked them and he insisted we eat every single one. When I was 14 years old my brother, who was 5 years old, refused to eat his butterbeans and his father made him sit at the table from 6pm-10:00pm. I was horrified by this. This was cruel! But my little brother stood his ground and he was finally sent to bed. There were still three butterbeans left on the plate.

For many years I had placed my family on the highest of pedestals taking pride in our Irish Catholic heritage and I was taught that a Reardon was always right. In my mind, no matter what, we were the greatest family in the world and there was none like it. Everyone wanted to be just like us--- (dysfunctional). All I really wanted was for my parents to love me, but they never said "I love you"! That is what I sought and I learned that my drinking behavior centered largely on this issue. When I visited, the time normally did not last more than a couple of hours and then I was off the hook for the rest of the week. I lived in my parent's strict "box" for a few hours in order to stay connected with them because I needed their love so very much. While they could never respond, I never left their home without saying, "I love you Mom, I love you Dad" ... yet I never heard those simple, yet beautifully loving words from them for which I so hungered.

I continued to get on the Internet and go to Doll's twice a week. I met other girls at Doll's on Saturday nights, along with

Teresa, Marti, and Ivan. We were a mixture of transgendered females and lesbians. Doll's was a lesbian bar from dinner time to closing with a handful of gay men from time to time. The more I went to the bar, the more comfortable I became in that environment. I started to get to know all the "regular" girls in the bar and even became a "regular" myself. I would typically arrive on Saturday just after dark in the winter and around 6:00 p.m. in the summer months. I checked my neighborhood very carefully to ensure I would not to be seen all dressed as a woman. I now had two neighbors because a second house was built on the other side of me. There were now three houses on the gravel road which was the maximum allowed by the county. Sometimes I would have to wait until my neighbors went inside before I could leave my house. We were alone down in the woods, but each house was arranged so that you could hear and see one another. The road was a dead-end, which meant one way in and one way out. I had some very close calls as several times my neighbors were turning onto our road while I was leaving.

At Doll's I had pretty much the same routine. I would have dinner, drinks, play pool, and dance until 2am and then the drive home. I got up every morning with the feelings of guilt, shame, and anxiety having had intensified. I reflected back on the day before and I could not figure out why I felt all this guilt. I continued to feel it every single day. I knew that I was compelled to dress as a female but I had never done anything wrong to anyone. It was very lonely, living in the country by myself. I would go to my job in Richmond Monday to Friday, work ten hours and go home, dress, or go surfing on the Internet looking for people like me. It had gotten to the point where I was always male in public and female in private and I dressed accordingly; I felt like I was living as two different people. I showed the world this wonderful, accomplished male who was educated and successful, while I was sincerely dying on the inside. I was taught that being this way was the road to hell. Truly it was like living in hell.

The guilt, shame, and anxiety had intensified and was beginning to last longer each day, so I prayed on my way to work for help. I finally realized this business of living male during work then coming home and dressing as a female was becoming unbearable. I went upstairs, got ready for bed in a very nice peignoir, opened my nightstand drawer and pulled out my 9mm Ruger. I lay in bed and felt how badly this world sucked and felt that I should just move on to the next place. With that, I loaded the 9mm with a clip of 16 rounds, pushed back on the barrel to cock the pistol and place a round in the chamber, flipped off the safety and pointed it to my head, applied pressure to the trigger, one flinch I would be gone. Suddenly, Zeb came flying upstairs, sat down next to the bed and stared at me with his beautiful brown Labrador eyes. I could not pull the trigger. What would happen to Zeb, my faithful companion who I loved so very much? Zeb truly saved my life that night. About two weeks later, this exact event happened again. When I put the gun down with Zeb there the second time, I made a decision that I needed to live my life the way it was meant to be regardless of the potential possibilities of losing my wife, children, family, job, house, and whatever else society felt entitled to take from me! It was just too much for me to ask myself to live a double life, a life that was not honest and was not who I was born to be.

Chapter 3- Reflection

I spent a great deal of time after work each night searching the Internet for some answers. I had learned about a couple of surgeons that were in the United States and actually met a girl in Richmond who had gender reassignment surgery. She discussed the surgery with me and actually showed me her results from both the gender reassignment surgery and facial surgery. I was amazed because I could not tell that any surgery had been performed. She looked as if she was born a genetic female. This gave me hope for the future. While I did not know how, I did feel that at some point it must be done.

One night I searched the Internet after I had been drinking all evening and praying to God for some answers. I searched transsexuals and Catholics and found nothing, then after a couple of hours of doing this forwards, backwards and sideways. I searched Catholic Diocese of Richmond and transsexuals. I rolled through the pages and clicked on many of the suggested sites and somehow from somewhere came up a Catholic Nun in New Orleans. I do not know how I got to her information but the paragraph read that she was a Catholic Nun and minister to the transgendered community. I think the information had to have been sent from heaven because of all the internal pain and conflict that was in my life. For me being at the end of my rope I had to have divine intervention to take place. It was my last hope and since I was having such a struggle with myself and religion, finally at 1:30 a.m., this miracle was presented to me. I was raised to believe that being gay, lesbian, bisexual, or transgendered was sinful and one could not gain the fruits of heaven and would live a life that only terminated with fire, brimstone, and hell for eternity. This was a huge burden and caused unmitigated fear within me. To me, transgendered meant that I would lose everything: family, friends, home, car, job, etc. I would become homeless, and be forced to live on the streets, eat out of trash cans, and at the end, burn in hell, simply for being born in the wrong body! I am transgendered and this was an awful way to have to live but I had to face the consequences and could not contain this secret and live with myself. It was my belief that many transgendered people commit suicide at this point in their lives. It was either die, live a lie, or take corrective action.

I contacted "Sister" via email and explained that I was Catholic, transgendered, and I needed help because I was predestined for hell. Further, I needed help with my faith. We emailed and spoke on the phone several times and I started to have some hope for my life. After a couple of months I talked with her about my visiting New Orleans for a retreat. We agreed on the last week in June 2005. I requested and was granted vacation time from Philip Morris for this week and made the appropriate flight arrangements for New Orleans, LA.

I was very nervous about going there because I had never met her and knew there were a many scams on the Internet. I prayed I would not be killed, harassed, or become an example for some self-righteous hate group. There was no way I could not go down to the local Catholic Church and inquire about the legitimacy of this group and of her. One of my greatest fears was to be beaten up because one time when I was 15 years old I did not make it home at the time my father told me to be there from a high school dance. Before leaving, I asked my Dad if it would be alright to take my date to Julian's, a Pizza Restaurant on Broad Street, after the dance and I would be home around 2am. My father said to me, "No, you have to come straight home". So, I conveyed the message to my date and two other couples who were going with us that I could not go out afterwards. The girl that I took to the dance was named Maria and lived two blocks away and my parents knew her parents very well. We had gone to grade school and now high school together the entire time. Her father picked us up after the dance along with the two other couples and instead of taking us to Julian's, he took us all home. One of the girls lived out in the country about 12 miles from my house and he took her home first and then her date. My fear was growing because it was past the time that my father had told me to be home. I sat very quietly in the car as Maria's dad dropped off the next couple. Since she lived only two blocks from my house, it only made sense to drop everyone else off first. Finally, it was my turn to be taken home and I was scared that I would be in trouble but thought that I could explain to my dad that I indeed had come straight home without going to the restaurant.

It was 2am and I was an hour late as I walked up the cement sidewalk toward the brick ranch style house, up the brick steps and stood at the front door. I reached into my pocket and pulled out the key to unlock the bolt lock while placing my hand carefully around the handle and applying pressure with my thumb on the latch opened the front door. Closing the door quietly, I turned and took three steps on the white tile foyer floor and met my father face to face in the dark as he appeared from around the bedroom hallway with a black belt in his hand.
"I thought, I told you not to go anywhere after the dance and to come straight home"!

"Dad"! "I came straight home and did not go anywhere" and I was immediately cut off and bullied backward toward the living room. "Take down your pants right now" and the beating began. His rage was intense and seemed out of control as my father beat me with a belt until both legs were purple, blue, and white with marks that welted in the form of the belt. I tried to shield my legs from the belt with my arms so they too were welting with the marks from the belt, the beating seemed to go on forever. Blood and pus was running out of my legs when finally it came to an end. "Get in the bed" was the final sound of this night. My mother, two sisters and three brothers had to have heard this commotion because it was very loud, but no one ever said a word.

I woke up at 530 am to deliver the Richmond Times Dispatch to my customers and the blue jeans that I wore was painfully rubbing against my torn legs as they were still throbbing. I was filled with a great deal of guilt and shame over the course of the next week and wore long pants and long sleeve shirt during the very hot period in June. All my friends were wearing shorts and tee shirts and asked me why I was dressed for winter and they told me it was too hot to wear long pants but I never revealed to them the reason. I pledged at that time no one would ever beat me like that ever again, and I guard that even today and no one has since. There were periods in my life that I cried about this many times, especially while drinking, and never told anyone until I finally shared this with Kathleen some 18 years later. This took away all the good times I had with my father, baseball, Woody's Ice Cream on Brookland Park Boulevard, the Richmond Braves baseball games- everything. I learned to live deeply in fear and to keep a careful eye out of those that could suddenly change toward rage. So, I knew I had to be very cautious on this trip.

Oh my goodness, today, I realize that my father was treated the same way he had treated me. It was even tougher on him than it was on me. I understand now that my father did the very best he could and only wanted the best for me. His childhood was difficult and he learned that this was the way to express love. His fear, as a parent, took the form of rage which was deeply rooted from his own lessons in life. I forgive my father for his actions and I forgive myself for carrying the resentment with me for a very long time. This realization took me many, many years to understand this expression of love. I am very grateful for the lessons and miss him so very much.

Finally the day before my trip arrived I packed my bags with female clothing. I had arranged for Zeb to be taken care of by my next door neighbor. I had my flight tickets in hand, and I was rearing to go! The next morning, I dressed as "John", made sure all of Zeb's arrangements were confirmed, and handed over the keys to my house to my neighbor. I left early, drove to Regan National Airport in Arlington, VA and boarded my flight to New Orleans. The plane was packed and I was able to sit by the window so I could look out. A very nice Afro-American male sat next to me and we struck up a conversation along the way. I told him that I was going to New Orleans for a vacation; of course I never revealed the real purpose for my trip. I often wondered if he would have been so nice and talkative if he had known the true nature for my trip to New Orleans. He was from New Orleans and pointed out his neighborhood on Lake Ponchatrain as we descended toward the airport.

Once I arrived in New Orleans and retrieved my bag I waited out front so Sister could pick me up. As I waited, I looked for a green Toyota Tercel with a sign that read, "Elizabeth". Elizabeth was my female name, and I used it for about 10 years, "Elizabeth Diane". Elizabeth after my first high school girlfriend and Diane for my wife. I saw Sister slowly drive by once with my name plastered on the windshield and carefully examined the situation before flagged her down the second time she came around. I finally met her, she looked to be in her sixties, and she did not look like a nun because she was dressed in every-day garb. She was very welcoming and I was honestly elated to meet her and felt very at ease as we drove to her home in the 9th Ward of New Orleans.

Sister lived in a townhouse in a predominately black neighborhood. We parked the car in the designated area under the awning, opened the back gate and went through sliding glass doors that opened into an eating area and behind that through an opening in the wall was a small dark kitchen. To my left was the den, which contained a sofa, two chairs, and a television. As I walked towards the front of the house into a small foyer, to the right was a nice sized living room which served as the chapel. In the chapel were statues of Christ and the Virgin Mary. There were two bookcases filled with books and a sacred area where the Body and Blood of Christ were kept. Upstairs were two bedrooms, the master and one smaller bedrooms and a bathroom. Sister showed me to the bathroom, and then to my bedroom, which was in the back of the house. I immediately cleaned up and changed into my female attire, a nice Ann Taylor brown skirt and matching tank top including makeup and wig.

I thought I looked good until Sister asked me why "all you trannies" liked to wear short skirts. I really didn't know how to respond to that question because it was not that short but realized back in my Catholic school days, girls were constantly being reminded that their skirts needed to be knee length. While I privately found it humorous, I realized I did not have any skirts that were knee length with me. I thought that my fashion faux pas may somehow land me in trouble.

I discussed with Sister that I did not necessarily like the name Elizabeth Diane and I really needed my own identity. I told her that I had thought for at least 6 months that I should officially name myself Kaitlin Sine Riordan. This tied me to my Irish roots and the change in the spelling of my last name would keep my family out of my gender identity issues. This would enable them to live their own lives without being tied back to mine; at least I thought so at the time. Sister agreed and from that moment forward, Kaitlin Sine Riordan was born!

As Sister explained, there would be no television or phone calls while on this retreat. I was a little amazed, so I called Diane, who I had asked to be alert to hear from me during this trip, and explained I was on a retreat and could not call. Unfortunately she did not understand at all so Sister agreed to contact Diane and explain in detail. Also, the retreat was a quiet time to reflect, meditate, and pray, which also meant that talking was kept to a minimum. I followed Sister's rules as she prepared dinner. She never wasted anything; in fact, she used every bit of food and froze the leftovers. She even washed out her plastic zip lock bags and reused them. It was interesting for me to see the way she took great care to use everything to its fullest. She had a very low income and what little extra money she was able to obtain came from ministering to transgendered people, but she knew how to stretch everything out to make ends meet. She had total faith and trust in God to provide her with what she needed and I could see her walk of faith in clearly her actions and how she lived her life!

We had dinner, talked about change and my feelings. Sister understood the feeling of damnation I had due to being transgendered. We discussed that God put each of us on earth for a purpose and that He loved us regardless, we are all equal in His eyes. Sister made reference to teachings in the Bible about God being an all loving God. She taught that through prayer and meditation, it brought one closer to God, and able to understand we are all His children. My assignment was to pray and mediate in the chapel with God, and understand that I am one of His children and I am loved. I washed the dishes and dried them by hand while Sister went about her work on her computer. Afterwards, I followed her direction given to me over dinner. I spent the remainder of the evening in the chapel, which gave me a sense of healing. That night I went to sleep easily and slept peacefully for the first time in a long, long while.

The next morning Sister and I had breakfast together and she provided my assignment for the day and scheduled a time for discussion in the afternoon. I spent the morning in the chapel relaxing and looking through the books on her shelf. Prayer and meditation was a big part of my day as I reflected back on my life and asked God for His blessing and help. We discussed the meaning of change during the afternoon session. I learned that in order for change to occur, it is imperative to leave the old and start the new. In my case, I didn't need to forget my past but instead, I needed to learn to accept who I was and move towards being my true self. If I worked with God and tried to understand God's will, then perhaps the feeling of loneliness would subside.

She handed me a booklet that was 40 pages typewritten, single space, which was entitled, Stories of Struggle and Transformation- Understanding our Transsexual Sisters and Brothers. It was remarkable to me that their stories, feelings, thoughts, fears, and anxieties were all similar to mine. Actually, it was a document that described me as I related perfectly with these ten Catholic transsexuals. Their story was my story, truly an amazing revelation which helped me to understand that I was not alone.

On Sunday we attended mass at St. Paul's Catholic Church. I was very nervous because I had never attended as a female. I was anxious, nervous, and had a fear of rejection. When we arrived Sister introduced me to the members of the church and explained that I was in town visiting from Virginia and here on retreat. This church served the Black community of the 9th Ward. I still felt apprehension and tension as we went inside and sat down in a pew about four rows back. The Mass was wonderful with what I call Southern Baptist singing and clapping along with the traditional Mass. It was intensely inspirational and I was filled with peace and joy, nothing like I had ever experienced! For the first time, I attended Mass as myself, just as God had made me. After the service, Sister introduced me to the Priest and Choir Director who were both very loving and accepting. They personally welcomed me to the Church and New Orleans.

After Mass we went back to Sister's house and made a big New Orleans style lunch, Creole red beans and rice with bread. We talked about the Catholic faith and how there should be no reason why I should not attend Mass. I learned from Sister that the Vatican does not condemn transsexuals. In fact, the official doctrine of the Church is that we are all mentally ill and because of our illness, we have the right to enter heaven. That was very interesting but not the reason why I should go to mass. The reason for going to Mass was to pray and stay connected with God and celebrate the many blessings that He has bestowed upon me. Later, I took a long walk through the neighborhood and reflected on all that had taken place during the week. I waved and said hello to several of the neighbors as we passed each other on the sidewalk. It made me feel so good and "alive", like a real person to simply be myself and walk among society and do so-called "normal" things and to be accepted while doing them.

I had a moment of clarity and a huge spiritual awakening while on my retreat. The five lessons I learned with Sister were:

1. God accepts and loves me as His child, exactly as I am;

2. I am not going to Hell because of the way God made men after all, we are all created in His image;
3. God will provide what I need if I remain connected to Him;
4. Prayer and meditation are one of the keys to staying connected and must live my life honestly;
5. Honesty will lead to humility and from there to peace.

I had found my peace with God as my Higher Power and accepted myself. Now I was terrified with what I knew was to come next ... coming out. Still I managed to maintain the calm that I had gained. The guilt and anxiety that I carried for so many years, especially each morning when I woke up was slowly dissipating. I felt I truly had become the woman I felt I was born as, Kaitlin Sine Riordan, and I was strong enough to scream it from the highest mountain tops ... or was I?!!

The next morning I was to fly back to Regan National on the Potomac River. I packed my bags for the next day, prayed in the chapel and thanked God for his love and acceptance. Sister helped me realize that I needed to pray with God and that everything would turn out fine. I slept very peacefully during the night and woke up early to catch my flight back east.

When I awoke, I dressed in my dreaded male attire once again, just as I had my trip from DC to New Orleans. I did not want to dress this way but I was afraid to dress as my true self because my Virginia driver's license and ticket read John, Jr., male. Sister took me to the airport in New Orleans and I boarded my flight. I remember I had a window seat near the back of a 737 and looked down on Lake Ponchatrain as I left New Orleans. I felt very calm and peaceful as I reflected back on the retreat. I really felt that God was with me and I need not worry about the future. It finally felt good to accept myself for who I was and to feel with the utmost certainty that the hell-fire and damnation I was brought up to believe was **not** going to take place. I carried a very serene feeling with me throughout the flight. I do not think I spoke to anyone the entire time because I was deep in my thoughts and in peace.

As the plane approached landing I could see our Nation's Capital, the Washington Monument and the Potomac River and I thought what a wonderful Country we live in. My hope would be that one day, all people would be just as accepting of each other as I felt with myself in that very moment. The plane landed, I retrieved my bags, found my car and drove to Richmond. I had never experienced a more wonderful drive from Washington, DC to Richmond on I-95. I walked into the door and was greeted by the ever faithful Zeb, who was so happy to see me! I lay on the floor and held him for the longest time. I grabbed a beer and Zeb and I played ball outside and I talked to him about my trip.

The remainder of the afternoon and evening was a reflection on my new found hope and peace. I played some more with Zeb, unpacked, watched television, and finally went to bed with Zeb by my side. The greatest feeling ever was waking up the next morning feeling whole, without the feeling of great terror, guilt and anxiety. This was the reason I had woke up every morning for the past 20 years feeling this way because I had not accepted myself or nor did I understand that I was loved and accepted by my Higher Power. I enjoyed this day and was off the reminder of the week. Privately I continued to dress as myself, while I continued my charade in public. Nevertheless, I remained happy that I understood myself, which was the beginning of the release of my bondage of self. I had no idea there was a lot more to come during this week. I was living in the moment without even realizing it.

Chapter 4– The Luck and Un– Luck of the Irish

I started electrolysis with Jodie, who came highly recommended by some of the other transgendered girls from Doll's.   I started with the facial hair removal above the mouth and lip. It was very uncomfortable and I disliked the experience, but it was the only way to permanently remove the hair from my face. In the beginning, I scheduled an hour on Saturdays and added a day during the week. Electrolysis was expensive at $70 per hour and the most expensive cost of the transition. It took years of electrolysis to remove all the facial hair, one electric shock and pluck at a time.

I was still lived in Maidens, VA during 2005 and visited with Diane in Concord, NC about once or twice a month during this period. We were still married and I loved her very much, we were still best friends, or at least I felt that way. I knew I had to talk to her about my situation, that I believed I was a female trapped in the body of a male. In the late summer of 2005, I went to see her to have the hard conversation about my thoughts and feelings and what I had decided I must do. I was engrossed in the projecting and visualization of this conversation the entire drive from Richmond to Concord which was 279 miles from my home to hers, which made the trip seem short. When, I arrived we had a nice dinner with her mother, talked about what was going on in our lives especially with our jobs, and went off to sleep after playing in the backyard with the dogs.

Saturday morning we followed our normal routine. We had breakfast, went to some yard sales and came home to play with the dogs and sat with Mom and relaxed. It was not until about 3:00 p.m. that afternoon, I got up enough courage to ask Diane to take a walk with me because I had something I really needed to talk with her about. I attached a leash to Zeb and she did the same with Oddie and we walked out the front door, down the three brick front porch steps onto the cement driveway, up the incline to the black tar road. The dogs walked off on the side of the road in the grass as we stayed on the side of the road and let out the 25 feet of rope for them to explore. We walked almost a block and a grumpy old lady came out of her side door and yelled at us "keep your dog's, off my property". I thought it was funny as they were walking in the ditch and Diane yelled back at her "you need to go back inside". Then Oddie squatted down and dropped a pile in the ditch and we kept on going, laughing, crossing a main roadway and up the second block.

I turned the conversation to a more serious note by discussing my retreat in New Orleans with Sister in great detail and further explained "that I could no longer hide my true identity any longer." "I feel like I am a female. I feel a little bit more at ease with myself coming to this realization."

"I am really afraid to transition but I think I need to accept who I am. It makes me feel better about myself. I really do not know what to say but I know that keeping it in would only make matters worse: I am telling you this because I do not want to hide it from you".

Diane had known from the start in 1992 that I cross-dressed, went to Tri-Ess meetings, and even that I was going to Dolls. She warned me all the time to "be careful and not get caught" so this conversation really did not come as a tremendous surprise. Maybe this was one of the reasons she wanted to stay in Concord when I transferred to Richmond. I am not sure nor have we talked about it. We were both very concerned about our marriage and relationship and I told her "I still wanted to be married".

Diane explained, that continuing our marriage would not work because, "I need to be with a man not a woman." We walked and talked about this situation and she said "We should get a divorce." It was with a tone of sadness, empathy, and kindness from a friend's heart. It made me feel sad and I told her "I do not want a divorce, because I really do love you." I was hoping that love would be enough to sustain our marriage.

"If you do this, I think that your family will not react very well."

"I think I know the consequences that face me with my family. I feel that I would be disowned and cast from the Reardon family and I think that when I legally change my name I should spell my last name Riordan so that I am not embarrassing to them."

"You know that your Dad is not going to have anything to do with you and he will have a fit."

"Regardless of all the possible negative consequences, I have to live my life as my true self; the internal turmoil is too great."

We had now turned around and walked back past the pile that Oddie dropped and laughed again and Diane said, "I wonder where she is, that old bat." Once on the cement front porch we opened the storm door and walked in and let the dogs loose. It was solemn for a while and I told Diane I was going to the store and would bring her back a Sun Drop soda. I drove my new Toyota grey Camry SE about a half mile to the convenience store and bought a 12 pack of beer and the 2 liter soda and proceeded to drink in its entirety the remainder of the afternoon and evening. We cooked out on the grill, played with the dogs, and watched the news; basically we went back to living as if the conversation never took place. Diane was my best friend I was hoping that we could work everything out.

After breakfast on Sunday morning, I drove back to Richmond with good 'ole Zeb in the back seat. We arrived in the late afternoon and I played ball in the yard with him, drank beer and watched the sunset below the tree line and through the large oak and pines. I thought about the conversation I had with Diane and wished that it was not true and wondered why in the world am I this way. I cannot explain it; I just know that it is true because of the deep conflict that is internal. I do not want to be this way; life would be so much easier without such a distraction. I talked out loud to Zeb and asked, "Am I mentally ill? Is this why my son is schizophrenic; is it something in the genetics?" This question I asked but I knew I was just "normal" as Zeb looked at me as if he did not understand. "I don't understand either, that makes two of us. Come on, let me feed you."

I put my "John" on for work Monday morning and the conversation stilled lingered in my head and just prayed on the drive to the plant for a great day and that everything would work out. I just need to get back to work and focus on that for today which is what I did but once home the thoughts were ever more present. Tuesday and Saturday evening I was out in town as Kaitlin. I was starting to stay out later, drink more, and now began to notice more police late at night, more so than I remembered. I thought that I really need to be careful and try not to exceed the legal drinking limit.

One Saturday night I had stayed at Doll's until midnight and drove the 28 miles to my home in Maidens. I felt fine to drive, as most people who have had too much to drink would say, and I already had one DUI in North Carolina in 1999. I think I drank at least 10 beers that night and really do not remember the drive west on I-64 but sure things were fine. I got off the exit for Goochland and proceeded down the tree lined, two lane country road, which was the worst part of the trip. This road was dangerous because it was narrow, very dark, and I always had to be on the lookout for deer. I needed to get a cigarette out of my purse so I reached over and fumbled around for them. Just then I came up on a curve on the country road and since I had not been paying attention, I rounded the curve and crossed the double yellow line by at least half the car width. I jerked my steering wheel to get myself back in the lane, then looked up and there he was, a deputy sheriff sat on the side of the road, in his menacing vehicle in the woods, his vehicle actually faced mine, and I saw him look right at me.

My worst nightmare was about to be realized! Here I was dressed, and my license read John and male. Dressed like a female, half drunk, I had crossed a double yellow line, late at night in the middle of nowhere and there was not a soul on the road but me and him. Holy s---! I saw the horrible blue lights and then the backup lights come on the police car in my rear view mirror. I trembled with fear and my life whole life flashed in front of me and immediate thought was that this county deputy would get me pulled over, see my license, and pull me out of the car and beat me half to death, rape me, then kill me and leave my body to rot ! My next thought, and possibly more rational but still frightening was of being arrested for DUI, taken down to the county jail, and being humiliated and beaten. I have had enough of that in my day. So I did the only logical thing a girl in my position thought to do, I hit the gas and I hit it hard! I put the pedal to the metal and got gone, took off to about 90 miles per hour around that curved country road, down an include and back up, around another curve and never slowed down and turned on two wheels onto a one and a half lane gravel road. I rounded two sharp curves and was throwing gravel out behind me before coming up on the only stop light in the county which was red. It did not matter what color the light was because I was going through, turning left up a main highway and then left onto my tar then gravel drive down into the woods. I slammed on the brakes, turned off my headlights in front of my house and slide several feet before stopping. I really have no idea how I got home without being stopped, only that I was there and could see and feel my heart pounding through my blouse. I got out of the car in a hurry and looked down through the trees from the porch of my house and I could see the stoplight and I saw the police officer's car stopped, I'm sure he was wondering where I had gone. I went into the house and did not turn off or on any lights, changed my clothes, grabbed a beer and went outside with Zeb in the dark and we played ball for thirty minutes. I sat on the steps and was a nervous wreck because one of my worst nightmares almost and should have happened.

I decided right then and there I should move to the city and walk to the bars so that I would be safe. That was my best thinking at the time. I did not think alcohol was the problem only that where I lived would get me in trouble. I had always loved the Fan District of Richmond and knew the people living in the area were, for the most part, open-minded. Richmond and the state of

Virginia is very conservative but I wanted to move into a small area of about 15 blocks in the historic area were people were liberal minded, forward thinking, and open to the gay, lesbian, transgendered population. Now that is insanity and later I put together that plan.

Chapter 5- Siblings

It was Fall 2005 and since my trip to New Orleans, I knew that I was going to have to talk with my parents, brothers, and sisters concerning my gender identity. I decided to start by talking from the oldest to the youngest of my brothers and sisters. Because I was the oldest of six children and 33 grandchildren, I was the one whom they all depended on to keep the family unified. I began with my oldest sister with the thought that she would be the most understanding, and possibly even accepting of all.

My sister lived alone in the west end of Richmond in the suburbs on one of those street where most of the houses looked similar in construction and appearance, although each house had one feature that was distinguishable. Her house was a beautiful two story Georgian style wood and siding home. I walked into the foyer and to the right was the great room which was the length of the side of the house and furnished in antiques and antique reproductions. The floor had white carpet throughout which lead to the back of the house where the kitchen and stairwell opened out into the green grass backyard surrounded by a wooden fence. The kitchen was decorated with antique signs from the past 50 years. Everything was very neat and clean. The backyard was about a quarter of an acre with a hot tub sitting on a deck that was tucked away in a corner of the backyard. The yard was Immaculate and well-manicured with a white picket fence that separated the front from the back. To top it all off, she had a beautiful Sheltie dog named Casey.

My sister was just 23 months younger than me, graduated from a women's college in Farmville, VA, and worked for the telephone company. She had sandy blonde hair down to the nape of her neck. She stood 5 feet 4 inches tall and had a little roundness to her body. She wore contact lenses most of the time which did not hide her beautiful blue eyes. A devout Catholic, she attended Mass every Sunday and followed the laws of the

Church exactly as they were taught, dressed conservatively and was very protective of the family, especially her brothers.

We walked out the back door from the kitchen onto a treated wooden deck to an outdoor table and chair patio set. Taking our places at the table I handed her a Michelob Light from the 12 pack that I brought with me. It was starting to get dark and she got up and turned on two spotlights that illuminated the deck and backyard. Casey ran around our feet, jumped up on us, before taking off around the yard and then back to us again. I started the conversation by just blurting out the purpose of my visit.

"I need to live my life as your sister because I am really a female."

She looked at me for a moment and her eyes changed to a look of grave concern. They slowly closed to look at me with a squint. After a pause and regaining a more normal look she stated, "Going out with you to a bar dressed as a girl was cute but that is it. You need not take such drastic measures."

"I came to you first because I thought that you would be the most accepting of all and I did not think you would have a problem with it."

She rose from her chair in a manner of disgust and with tears in her eyes cried out, "John, you are my big brother and I look up to you, you cannot do this."

"I just thought that you would be supportive."

"I don't know if I can be or not."

She was upset, "I want my big brother and I have trusted you. You cannot ever let Mom and Dad know how you feel. It will hurt them a lot. Just tell me why?"

"I am not sure why, I just know deep down in my heart that it just is."

I offered her the book, "True Self" and she took it and there was no further discussion about the book or of me. I had two copies of the book and she still has one today. I felt really bad that I had ruined her evening but thought to myself I really do not know how to move forward only that I had to in order to gain sanity within my heart. I did not like the fact that this curse would be so sad to those I truly loved and I wondered why I was born this way. I finally said goodnight after quickly drinking a few more beers and left with a feeling of uneasiness and sadness as if I had let her down. While she did show some empathy, she was confused on whether to support me or not so she stayed away from me until Christmas and then for a couple of years after the Holiday's. I thought as time passed she would come around but as more time passed, sadly, she grew further and further away.

Several weeks had passed before inviting my sister Ann over to my house and it would be another two weeks of so before she could actually make the trip out to the country. It was late October of 2005 and my sister could finally come to my house in Maidens, VA. It was bright outside, on a hot and humid mid-fall Indian summer afternoon at 3:00 p.m. I was sitting on the brick steps of the front porch and spotted her white Toyota Camry station wagon appear at the top of the long narrow gravel drive where the big oak tree splits it to form two lanes heading my direction. She drove right up to me in the circle driveway out front and I met her at the car and we gave each other a loving hug. She knew what I wanted to talk about but her body language showed no hint either way as to how she felt.

Ann is 5 feet 3 inches tall, short styled dark brown hair down to the nape of her neck, pretty green eyes. She is petite, slim and trims from teaching spinning classes at the local YMCA, a soccer mom, chasing and keeping together her husband, four children, two cats, and one dog. She is always running from school, to the mall, to church, to the gym and everywhere else. She has the gift of debate, very opinionated, talks really fast, but is the most opened minded of all my siblings. Ann walks with confidence and conviction and tells you exactly what she thinks.

She is a graduate from William and Mary with a degree in History and graduated from Marshall-Wythe Law School. A former prosecutor for the state of Virginia and now many years into the sabbatical from her work to raise the children. She is married to Jacob, the son of a South Boston tobacco farmer, a graduate of the University of Virginia and Marshall-Wythe Law School at the College of William and Mary. Ann and Jacob are very talented attorneys and own a beautiful home in an elite neighborhood of the west end of Richmond.

Diane was in the house visiting her home since she was on vacation for the week from her job in Concord, NC. I called in and Diane came to the front door and the three of us stood in the foyer which was at the foot of the solid oak staircase that went to the third of four floors which was part of our beautiful all brick Georgian style home. I stood very nervous about speaking with Ann because all I wanted was for my family to love and accept me.

We walked into the family room just off the foyer. The space in this room took up a third of the entire level and the floors like the kitchen, bathroom, dining room, and foyer on this level was made of tongue and grove oak. A Karastan rug separated the two matching sofas and ottomans that faced each other with and entertainment center in plain view. A high-back Victorian sofa chair sat in the corner next to a 1920's solid oak three drawer dresser chest which was placed perfectly between the two large windows looking out in the front yard. In the back of the room, French doors opened up to a deck that was a story off the ground overlooking a pond that was supplied by Courthouse Creek and our three beautiful acres of hardwood trees as the leaves were turning orange and yellow this time of year. I had trained Zeb to stay on our land and he never ventured off or wondered away. On occasions he would chase after the deer or the wild turkey's but always stopped before crossing the line. My house was secluded and I could walk up the drive to the main road and look through the trees and see the James River.

Ann walked over and sat on the sofa while Diane and I went into the kitchen to retrieve a glass of ice tea for her and a beer for me. I handed Ann the tea and sat down next to her and Diane sat across from us on the other sofa and listened to the conversation.

I opened the conversation. "The purpose of this visit is for me to explain to you that I have gender identity issues. I am truly a female trapped in a male's body".

Ann stated, "I just want to crumble and fall apart. You cannot do this because it would hurt our parents too much and would probably kill them."

"I know that Dad was really hard on you and not so hard on the girls. Is that why you want to be a girl because Dad would be easier on you or is that what you are feeling?"

"No, it has nothing to do with our upbringing, but everything to do with my feelings inside. I have felt this way since I was about five years old and did not believe it myself, but I have lived in a great deal of confusion and I know now deep down this is who I am."

"I feel sick to my stomach right now. I think you should explore this with a therapist."

"I have a therapist and his name is Dr. Bear's and you can come with me to some of the sessions."

"Maybe", stated with anger in a condescending tone.

I recommended and gave her the book entitled, "True Self". "It is a good book that helps others to understand the feelings of being transsexual".

She took the book and said, "I will support whatever you do but you will always be my big brother. But, you need to do what is right for you but make sure it is the right thing, again make sure it is the right thing". The support was very slow in coming.

Ann stood up from the sofa and walked into the large kitchen and placed her empty glass in the left stainless steel double sink. She looked very sad as she quietly said a few words to Diane before the three of us met in the foyer. I walked with Ann to her car without a word and we hugged and said to each other, "I love you". Ann sat in her car and rolled down the window saying, "I hope you know what you are doing", then drove up the gravel drive. I stood there watching as she passed the big oak tree at the top of the hill with a tear in my eye and then she was out of sight.

Diane standing on the porch, "She is right, it is going to kill your parents". I walked into the house and found another beer.

Diane reiterated the fact, "You need to consider this carefully. It will be devastating to your parents".

"So, what am I supposed to do, pretend that none of this exists? I have been doing that all my life and I cannot take it anymore."

I went back outside with Zeb, sat on the porch, and drank into the night. I felt both calm and realistic that my journey needed serious consideration and the painful realization was I would lose the majority of my family and my parents, possibly forever if I undertook this journey. It was a happy / sad feeling of a new beginning coupled by one of heavy loss. A feeling that made me sit and think for a long time about myself, and take a deep personal inventory and search for the truth. I thought about this conversation for the remainder of the year and did not see Ann again until Christmas. I continued to work during the day and go out to Doll's on Tuesday and Saturday night's. I dressed as a female at home and played with Zeb. I called Ann from time to time, as she was reading the book I had loaned her. She had many questions and commented on the feelings that were discussed in the book. Ann realized my journey was for real.

I decided to speak with the oldest of my three brothers next who was six years my junior. He is 6 feet tall, broad shouldered, light brown hair cut short on the sides with enough left on top so that he could brush it over to one side which gave it a semblance of a part. He dresses in Khaki pants and polo alligator shirts with loafers when he is not wearing a blue or black Italian suit outside of his white starched shirt and tie.

He graduated from the same all-male military Catholic High School as me. He was the highest ranking officer in the Corp of Cadets and went on to finish at Virginia Military Institute. He fulfilled his military obligation in the U.S. Army and started as a 2LT in infantry. Later he was promoted to CPT while with the U.S. Army Reserves in Richmond. During this time he also attended T.C. Williams School of Law and obtained a law degree.

He has practiced civil law since he joined a Richmond Law Firm and helps the elderly in his community. He has five children, one boy and four girls and is married to his high school sweetheart.

I invited him to my home and he drove over from Richmond on a fall afternoon the first week in November. I saw his blue-gray Ford Galaxy automobile approach from the top of the hill onto the gravel filled road and followed the path that my sister had a few weeks earlier. He got out of his car and greeted me like brothers greet each other with a handshake. Zeb barked at him and I had to throw a ball for him to chase before he calmed down. It was only the two of us and he had an ice tea and I drank my beer. He sat across from me in the family room on the sofa and placed his legs on the ottoman momentarily but took them down when the conversation started. I really did not know what to expect from him although I knew he was very religious, and at one time, seriously considered becoming a Catholic priest. He is an Opus Dei type Catholic but nevertheless, I still felt I needed to have this one-on-one conversation with all my brothers and sisters.

I was dressed in blue jeans, a sweatshirt, and clog's, the same way I dressed when talking with my sisters. My hair was growing out at this point as it had not been cut in four months. I would visit my parents during this period and my father would point out that my head was getting "a little shaggy" and in need of cutting "like a real man".

I spoke openly with my brother about my situation and explained how I had always felt different and that I really was a female inside a male's body. He listened very intently and told me a story about his best friend that had gone through the gender identity issue.

"Your story is similar to his." I talked with my friend for a long time about this issue and helped him find good counseling." "I can help you find the same kind of help at the Medical College of Virginia or John Hopkins University. There is a way to find a "cure" for your problem. Changing your gender is not the answer. You are sick and need treatment for this illness."

I explained that, "I already have a well-respected doctor with whom I am in counsel and his name is Dr. Bears." I shared my experience with Sister on retreat in New Orleans and I told him that "I have come to an understanding that God loves me and I am still a child of God regardless of my gender or gender identity issues."

After asking me who, what, when, where, and how I found this help? My brother took a deep breath, as if to clear his head and immediately said, "I do not have any faith in your doctor or in Sister and these are not the right kind of people who can help you."

"Oh, yea, I forgot I am sick."

He further stated, "My friend that I spoke of earlier from high school is a Catholic priest and I assisted him with this issue and know that with proper treatment you can be cured just like he was and that your feelings can be suppressed and you can return to a normal life."

My brother left me feeling bitter and angry. I despised the fact that he said, "I was sick, could be cured, and needed to pray to get closer to God and to fear Him."

I told him, "quite the opposite is true and my feelings were that my God was one that did not want me to live in fear." Although, this conversation did regress me back into the old way of thinking, one of shame, guilt, and fear. It was definitely a place I did not want to ever visit again. I already felt tremendous fear about being killed because I was not aligned with society and once everyone discovered my true self they would laugh, jeer, and humiliate me to the point of making me a societal outcast to the entire human race.

Still, I could not live this lie and had to be true to myself in order to have some type of internal peace. I began to experience huge resentments towards my brother and thought of him as a right winged conservative hypocrite. I carried this resentment with me for the next three years. I drank into the night, got up early, went to work, prayed and tried to forget about our conversation. If nothing else, I at least told him my truth.

The second of three brothers was nine years younger than I and went on to graduate from Virginia Military Institute. He served in the U.S. Army as a 2LT and worked in bridge demolitions. Once he finished his military obligation, he married his high school sweetheart and they had two beautiful twin boys that had his features which visually demonstrated that they were his. He joined his father-in-law in an upscale men and women's clothing store in Richmond and has worked there for over 20 years. He stands 5 feet 10 inches tall, black hair moderately short, dark brown eyes, and dark skin completion. Outside of work he wears blue jeans and flannel shirts and drives an old silver Toyota pickup truck with tools in the back. Empty beer can clang from one side to the other against his chain saw in the back of the truck. He lives on 14 acres of land with a nice two story home and a stable that houses three horses, one of which belongs to his wife. He hauls hay, cuts wood, and repairs the fence while his children play with the German Sheppard near the one acre pond on the back of the property.

My brother was the jokester of the kids. He woke up every morning in a bad mood and hid behind the cereal box when he had breakfast and dared anyone to look at him. He was quite humorous with a very quick wit and was basically a very happy kid. I remember that my father took away his happiness when he beat the hell out of him for a reason unknown to me. I just remember how sad he was and how badly he was beaten around the age of five to the point that my father felt so bad he took him for a walk, a walk that all the kids wanted to take with Dad. We wanted his attention in a positive way not a fearful, "yes sir, whatever you say sir" kind of way. This event reiterated the fear that I had about me and reinforced that I had to do as I was told and leave the creativity and my secret suppressed and not be who I really am. Speaking of my true feelings would be very dangerous. I was dressing very privately, whenever possible in my mother's clothes and had to remain extremely careful.

By the time for my conversation with him, word had gotten around among my brothers and sisters, and my second of three brothers knew the reason for my call and the reason for a conversation. He never responded to my calls, so eventually I dropped it. He had always minded his own business and did not want to get involved with our problems but he was very helpful towards our parents. He lived up the street and over one in the country near them and would drop in at a moment's notice. I saw him at Christmas but a conversation was non-existent as he left early. A certified letter was sent to his home inviting him to come to a therapy session and it was returned and stamped "return to sender" in every single space available on the front and back of the envelop except the area where it was to be returned. His message was loud and clear. It has now been seven years since we have spoken. I still have hope that one day we can talk.

Later that month, I stood in my front yard with Zeb, a week before Thanksgiving 2005, and waited for my brother David and my sister Ann to come over to my house. It was dusk so I went inside momentarily and turned on the southwest corner of the house spot light which illuminated the circle driveway and front yard. This time of year it starts to get dark in Virginia around 5pm and since I was on vacation this day I awaited with trepidation because I respected my brother a great deal. By the time the spot light started to take its effect, I heard a vehicle turn from the main road onto the gravel drive and then two head lights heading in my direction. It was his red Toyota Van approaching and in the driver's seat was David's wife, Melanie and sitting next to her was Ann. They did not come full circle to the front but parked on the side and as Melanie and Ann opened up their doors and got out, I wondered about David. Then I heard the sliding side door of the van open and David emerged. First, I saw his light brown hair, short on the side and pushed up on the top as if he had been pushing his hand through it and then he turned and looked at me. He had a beer in his hand and proceeded to chug it and stepped around the van and threw the bottle at me. The bottle flew over my head and missed hitting me by two feet. His eyes were wide open and glaring at me as if he were to kick my ass, right then. Melanie yells out to him, "David, you need to calm down!"

David walking towards me standing 5 feet 11 inches tall, blue eyes dressed in blue jeans, bluish gray V-neck sweater and laced brown earth shoes. Medium build and his weight proportionate with his body and he is trim. At this moment the three were together as David walked up directly to me and angrily asked, "what is this all about?" as if he did not know.

His wife Melanie, who is a petite woman about 5 feet 2 inches, mother of their three children, two boys and a girl, light brown straight with some curly hair, green eyes, blue jeans and a sweatshirt said again,

"David, calm down and let's go inside and listen. You need to keep an opened mind."

"Ann, that sounds like a good idea."

David, as was the tradition of the Reardon men, also attended Benedictine High School. David went on to graduate from James Madison University in Harrisonburg, VA and passed his CPA exam on his first attempt. He immediately went to work for a prestigious accounting firm in Richmond. He was my youngest brother, twelve years my junior. When I moved out of my parent's home at 18, David was only 6 years old. He was spared most of the rage that took place with me in the house. We had always gotten along very well, and helped each other out over the years. We laughed and had partied together, played golf, attended NASCAR races at Richmond International Raceway, and I even coached his team one year in little league baseball. David has always been very kind so his action was completely out of character.

We walked into the house onto the hardwood and turned left through the dining room and past the large rectangular solid oak table, oak corner hutch, and Diane's grandmother solid oak 1900 antique chest. All the furniture in this room matched perfectly in a dark oak finish and looks beautiful against the natural solid oak floors. We walked into the kitchen for ice tea and a beer for David and me. Then through the kitchen into the family room and sat on the sofas, David and Melanie on one side and Ann and me on the other.

Melanie was the peacemaker in the conversation and reminded David to "keep an opened mind." I could see that he was openly hurt and very angry with me but he tried to listen and comprehend but it was beyond his scope for the moment.

I explained to them my true feelings and that "it started when I was a child and as a child I did not understand these feelings, but I knew that something was not right." "Early on in life, I felt that I may be a girl trapped inside the body of a boy, but suppressed these feelings."

David asked, "when did this start?"

I told him about "playing in the dress rack when I was 5 or 6 years old" and "I would look under the mannequin's skirts to see what was there."

Ann said, "You did not tell me about that. How did you feel?"

"It was all consuming and I thought about it all the time and I buried my feelings into school, baseball, and delivering papers early on. I suppressed it because I did not want to get a beaten or be sent off to a mental ward. I just knew that I could not talk about it or take action when anyone was around. Now that I am 50 years old, I have to come to terms with this and not live a life of a lie. I have struggled with attempting not to be this way, how I thought I could suppress my feelings, how I thought something was wrong with me mentally and even held a gun to my head twice here in this house. I went for spiritual help in New Orleans to see Sister and I came to understand that God loves me for whom I am."

"Why do you think this is happening?"

"David, I do not know why, all I know is that God made me this way." I know that to be the truth."

David said, "You do not need for Mom and Dad to know about this."

"Well, at some point I need to tell them."

"I would not do that."

"I have to."

I offered them the book *True Self*, and Ann spoke up. "I am reading it now and it's a good book."

David, just like my brothers and sisters, really did not understand and had a very hard time from the onset. Melanie was willing to understand but David was not there. He wanted his big brother and felt frustrated and disgusted with this whole idea and was in disbelief. David was not pleased at all and decided he had heard enough and got up and headed for the door and told Melanie and Ann to come on "let's go home." So Melanie and David walked to the van while Ann stayed back a moment and said, "This is really hard on everyone, I hope you know what you are doing." David, he was really upset before he came over. He did not want to come but Melanie made him and he did well to keep his mouth shut. Bye, talk with you later."

Melanie behind the wheel and David in the passenger's seat with Ann in the back pulled off without a wave or a smile and floated up the drive slowly out of sight. I was standing in the night with the spot light on talking to Zeb and saying "no one can understand". I threw his tennis ball and he ran for it as the feeling of sadness, guilt, and shame came through me and vibrated my inner being.

"No one can really understand, not even me." Zeb and I went in the house and I feed him and then I drank my dinner late into the night, the great escape.

Chapter 6 – The Grand Inquisition and Last Supper

By Christmas of 2005 I had spoken with all but one of my brothers and sisters and in essence they all knew of my situation. My parents did not have a clue about my real issues at this time and none of my siblings were about to tell them. It was 11:30 a.m. on Christmas morning, alone in my master bathroom; I stared in the mirror and wondered what to wear to my parent's house for our family Christmas gathering. I decided on a pair of brown Calvin Klein corduroy boot cut jeans and a long sleeve pullover Philip Morris polo top. I lightly dusted powder on my face, donned a pair of brown matching socks, and slipped into my clogs. I went down the stairs for a beer and out the front door to play with Zeb and the new tennis balls he had received for Christmas. I felt confident and happy about it being Christmas and the day that was ahead of me. My thoughts were of me subtlety introducing my real self physically to my parents. A couple more beers of liquid courage and I would be ready to drive to my parent's house which was about eight miles away over in Hanover County, near Rockville, VA.

It was a cold, but a sunny afternoon and the drive through the country was very pleasant. Once over the Interstate, the drive takes almost 10 minutes through the winding roads, past the open fields and large based oak trees. The gravel driveway was lined with my brothers and sisters cars. With gifts in hand I walked through the garage door and into the back door and into the kitchen. The smell of freshly baked bread and ham instantly hit my senses. I greeted my sister and proceeded into the family room, bypassing the dining room where it had been set up for family dining. We always had ham, mashed potatoes, greens of some sort, and homemade bread for Christmas dinner at my parent's home. All of my siblings and their families were present. It was a full house to be sure!

We all mingled, joked with the children, and played with dad's dog Wolf, a German Shepherd. Finally, it was time for our great Christmas feast. We filled our plates and some sat in the dining room, others in the kitchen, and still more in the family room. Everyone caught up on each other's lives, but there was one huge elephant in the room and that elephant was ME! Not a word about my situation was mentioned the entire time. The conversation was around my work, my home which was now up for sale, and of course religion always entered into the picture from someone in my family. Someone was always being baptized, first communion, confirmation or being of service in the Catholic Church. The subject would always come up about me and when was the last time I had attended Mass. I simply skated past the questions and explained that I had gone on a retreat in June to New Orleans and was seen at Mass some this fall. I would go to Mass because it made me feel better but also so my parents would see me there and think everything was fine in my life. I would take my son, John in hopes that his schizophrenia would be cured because I believe in miracles, but on this day he was with his Mother, brother, sister, and girlfriend.

After our family feast we all gathered in the combined family and living rooms, to exchange gifts. I had given my mother and father nice sweaters and they both loved them. My mother always did the Christmas shopping and I always received a nice shirt. Typically flannel, cotton, or wool; this year my shirt was flannel. My dad's gifts were always money, normally a couple of hundred that he gave to each set of the households. The mood of the house was very warm, loving and cozy.

One of my niece's came up to me and asked "are you wearing girl pants;" I just kind of chuckled and blew her off by saying "oh, go on." We all had dessert and continued our conversations that had lingered over from dinner. I told my parents that I had something very important to discuss with them very soon and probably within the next few days, so we made arrangements to get together for that important conversation. After about an hour I declared myself excusable and drove home. I thought about what my niece had said and wondered if anyone else noticed. Soon thereafter, I found out that she had a conversation with my father concerning the way I was dressed. Fear about my conversation with my parents started to intensify.

Now it was January 1, 2006, I consulted with Ann and she recommended that I take along another person when I sat down to speak with my parents. Her reasoning was because "I do not want anything to happen to you physically because Dad will be mad." I agreed with her and we asked her husband Jacob if he would accompany me, and he agreed. On January 2, 2006, Jacob met me at my home and we drove over to have the conversation with my parents.

I drove my new phantom gray Toyota Camry SE with Jacob sitting in the passenger's seat to my parents' house. On the ride over we discussed that I needed to remain calm and just tell my parents the truth. Jacob said, "If it starts to get rough in there we are just going to leave. I think that it is a good idea for you to bring me along, who know what is going to happen."

"Yes, unfortunately, I think you are right and that is why you are here. I am very uneasy about this conversation but I need to let them know how I feel. I hate it but I have to for my own welfare".

We pulled into the gravel drive which was lined with railroad ties from the state road to the house. Wolf was outside and he barked as if we were intruders but calmed down once he saw it was me and I patted his head. He smelled Zeb on me and wagged his tail as Jacob opened up the side door leading into the garage.

Walking through the garage passing my father's Chevrolet Impala we progressed to the steps that lead into the kitchen and I knocked on the door which is different for me because in the past I would just open it and walk in. I heard my mother say, "Come on in."

"Oh, it's John and Jacob," as if she was surprised.

"Hey Mom, Hi Dad; what is happening?"

82

My Dad stated while wearing his gold sweat suit with red USMC lettering and carrying the newspaper in his left hand. "I don't know, you said you wanted to speak with us privately." He worked his way behind the kitchen table and stood in front of the big picture window that looked out on the 10-acres of land that he owned. My mother was now between the kitchen counter and table standing.

"I do".

"Then why is Jacob here?"

Immediately my parents were taken aback because they did not understand why I needed to bring someone with me and my Dad stated, "Then you should speak with us alone."

I explained, "due to the very sensitive subject matter, it would be best to have Jacob present."

My father asked, "What is that? You don't need anyone to come with you to have a private conversation with us."

I positioned myself at the table and sat with my chair backed away a little more than usual, right next to the back door with my coat in my lap and my car keys in hand just in case I needed to make a run for it. My parents sat down which offered a little bit more of a buffer for me. Jacob leaned against the kitchen counter which was only five feet away and listened. There was a noticeable pause as I carefully thought about what my next words were going to be and then to break the silence.

Jacob said, "Jack, you need to keep an open mind. That is why I am here." My mother and father gave him this blank look like "this guy is crazy." I could feel a difference in my whole body; I was filled with great fear. I did not know how to sugar coat my words and I softly said, "I feel that I am really a female."

After that announcement, there really was not much conversation. The silence lasted only a few minutes with my father's declaration, "it is not possible! You are wrong and need to get some help." They were very confused, quite shocked and really did not have much else to say.

Jacob tried to explain that "this type of thing does in fact occur every day, all over the world and the best thing to do would be to please try to remain calm, rational and keep an open mind."

My parents ignored his statement and I could feel and see the frustration, disgust, and concern on my parent's face. I said, "This is not about hurting you but something that I had been living with my entire life, since I was a child playing in the women's clothes racks in the department store."

"It is not possible" my father insisted and sited some of my childhood accomplishments. "You were good at playing baseball and football and I have never seen you do any 'girl' things. This is just not possible, something is wrong with you." We just looked at each other for a moment and my father said, "We will talk about this later." So, I got up and opened the door and told them that "I will see you later." Jacob followed me out the door and into the garage and we drove back to my house.

Jacob said, "I think that they are shocked and will need some time."

"Yep." The remainder of the ride home was in silence while we listened to the radio. Once we were at my house, Jacob immediately got into his black Lexus and said, "see ya" and abruptly left to go back to his home in West Richmond.

I was at work and sitting behind my mahogany desk and the phone rang on this cold Friday, January 6, 2006. It was 10:30 a.m. in the morning and the caller identification digitally displayed it was an "outside call." I picked up the phone and answered, "Philip Morris, Reardon speaking." It was my mother and she said, "Hello John."

"Hey Mom, how are you doing?"

"Fine, your father and I want you to come over for dinner tonight."

"Ok, I will be there by six."

"Alright, we will see you then, bye."

"Love you, bye".

She did not have to say a word as I knew it was the moment of truth, the real conversation about my feelings, alone, just the three of us. It was difficult to focus on my work that day but fortunately for me I had a busy schedule with meetings and a presentation. This occupied my time to 3:30 p.m. that afternoon which help me from completely worrying about the evening meeting. At 4 pm, I locked my office door and walked out to my 1995 F-150 Black 5 Speed Truck that was parked directly under my office window. I would drive the truck to work a couple of times a month to keep it in shape while traveling the 32 mile down the interstate. Fortunately the traffic flowed swiftly out of the city on this day, a gift on a Friday afternoon. The sun was blinding as I turned down the winding country road towards my house and thought about the next few hours. I parked my truck in its normal place off to the side in the oak trees off the circle driveway. I had about an hour before leaving to my parents' house.

Zeb greeted me at the door and rushed outside to relieve himself and I threw ball to him for the next hour and I did not realize where the time had gone or even what I was thinking. I did not even drink my normal "coming home from work" beer. The time was soon gone. I had gotten lost in my fear and anxiety and had obviously given Zeb a good workout as his tongue was almost hanging on the ground. Onto the hardwood we walked and into to the kitchen I fed my faithful companion as he lapped up all the water in his bowl before eating and then I heading out to the next county. I was in my work clothes, navy blue dress pants, a Philip Morris logo white shirt with button down collar and pocket, and my PM zip up winter coat as there was no time to change.

When I crossed over into the next county, I felt as if, I was in another country. I slowly drove up past the railroad ties, walked through the garage where Wolf met me at the door, and knocked on the door and opened it into the kitchen. I was on time at 5:55pm as dinner is always served at 6pm no matter what. It had been this way my entire life. I heard my father say,

"Don't let Wolf in", but it was too late so he came into the kitchen and had him lay down by the door. The 110 lb. German Sheppard was now blocking the exit and I took note of it.

My mother was behind the counter wearing her apron and taking the roast beef out of the pot and placing it on a platter. She proceeded to slice a few pieces and set it on the table along with the carving knife and a long double prong fork. The table was set and she told me to sit down at the place with my back to the door, below the wall mounted telephone and next to the dog. Out came the mashed potatoes, gravy, green bean, and her famous homemade rolls. It was my favorite dinner that I would request in the past, when asked for my choice in dinner and it struck me oddly that this could be "my last supper".

My father took his place at the head of the table, the same spot I sat in 4 days earlier, and my mother sat directly across from me. The brown wood and laminate table was the same one from my childhood. It was at least 35 years old and only the chairs had been replaced over the years. Once my mom sat down she jump right backup to quickly grab the pitcher full of ice tea and promptly poured my father a glass full in HIS oversized glass. Then she poured some for me and finally for herself. We said, the Catholic, "Bless us O lord" prayer as always before we began to eat.

There had never been a television in the kitchen before and on this night my parents had a small 13 inch on a small table turned onto the news while we were eating. This I had never experience before with them because in the past we had to turn off the television and come into the kitchen or dining room to eat. We talked over the news and my father asked, "How is work going?" And so I told him while wondering when the real questioning was going to start, that "I am working with all the employees in the plant and in all departments on continuous improvement and team building. I am working with developing and educating the workforce on Lean Manufacturing thoughts by driving decision making down within the organization, helping the teams to problem-solve."

"You have done well with Philip Morris, you should keep working hard."

My though was now I know where we are going with this one but it was not the case.

"Yes, Philip Morris is very good to me and I do love my work."

Then the conversation turned from my work as my mother brought up that "Fox News was the best news and that they seemed to always get it right." I'm not sure where that came from but it took the focus off of me, as they rambled about this topic. It filled the time during dinner for a while and then my father told me that "your brother has been over here and we had a nice talk." Then the topic went into the fact that my two brothers were doing very well and always the mention of graduating from Virginia Military Institute. I reminded him that I "graduated from the University of Richmond and had an MBA from Pfeiffer University" and worked for the best company in the Richmond. This is how dinner went as finally my mother pulled out a chocolate pie that she baked that morning and it was delicious.

My father got up from the table and I picked up my plate and utensils and placed them in the sink and walked back over to the table and picked up the platter, empty bowl of mashed potatoes and placed them next to the sink on the counter. My mother told me to "leave the dishes right there and come into the living room because we want to talk with you."

I walked past the stove that was built into the center of the kitchen between the walking space of the cabinets that completely lined the room and then by the wide refrigerator heading straight through the door and into the living room. I was now off the tile kitchen floors and onto the oak hardwood floors that was throughout the remainder of this two story brick farmhouse. On this level was a dining room, living room, parlor off from the foyer, and huge master bedroom and bath. Up the oak staircase were three bedrooms and a large bathroom. My father kept his office upstairs in the front bedroom where he kept his weight lifting trophies, papers, and memorabilia.

I was surprised walking into the living room because the furniture had been totally rearranged from just four days ago. It reminded me of the days when I was younger living at home that my mother would ask me to help her rearrange the furniture. She used to talk about how I was the only one that would help her with this project and she would laugh and smile. It would make me smile too because it was a happy time for the two of us. But for today, the furniture was strategically placed so that my father could sit in the sofa chair with his back to the picture window while the sofas flanked ahead of him one on his left where my mother sat and one to the right which was place.

Prior to being seated my father emerged from the master bed room with a notepad in his hand. As he took his place I could see that the first page was filled neatly with words. Then the conversation began with, "your mother and I invited you over tonight to talk with you about this gender thing and you telling us you were female. I have prepared myself for this talk and have taken a few notes." He looked down at his pad and said, "First, I want to read you something from the Bible, Romans 1: 24-32." After the reading, I realized that this was not a conversation but a lecture on "deformation of the body was an abomination to God." That it was "sinful of me to live in the flesh" and that "you will be punished for any action of this type. What you need is help from a priest and profession to help you with this gender thing". I listened with the upmost respect because I felt like anything other would set off the fuse. I just listened and was starting to feel bad, I knew this "conversation" was going to be rough and I wanted to explain.

"Now, I want to read to you, 1 Corinthians 6: 12-20". This lecture concerned the biblical quote, "Every sin that a man commits is outside the body, but the immoral man sins against his own body. Or do you not know that the temple of the Holy Spirit, who is in you, whom you have from God, and that you are not your own? For you have been bought at a great price. Glorify God and bear him in your body." I listened again to my dad's interpretation of immorality.

I tried to explain that I am a child of God but there was no listening to me, none. My parents did not hear one word that I spoke and then the questions began, one right after the other and all I could do was to begin to answer each question and then being cut off from by being asked another or made a statement.

"What makes you think you are female"?

"When did you start to feel this way"?

"Why do you feel this way, we have never seen you behave like a girl"?

"What happened to you when you were on that cross country trip with the priests, did they try to mess with you"?

"You were a good Cadet, recipient of the Religion award your junior year".

"You are a man, God made you a man".

"You were good at baseball and played football, you are a man".

"You have three children and married".

"Now, I think you were the problem, not Kathleen".

"You need to pray".

Your brother told us he has experience with this and can help find you a good Doctor to help cure you".

"You are sick".

I did manage to invite my parents to come with me to therapy and discussed who he was and they totally discounted him. I told them I had called the psychiatric hotline and explained my issue and Dr. Bears returned my call. They immediately wanted to know where his office was located and discounted his abilities from the start, without even knowing his credentials.

This Dr. Bears is not good for you, you need a real Doctor".

This line of questioning after the lecture went on for over an hour and the most I could get out was only three words per question if that many. The question were the same only asked in different ways and the words were starting to run together and getting louder and louder in my mind as if I were schizophrenic and it seemed like these words were all around me.

I stood up, "I cannot handle this anymore, I know that I am a child of God and that I was born this way. You will not let me say anything. I have to go".

My father told me, "You cannot ever come back to MY house dressed as a female!"

I walked out, got in my car and was home at 9:45p.m. I talked to Zeb and drank away the physical coldness of the night and of the mind. I cried, cried, and cried out, "No one will ever understand. I have lost my family and it was my last supper".

My house was for sale in Maidens, VA. I hired the same real estate agent to help me find a house in the Richmond Fan District which is just west of downtown. The Fan District is one of many historic areas of the city. I wanted to move closer into town to be near my work and to able to walk to the bars without the risk of the police catching me drinking in my female attire. I felt that it had become too dangerous for me to dress and drink and be so far away from home. Besides, living in the Fan District on Park Avenue where I decided to purchase a home was a very prestigious and progressive neighborhood.

Now divorced, three mortgages, which exceeded my income, I thought that I had arrived. The pressure I felt with this move was immense because I had more on my plate than I could handle. My family had disowned me, and I was doing things that seemingly did not make any sense, just to feel good about myself. All I wanted was to be loved, feel in control and to feel important. Whose business was it anyway if I were a male to female transgendered person?! That is who I was. Like it or not. Zeb and I moved to the Fan District into a beautiful old Victorian house and a short time later my son John came to live with us. That only lasted about six months. John was in the group home in Powhatan County and I brought him home with me every weekend until we both decided it would be fine for him to leave the group home and be in the city where he could ride the bus and be able to move about freely. That did not happen as John

90

found himself and girlfriend and decided to move in with her. His schizophrenia seemed to be in remission however, we continued to go to the doctor together every month for evaluations and care. Unfortunately I had no idea my son was drinking and using drugs during this period and neither did his girlfriend.

I had begun living my life as Kaitlin full time outside of work when I moved to the city. I only dressed as a male for work, which was normally Monday thru Friday from 6:00 a.m. to 6:00 p.m. I came straight home from work and immediately changed into my female attire. Regardless of going anywhere or even to sit on my front porch, I was Kaitlin and I introduced myself as Kaitlin to all my neighbors. I only dressed as a male to go straight to work and straight home; I did not go anywhere else. I would sneak out to the car each morning as "John" and hoped none of the neighbors would see me. This was a total reversal from the time I would sneak out of the house as Kaitlin. I truly was living a double life and it took a lot of work to maintain this lifestyle. It was crazy and very time consuming at times because in order to do anything after work I had to come home first and change my total appearance. Many times I had my therapy sessions after work and had to plan accordingly and rush to change. I would park my car as "John" and sneak back into the house so that Kaitlin could emerge, which made me feel much better. Every day when I would get home from work I would first grab a beer and go upstairs to make the transformation and then back for more beer. I would then go out on the town to drink, have dinner, and see some friends.

Normally on Tuesdays and Saturdays it was Doll's. During the other days of the week it was Joe's Inn or another bar or across the street to the Berry Street Deli or café which sold beer. They all knew me by name and there where many people that knew me but I could not remember who they were or where I had met them. Obviously, I was too smashed to remember. I just know that I would walk Zeb through the city streets and people would come up to me and say, "Hey Kaitlin how are you?" and I would not have a clue as to who they were. I acted as if I knew them and made them feel like a long lost friend. What a talent, I had certainly become a huge people pleaser. I got by on calling these people "sweetie", "dear", "honey", or some other endearing name and acting really happy to see them all. Nevertheless, Kaitlin was alive and well all over the streets of the Fan District!

I found myself in a very bad financial position. I had two homes with three mortgages and I started by paying one mortgage one month and the other mortgage the next. As the year progressed, it all began to catch up with me. It was just like that old adage, "robbing Peter to pay Paul", in a nutshell, that was exactly what I was doing. Unfortunately during all this, I continued to use alcohol to mask my constant pain. It was April of 2006 and I was expecting a phone call from my parents to invite me over for the annual Easter celebration my family had each year. It was much the same as our annual Christmas celebration with ham, mash potatoes, homemade rolls, but instead of gifts, there would be a huge Easter basket full of goodies. However this year, that call did not happen. Nor did I receive a call for the family gatherings on Independence Day, Labor Day, Thanksgiving Day, and Christmas Day. I called my parents on each one of the holidays and wished them a very happy holiday and added that I loved them both very much. However, it always ended with my father telling me I was very sick and needed to get help and then hanging up. Those were always his last words to me, always.

On Easter of 2006 I got really drunk and only remember that I was walking Zeb on Monument Avenue in Richmond and I fell or tripped over one of the cobblestones in the street and hit my head on the cement curb. It was 12:30 a.m. and a very nice gentleman on a bicycle stopped and asked if I was alright. I must have been a sight to him, but I was completely ungracious and shrieked in my most girly voice and I told him to leave me alone. I do not know how long I had been laying in the gutter in my pretty pink Ann Taylor spaghetti strap Easter Dress, I do know that I still held Zeb's leash tightly in my hand and he was standing on the curb making every effort to help me. My cell phone had disappeared and I think it fell down the sewer since it was just a little to my right. I managed to get to my feet, stagger home, and looked in the mirror: my face and forehead were both badly cut and bruised. I just could not get over what had happened; the day of the rejection from my family. I went to sleep and was quite thankful I was off the next day since I awoke with a terrible headache. I went out to my cell phone provider later that afternoon and purchased a new phone, then stopped by Ann's house and called the doctor. I felt very, very ill. Unfortunately I made the decision to drink more until it was time for bed and the following morning I got up for work and felt even worse. The rejection I felt was immense and all-consuming and made me feel worthless.

My face was black and blue and naturally everyone at work was curious. I thought they were basically a bunch of nosy so and so's! I originally thought I'd make up a funny story or a horrific tale of beating back a would be mugger, but then I just felt so defeated and simply stuck with the truth. I explained that I was walking on Easter Sunday night and tripped the cobblestone street while walking my Lab and hit my face on the curb. Of course there were some who questioned that, but it was the truth. When I arrived home from work each day it took a fair amount of makeup to hide the cuts and bruises, but I was not about to go out as Kaitlin, all battered and bruised!

When I went to Doll's on Tuesday nights, I'd meet the other girls normally Teresa, Marti, Ellen and Ivan. I'd suggest starting a support group so that if any of us in our group ever needed help, we could call on each other, no matter what day or time. I added that I thought we should meet at some frequency away from the bar and drinking, especially so we could seriously discuss things we needed like doctors, lawyers, or just overall help with daily living and support for me in the hopes that I would have surgery one day. I talked at length with Michelle Hodges and she was very much in favor and we started to work together to make this happen. I named the group James River

Transgender Society. Michelle talked it up and we met each week to discuss the possibilities. Michelle came across a place called the Free Clinic where she started to volunteer and secured us a place to meet within the clinic. Michelle had made a flyer, distributed it, and asked therapists who work with transgendered people to recommend our group and all agreed. Since transgendered individuals were using the clinic for hormone therapy, she discussed the support group with each person that utilized the clinic for that purpose. I acquired a email list from a well know transgendered "drag queen" and distributed the information of a support group through her listing with her permission.

On the first Friday, August 2006, we held our first meeting of the James River Transgendered Society. I was the President, Michelle was the Vice President, and Ellen was our Secretary. There were 23 people in attendance for our first meeting. Most of whom were transgendered girls, but we did have a few others who joined the meeting as well. One such couple who showed up liked "playing" with children. We immediately explained this was not appropriate at all. We told them their behavior was illegal and that they would not be welcomed in our group if they were practicing pedophiles. Fortunately they never returned because the purpose of our meetings was for individuals who were interested in transitioning from male to female or female to male. We found out that a female to male group already existed in Richmond. So we primarily took on the male to female aspect of transitioning. We had endocrinologist, lawyers, electrolysis, female feminization women, therapist all attend our meeting to discuss and provide information concerning transitioning. One early topic was the nature of hormones and what it took to make the complete transition from male to female.

Robyn, who I met at our first meeting, discussed hormones therapy and the doctor she was seeing in Richmond. This was extremely valuable information not only for me, but for all in attendance. I found the information so valuable that I made an appointment with this endocrinologist immediately. His manner was wonderful. He was very understanding, and when I first met him he looked me over and discussed the importance of my ensuring my shoes, belt, and purse match, it was great. We discussed all my feelings, especially why I felt the need to transition. He started me out on low dose of estrogen and spirolactone, which is a testosterone blocker. He explained my need to raise the level of estrogen in my body and subsequently, lower the testosterone levels to be within the range of a genetic female. He added that this process would take a considerable amount of time, meaning it would not be an overnight process. Over time, he would increase the estrogen after taking blood and checking the hormone levels. He stated that once I underwent surgery, I could stop taking spirolactone. He directed me to take one aspirin with this medication to assist with any possibility of heart issues. I started hormone therapy in September of 2006 and as time progressed, he increased the estrogen intake until my levels were within the range of a female.

In the beginning our support group struggled over structure and individual power. It was amazing as we held elections for a variety of positions. Some of the girls who were involved early on in the development of the group were hurt when they were not elected, and they ran off referring to me as a bitch. Some even attempted to form another transgendered group in Richmond. A few did leave and held their own meetings, but JRTS survived and our meetings averaged attendance was about 25 transgendered individuals each month. On some occasions parents would attend to learn more about their child. It was very remarkable to have all this information gathered in one place. The group held an annual picnic in the summer and even a Christmas party. The core group remained intact, and works closely with the newcomers to ensure they understand what the group is all about and all the services available within the group and the community. To date, there have been seven of us that have had gender confirmation surgery from the group.

I was very much involved with planning and organizing JRTS during this period. On a regular basis, I would conduct meetings with various members of the group to try and organize by-laws and rules. A web site was developed by Kathy who opened up a whole new realm of contacts and the group was growing quickly. Members came from the mountains of Virginia, Northern Virginia, Virginia Beach, and northern North Carolina, and it was awesome to see the interest and synergy of this group. It took on a life of its own and the group is still growing today. Thanksgiving had come and gone and I now had a new family of friends.

Christmas of 2006 arrived and there were no plans except to stay at home and play with Zeb. I had purchased a pair of slippers and a beautiful brand new outfit for myself. There was no big family Christmas invitation, no family visits, no calls from my family, with the exception of my three children. We spoke briefly and I told them I was doing great when in reality I was dying inside, but I did not want to lay that on them. Zeb and I walked around the city and played with his new tennis balls. I walked two and a half blocks over to Joe's Inn, had a hamburger and a couple pitchers of beer. I talked with the bartender and other regulars about having a nice Christmas. It was my release, a means by which to eliminate my real pain of being ostracized by my family, the people whom I loved most in this world and who I thought loved me.

As I started back to the house, I stopped off at the Berry Street Deli to purchase more beer for the remainder of the day. Once home it was out the front door to walk Zeb through the neighborhood and into the cold late afternoon air. It was winter in Virginia and the sun sets early around 5:00 p.m. and we watched the street lights come on as the dusk settled into night. I had begun to feel sorry for myself as I watched families gathered together, laughing and enjoying themselves, through the windows of these old Victorian homes. I was in full "pity-party" mode when I asked Zeb what was wrong with my family that I could not come over or see them or even talk with them? I was the same person that I have always been. I was still the same loving person with the same capacity to give and receive love from my parents and siblings. Why did this have to be this way? Poor Zeb just looked at me with his soulful brown eyes, leaned in and licked my hand. I swear this creature was more than "just a dog"; he sincerely seemed to know what I was feeling and tried his best to make me feel loved and wanted when everyone in my life had abandoned me. No wonder Dog spelled backwards, is God ...

When our walk was over I sat down at the dining room table looking out the window. I sat and listened to the happy and joyous cheers coming from the passing cars and people walking down the sidewalks. I sat for hours and wrote, cried, and sat in a big pile of self-pity. I drank beer until it was time for bed and even took my drink to bed with me. Thankfully with all the drinking I was doing, I was on vacation during the Christmas week, and remained on vacation until after the New Year.

Chapter 7– Reflections in Tucson

During this time I decided to arrange another retreat with Sister from New Orleans. Sister had relocated to Tucson because Hurricane Katrina had destroyed not only her home in the 9th Ward of New Orleans, but the Catholic Church she was affiliated with as well. The devastation of her home was very disheartening; the water had flooded all the way to the second story of her home. The pictures Sister had sent me of the discoloration and water lines on the walls broke my heart. This was a place of great serenity and peace. A place I had come and made the realization that God loved me and I would not burn in the fires of hell for being transgendered. The retreat was a lifesaving experience and Sister's space was a "life-giving" place. I felt my life had been renewed after spending time with Sister and being on that retreat.

I returned to work in January of 2007 and rearranged my vacation schedule for the year to include a week in February. Since I had five weeks of vacation accumulated, it was very manageable to take a week off, especially in February. I immediately made all the arrangements for Zeb's care and adjusted my work to allow for my vacation retreat. I made my flight reservations in my required legal "male" name from Reagan National Airport to Tucson, AZ, which required a connection flight from Phoenix.

February of 2007 arrived in the blink of an eye and it was time to drive from Richmond to Arlington. I had my bags, tickets, and identification. I parked in the long-term US Air terminal parking lot and walked inside the airport terminal. However, for the first time, I dressed as my true self and appeared to those in the airport as Kaitlin. I waited in line at the ticket counter for about 30 minutes before I finally reached the counter and I had to use a credit card to retrieve my ticket. I got a "No Ticket Found" message three times, and thought I was in for a lot of trouble and the airport security was going to take me away and ask all kinds of unhealthy questions in a hot dark room. Finally, one of the attendants stepped over to help me and tried the same credit card with the same results. She stated she did not know what was wrong so I took my card back and went to the back of the line because I did not want to attract a great deal of attention to myself. I was flabbergasted and did not know what to expect. I waited in line for a few more minutes and noticed that there was another US Air counter about 30 feet to my left with fewer people in line. So I went to that line and asked the attendant for help. She explained that I was in the right place for planes leaving to Phoenix. We inserted my credit card and out popped my tickets to Phoenix and Tucson and I checked my bags. I was relieved for only a few moments; I turned away from the counter area only to see the line for the Homeland Security check point.

I could not see the end of the line down a very long and narrow corridor that had only white walls, blue carpet, and cones with black plastic material that guided you around the corner. I was very apprehensive as I waited in line for the TSA Homeland Security Officer to check my ticket and identification. I was shaking in my high heel boots, brown jeans and matching leopard print top. I wore a short wig that matched my hair color perfectly and since I had been growing my hair it blended very nicely. My face was smooth and made up to perfection from all the years of practice and patience.

Once around the corner there was the TSA Officer checking identification on a lecture podium stand. He was a white male in his mid-thirties and was guarded by another white male in his mid-forties. I was very tense and tried not to show any emotion. I was next and he was calling for me. I presented my ticket and State of Virginia drivers license. He looked at me, the ticket, and the license, me, the license. He said, "Are you John" and I said yes. He looked at the license and he looked at me again and said, ok have a good flight. I felt this enormous smile come over my face as I gathered my carry-on bag, ticket, and driver's license and sashayed toward the plane!

My next obstacle was the gentleman with his metal detectors. He was a black male, big and strong looking in his fifties. I took off anything that looked like metal and placed it in the plastic containers provided. I handed over my ticket and he told me to take off my boots which I did without hesitation and confidently walked through the detector without incident. Being pre-op transgendered I did not know what to expect but I was very pleased to have successfully gone through this check-in process.

I had to go to the bathroom really bad by this time and found the first women's bathroom while walking down to the gate. As I was walking I was wondered what would happen if they find out I still had male genitals. I wondered if I would be arrested if I utilized the ladies room. I conducted myself very properly taking care of my business and checking my face in the mirror. I walked to the gate and stopped to get a cup of coffee. I sat down and waited to board for a little over an hour and allowed for my inside emotions to catch up with my outside appearance.

Finally it was time to board and my seat was near the back next to the window; two ladies a few moments later joined me in my row. We said hello and did not speak for the first two hours in flight. Eventually, we did talk which made me feel more at ease. The woman next to me said she had just attended a teacher's convention in Washington D.C. and lived in Phoenix. Although we were a little late on our arrival in Phoenix, it was a nice flight nonetheless.

Since I was near the back of the huge plane which was full to capacity, it seemed as though it took forever to deplane. I finally disembarked from the plane which was at Gate B and quickly learned my connecting flight to Tucson was over at Gate A. I rushed down the corridor at Sky Harbor Airport to that gate and I could see my plane was already being backed up off the tarmac and getting ready for departure. There was a woman in her late seventies who was on the flight with me in the same predicament. We both looked in amazement at the customer service representative behind the counter when she said we just missed the flight by a couple of minutes. She offered no assistance whatsoever accept to tell us to walk back down the corridor to customer service and try to get tickets for the next flight. I spoke with the elderly lady as we walked down the corridor and discovered she was from Santa Anna, CA. By this time, she was in a bit of a tizzy, and truth be told, so was I! I felt very nervous because this delay was now going to cause me to have to interact with more people one-on-one, and I certainly was not prepared for that at all! All I could think about was my identification not matching my outside appearance and then I continued to fear what others would think of me.

I called Sister and told her what had happened and explained that I would let her know when I would arrive in Tucson. I told her my bags where on the flight which just left the terminal. I really did not know what to do so I went outside of the terminal and smoked a cigarette; I was beginning to feel that old panic mode come on. Outside I saw the rental car shuttle buses and thought about driving from Phoenix to Tucson, which is only about 100 miles. I puffed away on my cigarette and decided this would be my course of action because I would not have to risk going back through TSA security and explain myself all over. I stomped out my cigarette, went over to the US Air counter and sarcastically thanked them for causing my problem.

I flagged down the next shuttle bus to the car rental area at Sky Harbor and walked into the Avis Rent a Car building where I found a line of people waiting to rent vehicles. I waited patiently and thought about what I was going to say to the service representative. When my turn came I confidently walked up to the window and told the agent, that I needed to rent a car to the Tucson Airport. I explained right away that my name is Kaitlin, but my identification reads my male name, with the sex as male. I added that I worked for Philip Morris and I had used this company for my rental car needs when on business trips. He looked at me without even batting and eye and simply said "ok." Naturally his accepting attitude stunned me because I had braced myself for at least some sort of harassment. His positive attitude was a welcome relief to say the least. I rented the car in my legal name and paid $129 to drive to Tucson. I called Sister and told her I had rented a car and was driving to Tucson and would meet her at the airport in a couple of hours. She provided me with directions and told me to call her when I was almost there. It was still light outside when I found my way onto Interstate 10 and headed southeast to find her. I called Sister twice, once when I was 30 miles from the city and again when I got lost while trying to find the airport. Luckily for me Sister was very good at giving directions because she was able to guide me right into the airport via cell phone.

I finally made it to the airport after two and a half hours, dropped off the car at the Tucson Airport Avis rental center and walked into the terminal. The airport was small compared to Reagan National and Sky Harbor and I saw Sister walking down the corridor in the terminal. We greeted each other warmly, hugged, and she told me I looked very nice which was very comforting to me. We went together to the US Air baggage claim office and found my luggage waiting on me. My fear and anxiety had now subsided since I had now made it from Richmond, VA to Tucson, AZ and found Sister. I discussed my ordeals and the joy of making it without any real incident.

She drove me to her home in South Tucson off of Starr Pass Road and I got to see both the city and the desert once again. When I was 15 years old I took a three week cross-country trip, traveling in a station wagon with two Catholic priests and another boy who was 16 years old. We traveled from Richmond and stayed three weeks in Colorado, New Mexico, and Arizona. This was my first time back to this area in thirty-five years and I loved seeing the saguaros. When we arrived at Sister's home, it was beautiful, built in the Spanish tradition. As I walked through the gate onto the open back porch, I could feel the serenity of this place. There was a wall around the property and another wall around the backyard which separated it from the circular driveway. In the center of the circle drive was a statue of the Blessed Virgin Mary.

We entered the house from the back door which opened up to the family room. It was sparsely furnished, with just a sofa, chair, and a television. To the right was a sitting area with a sofa and chair and through a set of French doors was Sister's office and a small private side room. I could see the entrance to the kitchen and foyer and I inquired about the chapel. Sister directed me down the foyer, to the left, and when I found it, I thought it was very beautiful. There were three chairs, a small table, a bookcase, and the crucifix stood in the corner on a stand, surrounded by colorful material that made it the center point of the room. I went in and immediately thanked God for a safe trip to Tucson. Sister then showed me to my bedroom and bathroom. The kitchen had a skylight and was very neatly kept and naturally everything was in its place. Toward the front of the house was the dining area and from there was the master bedroom. The floors were square tile and only the bedrooms were carpeted. I loved Sister's home and felt it was immaculate!

We made sandwiches, sat down, ate and discussed our plans, goals, and objectives of this retreat. Before I left I had made an appointment with Dr. Toby Meltzer in Scottsdale, AZ for a consultation concerning sex reassignment surgery and that was to take place in two days. Sister knew about this appointment prior to my arrival and planned to accompany me, so we discussed the logistics of this trip. I spent time in the chapel with prayer and meditation for the remainder of the evening and then retired to my room and peacefully drifted off to sleep.

I experienced a very restful sleep during the night and awoke around 7:00 a.m., which was actually 10:00 a.m. on the east coast. By the time I woke up, had coffee, visited the chapel, and dressed, Sister was returning from Mass. I had on an Ann Taylor short skirt and matching top and as she walked into the back door I quickly quipped, "Yes, I know, all us trannies like to wear short skirts"! Sister shook her head, rolled her eyes. I wouldn't bet money on it but I think she did get a kick out of my remark. I mean the skirt was not that short, but it was not Catholic school appropriate either because it was certainly above the knees.

We both went about our day which consisted of prayer and meditation, and afterwards we discussed issues. I spent several hours in meditation primarily centered on our discussions, which were my feelings about transitioning from male to female. I had come on this retreat to get reconnected with my Higher Power and to pray and be absolutely sure this was the right path for me.

I discussed my feelings at length with Sister. I explained how I understood this would be a life-changing event for me of the greatest magnitude, but one that was the right thing for me and something I needed to live correctly for the remainder of my life. I spoke with her about the conversations I had with my parents and siblings and described the pain that ensued from their rejection. I felt as though I had no family and it saddened me, and I believe, drove me deeper into my beer bottle. Sister offered that my family may well have not been emotionally, mentally, or even intellectually equipped to handle such news. As I looked at it from Sister's perspective, I thought what she said made a lot of sense to me and helped me understand my family's abandonment of me. It made it slightly more tolerable, but still very hurtful and of course still unforgiveable. We discussed the need for the transgendered community, in many cases, to create their own family, in essence, to take care of one another. Although not biological, the community needed to act as a family in order to help each other. After our discussion that evening, I remained hopeful that one day my family would try to understand and become supportive of me and my decision to transition and live my life in truth.

Outwardly I appeared to be a normal white male, but I was actually a female living in a white man's world. My transition would place me into a minority category. As I transgendered from a male to female person, it took me out of having any so-called "status". Therefore, in the real socio-economic world, my status in society would go from very favorable to virtually non-existent. I would be the same person, but with a completely different status in a blink of an eye. I realized what this change would encompass, but still realized deep in my soul I had to lead the life and be the person I was truly born internally. This would be the only way for me to have inner peace, outward happiness and complete balance in my life. I prayed and meditated concerning all of these issues and knew that it was the correct course of action and I understood the risk of losing everything I had worked so hard to achieve. Regardless, I knew that no one could ever take away my education, experiences, hope, and courage of being me.

The next morning I dressed in a pair of nice pants and a blouse and attended Mass with Sister. She introduced me to many of the parishioners who attended daily Mass and each one was very open and welcoming. This Mass was more traditional in nature and the message was about love, kindness, and acceptance. I was extremely overjoyed to have a sermon not based in fear, but only in peace and love and in a very lovely setting to boot. The church was relatively small and seated approximately 350 people. It had oak pews with padded kneelers and nice burgundy colored carpeted floors. After Mass I was introduced to more parishioners and the parish Priest. It was a very nice Mass and I felt able to get connected with my Higher Power.

After Mass, Sister and I returned to her home and together, prepared our meals, ate, and washed and dried the dishes. Sister gave me an assignment and we continued our discussion concerning my transition, my family relationship, transitioning on the job, and all the aspects of the surgery. Prayer and meditation in the chapel continued to be a must for me because it was a very quiet, safe place where I felt I could become connected with myself. We talked about the time-frame for my surgery and about Dr. Meltzer performing the surgery. I told her that I had done my research and found that Dr. Meltzer was known as the best surgeon in the country for sexual reassignment surgery. I further explained that the facility was very nice and was only 100 miles from Tucson. This close proximity would enable her the opportunity to come visit during the two week process of surgery and recovery. Sister thought about this and voiced that she thought the idea was a good one. Before I could even have the surgery scheduled, I still needed to live full time as a female, which meant that I had to transition on the job with Phillip Morris, USA. I prayed and meditated about the job transition and asked my Higher Power for assistance because I knew that I could lose my job. The prospect of the loss of my job sent my mind whirling, from worrying about becoming jobless and then becoming broke, then to becoming homeless! Sister eased my fears by informing me that she had had retreats in New Orleans and even here in Arizona with women who successfully transitioned on the job and all were doing well. This helped me, but I worked in a traditional conservative tobacco company in the "Capital of the Confederacy" no less, and the outcome really scared the dickens out of me! However, this was a prerequisite for surgery and had to be done just to qualify for surgery. I had been working with a therapist in Richmond and felt as though one of the two letters of recommendation required for surgery could be obtained from him, along with the one year, of "real life" experience. In order to have surgery one must follow the Standards of Care which is an internationally accepted protocol of treatment for those diagnosed with Gender Dysphoria by the Harry Benjamin International Gender Dysphoria Association. This included the real life test of living full time 24/7/365 in the person's new gender role and two letters of recommendation from two qualified therapists that specialize in the area of gender identity.

Sister and I discussed my real life test at length and further discussed how I had already had been living for the past year as a female outside of work. I shared my realization that living a double life had been very difficult for me: I sneaked into work as a male and then would sneak home as the real me, a female. I felt like I needed to approach my employer with grave caution, expect the worse, and if anything better happened then I surely would be blessed. I decided then and there I was going to "out" myself at work, in the very near future. I continued to meditate about transitioning on my job and continued to pray and seek

106

continued guidance with my Higher Power so that I would understand how all this would be made possible. While it all remained very scary, it was soon to become, through the help of God, my reality.

The next morning I visited the chapel and sister and I made breakfast while we discussed our trip to Scottsdale. My appointment was at 11:00 am with Dr. Meltzer, so we needed to be on the road no later than 8:00 am. We filled the tank with gas in Tucson and headed out for Scottsdale. I could barely contain my excitement as I looked out at the desert and mountains and noted how very beautiful they were in February. I gazed at the shadows left by the sun and noted the sun is much brighter here than on the east coast. Sister and I made easy conversation on our drive, and chatted about my doctor's appointment in anticipation of my life-changing event. Scottsdale is a very plush city and has very beautiful, well-kept, green palm and fichus trees, flowers and perfectly trimmed shrubs. Everything looked so new and clean in my eyes; definitely a great place for rebirth.

Dr. Meltzer's office and waiting rooms were astonishing! The floors were tile, caramel and white in color, and absolutely pristine. They were just that clean. The receptionist sat behind a black marble countertop encased in a wooden frame. The waiting room was decorated to perfection with black leather sofas and chairs, and accented with flawlessly placed black and silver glass top coffee and end tables. I had never experienced a waiting room so classy and sophisticated. The bathroom was equally as nice and the stalls were "showroom" clean. The same tile floors and black marble countertops adorned the bathroom. Beautiful silver faucets towered over the sinks. Towels for hand drying, while made of the finest paper, had the feel of linen. The towels were so nice, I felt as though I could have easily used it for a handkerchief; in fact, they were so nice I did not want to throw it away. The women who worked in the office were very nice, beautiful and at least half of them were transgendered; many were former patients as well.

I felt anxious as I waited to meet Dr. Meltzer because he was both world renown for his sex reassignment surgery, and he was the one who would make the decision on whether to perform the surgery. It was very exciting for me to be in his office and I was joyous with anticipation.

After what seemed like an eternity, one of Dr. Meltzer's nurses called me back into one of the examining rooms. She instructed me to get undressed from the waist down and put on a gown, with the opening facing towards the front of course. In less than five minutes, Dr. Meltzer and a nurse, who appeared to be transgendered, entered the room. He immediately began asking questions about my background and I first explained that I have felt this way my entire life, then went on to express all the reasons I felt this was the right course of action to complete me, the woman I truly was on the inside. He began his physical examination of my body and explained the surgery to me in terms that I could understand. He said that with his technique he could probably get about five inches of depth from vaginoplasty surgery. We discussed my current status with the Harry Benjamin Standards of Care and I told him about my therapist in Richmond. He told me that he would do the surgery provided I follow the Standards of Care which meant living full time as a female for one year and he needed at least two letters of recommendation from a qualified therapist. He was very encouraging and I told him that it was my plan to go back to Virginia and start my real life test as soon as possible. After he completed his examination, he had me go to his business office to complete the preliminary paperwork required for the surgery. The nurse instructed me to keep Dr. Meltzer's staff informed regarding my progress in accordance with the Standards of Care. I paid the $100 consultation fee and felt elated as I walked back into the waiting room where Sister sat patiently waiting. The first thing I told Sister as we walked out of the office was Dr. Meltzer said "he will do my surgery." Nothing else mattered at that moment in my life, and I was filled with hope and joy! Sister and I went off for a celebratory luncheon in Scottsdale. I was on Cloud 9 and noticed all the beauty all around me for the very first time! I was finally going to be free of this "birth defect" and free to be me. I it was truly a magical moment.

Sister and I hopped into the Ford as we went off into Scottsdale. We stopped at a beautiful restaurant and had a well-deserved lunch. We discussed the ride from Tucson, the appointment, and the gorgeous countryside. It was a beautiful sunny, yet cool February day in the Phoenix area with a slightly brisk wind. Tumbleweed blew in the bright sunshine as we made our way back on the Interstate and headed southeast to Tucson. We had a wonderful trip to Phoenix/Scottsdale and we marveled in our joy. About 40 miles into our ride, we were in the right-hand lane and we actually drove the legal speed limit of 75, when all of a sudden a piece of cast iron wheel approximately six inches in diameter flew up from a big semi several car lengths in front of us, then continued to fly to the car directly in front of us. We saw the piece of cast iron cylinder bounce and go under the car in front of us and back up again, and then hit the top of the passenger's side of our car! It came right at me and I ducked as it hit the top of the windshield and shattered the glass. Sister told me a week later that the repair man said if it had hit a half inch lower it would have killed the passenger in the car — me! I remembered seeing it hit and as it came towards me, I reacted to save my life. This reaction was a far cry from where I was emotionally and mentally only a year and a half ago when I wanted to take my own life. I felt great about myself; clearly I wanted to live again. I now had new found hope for my future!

When we arrived at Sister's home we were both a little rattled but the automobile accident did not dampen our spirits or our accomplishments one iota. I went into the house, put away my coat and immediately went into the chapel and gave thanks to my Higher Power for getting us home safely and for such a positive appointment with Dr. Meltzer. We made dinner together and planned for our final session of the retreat.

During our last meeting of the retreat sister and I discussed my surgery, my family, JRTS, rejection, aspects of change, job transition, attending Mass and the loving power of God. We discussed my flight arrangements back to Washington, DC and the drive to Richmond. My flight was from Tucson to Phoenix and then to DC. Flying back east meant that I would lose 3 hours of the day so the six hour flight was really nine hours of daylight. I was scheduled to leave around 9:00 a.m. so we planned to get to the airport by 7:30 a.m. I went back in the chapel to quietly meditate before I retired for the evening.

The next morning we were up early around 5:30 a.m. and I prepared myself for the trek back east. I wore the same outfit I traveled west in and made sure that I looked presentable. Sister and I sat down to breakfast and I told her I found her to be the most wonderful and amazing person, and I thanked her whole heartedly for all of her assistance. She was truly a blessing and helped me understand how loved I was which really made me feel it. My last 30 minutes in her home was spent in the chapel, in prayer and meditation. This was a place where I could feel connected with my Higher Power. Sister drove me to the airport, dropped me off in front of the airline entrance, and we said goodbye. It was sad for me to leave but I felt I took a true gift with me. I thought it was nice to be able to attend these two retreats with such a loving person that had a great grasp on life both spiritually and in the physical world. I knew it was time for me to begin another phase of my life and I felt one step closer to becoming the real me, the true me I was born to be. I also felt one step closer toward the start of my physical transition.

I arrive back at the ticket counter again and felt a wave of anxiety wash over me as I cautiously watched everything and hoped no one would burst out and say, "Hey look at that man in drag!" And subsequently riotously erupt into laughter or worse do something crazy, like throw something, spit at me, or attempt to beat me up! I approached the attendant, checked my bags, presented my male identification, and she handed me my ticket without incident. I was amazed that no problems occurred through the ticketing process. I walked through the corridor and up the ramp to a TSA officer who sat on a stool checking tickets and identification. He was a white male, slightly on the heavy side, and approximately in his late fifties. I handed him my ticket and my identification and he said with a big warm smile, "I never would have known without your ID". He told me to have a good day and safe trip and I wished him the same. Further down the corridor was the TSA officer who reviewed every ticket and ID with a fine tooth comb. He checked me out without even a single question. I proceeded swiftly through the metal detectors and off to the boarding gate. I was amazed at how nervous and cautious I became when in these types of situations. I just don't want to be ridiculed or have anything terrible happen because of who I am and my need to live my life peacefully as myself.

The flight to Phoenix did not last very long as we went straight up and came straight down. I had never been on a big plane that flew such a short distance and it was like a ride at Bush Gardens in Williamsburg. Once inside the Phoenix Sky Harbor I found my connecting flight and it was on time. I had a quick chance to use the ladies room, and made sure to use extreme caution and mind my own business. This was the part of the trip that scared me because I was still physically male and here I was in a "ladies" restroom dressed as a female but being myself. I imaged the morning newspapers if I were caught: "Male Pervert Caught in Dress in Women's Bathroom at Sky Harbor." I wondered if I would serve time for being me, so I made sure not to make eye contact and took care of and exited as quickly as possible. I boarded my plane for Washington, DC and really did not speak with anyone, but I felt the same peace and serenity that I had when I left New Orleans a year and a half earlier after my first retreat with Sister.

As the plane landed at Reagan National in the late afternoon I could see the Washington Monument across the Potomac River. It was a beautiful sight and I was very thankful to be back down and on the ground. I liked to fly but it scared me because it took away all my control and it was such a long way down. It took me about an hour to pick up my baggage and find my car. I literally walked all around the parking deck looking for my car.

The weather in DC was slightly overcast and rain showers were moving in. It was cold but not quite cold enough to snow; it was that in-between type weather. As I finally found my Toyota Camry SE, I began to realize that I just flew across country and back as a female and I did not have one problem. My anxiety and fear was far worse than the whole event. The drive down the I-395 was swift, but once on I-95 it was growling with stop and go traffic for the next 50 miles into Fredericksburg, which was typical DC traffic at 4:30 p.m. The sky darkened as I traveled the last 40 miles into Richmond and I could not wait to see Zeb. The trip was long and I began to think about how to approach Philip Morris with my public transition. I knew to be successful, my plan had to be rock solid and fail proof! I finally arrived home and my faithful and devoted Lab, Zeb, stood at the front door waiting for me. He was certainly a welcomed sight and I immediately gave him a big hug. I love Zeb with all my heart. He has always been there for me no matter what. I grabbed two beers and he and I headed out the front door to go for a walk. I thought it was quite interesting that the entire five days I was away I had not had any alcohol whatsoever and did not think about it or crave it at all. At that moment I thought I must not have am alcohol problem since I was able to go five days without drinking. Anyway, those thought quickly left my mind and returned to my walk with Zeb. Zeb and I finished our walk and I returned to the refrigerator for another beer. The reality of having to out myself at work was starting to take effect and my good 'ol friend "Mr. Budweiser" was going to help me make it through the night.

Chapter 8- Back to Work

The Monday morning arrived and I woke up promptly at 6:00 a.m. and prepared myself for work. I made coffee, picked the newspaper off the front porch, and threw a ball to Zeb in the backyard while I drank my coffee and read the newspaper. Zeb played with the ball while I continued to drink more coffee and scan the newspaper. Just before I left for work Zeb and I walked through Scuffletown Park, which was directly behind my house. Zeb knew the routine and prepared himself for an all- day stay inside, while I was at work. I always gave Zeb a big hug, told him to guard the house, and assured him that I would be back soon. In my heart I knew he understood as I turned and locked the door behind me every day.

I drove the three miles through the Fan District and down Belvedere Street to Maury Street where my office at the Blended Leaf Plant of Philip Morris was located. I thought during the drive and as I walked into the front door what it was going to be like when I approached the company about being transgendered and transitioning on the job. I took a really close look around to capture a picture in my mind to remember what the place looked like in the event of me being terminated. I felt like my days were numbered because I would soon announce my move to transition.

In order to have surgery, it is required to live full time in the gender that one will transition. Although, I lived my life outside of work as a female this did not meet the qualifications for surgery. I had to transition full time, and that meant on the job as well. I understood this was not going to be easy, not just for myself, but for my colleagues at work as well. However, I had grown quite weary of living a lie and felt the preservation of my sanity was more necessary that assuaging the feelings of people at my place of employment. I opened the door to my private office and sat down on my black leather chair at my large mahogany desk. The desk had a full credenza completely surrounding the right hand side and behind, across from where I sat was a mahogany book case. I opened my laptop, powered it up, and got started for the day. After I finished my normal routine of checking emails, I went upstairs for a cup of coffee and toured the production floor and spoke with all the employees with whom I came in contact. I loved the employees and felt that they loved me. I really enjoyed talking and listening to them and I offered advice on a wide array of topics. Mostly, the conversations were about the process and production, the day to day issues and problems they had with people, policies, and equipment.

I had been promoted a year earlier from an Area Leader in production on shift three to Principal Supervisor, which was a grade higher, to work hands on with employee's and develop teams. I attended the Lean Learning Center in Novi Michigan six months earlier and had been educating the workforce on Lean Manufacturing tools. We divided up the areas in the Plant and formed Business Units and worked with each unit in identifying and solving safety, quality, productivity, and cost issues while we guided each employee in the art of the independent decisions making process.

I conducted monthly training sessions with all plant employees on all three shifts. These training sessions included elimination of waste and implementation of the plant's 5S program, and tasks related to the plant's PDCA (plan, do, check, act) program. I was the leader of the Yield Team in the plant, with the responsibility to calculate yield loss problems in manufacturing when yield fell 7% over the course of 6 months. We utilized PDCA and identified the problem and quickly returned the plant to operating proficiency. At that time, the time when I was ready to announce my transition, I discovered a major issue effecting plant operation. I quickly discovered the problem was equipment issues, and raised the yield back to 106 %. This was a monumental endeavor as the problem was deeply hidden, but with persistence in development and listening to the workforce we figured out the problem together. This is what my job con-

114

sisted of and it was very important to the organization in lowering costs and gaining ownership from each employee. When I obtained my performance reviews during that timeframe, I was praised for my interpersonal relationship skills, my ability to organize, and for my ability to lead and change the mindset of the employees. Over the course of twenty-four years, I had consistently maintained a meets or exceeds performance rating each year.

After work, I sneaked back home and changed back to be the "real me," Kaitlin. I was always so relieved when I could leave work and not for the reasons everyone else was glad to be off that's for sure! I would always go straight home, take a beer from the refrigerator, let Zeb out back and change immediately. Kaitlin would emerge down the steps and into the back yard to play ball with Zeb. On many occasions I would have appointments after work with my psychiatrist, dentist, doctor, or just perhaps I just had to run an errand, but I always came home first and changed from male to female. It was very time consuming, but I never went anywhere after work until I had changed my identity to the correct gender. My comfort level with myself increased immensely the moment I came home and became me again.

After I played with Zeb and ran my errands, I sat on the front or back porch, drank my beer, and thought about the difficulties I would face with transitioning. I wondered how I could possibly make people understand me. I thought about my family every single day. All I wanted was for them to love and accept me. I could not understand why I was not allowed back into my parent's home as Kaitlin, my true self, or why my brothers and sisters would not speak with me. Eventually Ann and David would come around on a very limited basis, but their children were not allowed to interact with me at all. I felt like my family thought if they supported me then they would catch some sort of "transgendered" disease. I become obsessed with the fact that my family did not love me. I wanted my family to see the same person and I wanted to maintain my status and position in the family. I drank more and more, and blamed my increased drinking on this issue. I still enjoyed drinking and thought it was still a lot of fun with only a few problems at this point, plus it helped me maintain my sanity throughout the evening. I often walked down to Joe's Inn, had dinner, ordered a pitcher of beer to go along with my meal, and talked with whoever would listen. I made a lot of acquaintances in the restaurant-bar and many people knew me. I had gotten to the point where I only recognized faces and forgot their names. It was all about me and how ridiculous it was the way my family was treating me. Their own flesh and blood was disowned forever.

My support came from the members of James River Transgendered Society, the group I started and was President and the girls in Doll's. It was to the point that I sort of took ownership of Doll's in my mind, I was a regular and everyone knew me there by name. I became dependent on JRTS and partied in Doll's every Tuesday, Friday, and Saturday nights. I arrived at the bar at 6:00 p.m., had dinner and drank until 2:00 a.m. On Friday and Saturday nights I went to an afterhour's club that stayed open until 7:00 a.m. I walked home and stopped at the local diner for breakfast before going to bed. I slept until 1:00 p.m. or 2:00 p.m. and got up just to do it all over again the next day. Now I did come home between going from one bar to the next to take Zeb for a walk so that he would not be in the house more than 6 or 7 hours at a time. I had to take care of Zeb, he was my best friend and I loved him so very much. He seemed to be the only "person" that understood me and actually stayed by my side through my self-pity and the transition. While I know Zeb is a dog, I have grown to think of him as a human. He has been more of a "human" to me than practically anyone on this earth.

Philip Morris provided an escape for me because I was totally into my job, regardless of my gender. It was very rewarding for me to develop and watch people grow. My office was often a place where individuals would come to vent or discuss their own personal or company situations. It was a wonderful

116

feeling to help another person. From time to time I often wondered if these people would be there for me in my time of need. I knew the time was soon coming and it was always in the forefront of my mind.

I was a member of the Plant Leadership Team which set guidelines, policies, programs, and the budget for the Blended Leaf Plant. I had a high level of understanding about the process and the union employees that worked within. Also, I worked as part of a companywide team that established guidelines for measuring team development and I was one of three employees that audited the six manufacturing facilities and their teams. Because of this position, I traveled to Concord, NC, Williamsburg and Chester, VA from Richmond and audited teams and reported to the Senior VP of Manufacturing the status of each plant. I was a highly visible, high profile employee. I knew a tremendous number of employees after working for more than twenty years in all the plants. I understood that when I came out as a female everyone would know which, was more than 5000 people. I prayed for a positive impact, and hoped not to be terminated. The thought of termination was forefront on my mind every day, especially as I knew the law in Virginia allowed one to be fired for being transgendered. I also read many stories about people throughout the United States who had been fired or badly mistreated when they came out.

Chapter 9 – Key West, Florida

In April 2007, Diane and I took a vacation together to Key West, FL. Diane worked for Philip Morris and we had been planning the trip for six months, so I drove from Richmond to Concord, NC and stayed at Diane's house overnight. She has a lovely home in Concord, a white two story Georgian style house, which overlooks a beautiful pond. The front porch extends the entire length of the house and it's wonderful to sit and visit with such a beautiful view.

We were divorced by this time but remained very best friends. We discussed transitioning with Philip Morris and we shared the same fears about my being fired and losing everything. But we also laughed and reminisced about the past and our long friendship. However, she did not want me to fly to Key West as a female. I told her that I needed to and had to be myself. I was upset and retreated to the guest bedroom for the remainder of the evening.

The next morning we woke up early and I emerged from the bedroom as my female self, loaded our bags in the car and we left for Charlotte-Douglas International airport. We parked my Toyota Camry SE in long term parking and rode the shuttle to the terminal. Diane again complained to me about flying as a female. She was afraid, I think, of my being ridiculed and herself being embarrassed. We waited in line at the US Air ticket counter and finally made our way to the agent. I handed over my driver's license which still read John/male to retrieve my boarding pass and check my luggage. The female agent came out from behind the counter and pulled me to the side.

She told me, "I have a friend who is struggling with gender identity issues. Can you please talk with her?"

I gave the agent my cell phone number and told her," I would be glad to talk with her."

"Thank you so much, she would really appreciate it and so do I." The agent then hurried back behind the counter and said, "Have a safe trip." I smiled and waved goodbye.

Diane was somewhat amazed because there is some fear involved with traveling with a pre-op transgendered female with male identification. I was sure that it did not help that I too was in fear of being singled out, although I desperately tried to show that I was fearless.

My anxiety level tripled as we approached the TSA security checkpoint and the older man looked at my license, boarding pass, and information. He looked at me like now "I have seen it all look" and gave me back my papers. He flipped his hand in what I perceived as disgust and told me to "go on". My anxiety level was high as we walked through the terminal and over to the gate for our flight to Ft Lauderdale. I have never looked people in the eye when traveling in this manner because of the fear of being read as a male and I never wanted to cause any sort of disturbance. Patiently, we talked and waited for the time to board and found our seats which for me, were always next to the window. The flight from Charlotte to Ft. Lauderdale, FL was flawless and it gave me the opportunity to calm down. We flew through beautiful blue skies and I could see the coastal towns and cities from my window. When the flight attendant came around and asked "what would you ladies like to drink" I felt the confidence that there would not be any derogatory comments made, at least for the moment. I was relieved when the plane landed, the wheels touched the ground, and the brakes are applied, it gave me, a great sense of security and relief. The landing was smooth and Fort Lauderdale looked so beautiful with the green grass, palm trees and the gorgeous blue green ocean.

We had a short, 50 minute layover in Ft Lauderdale which gave us just enough time to find the gate for our flight to Key West and pick up a cup of coffee. The US Air plane was much smaller than the one we flew on there, and it was packed. The atmosphere and attitudes of the people on the flight seemed to be somewhat festive and non-judgmental which eased my travel anxiety immensely. I laughed and joked with Diane as we looked forward to our vacation. We had been to Key West one time before when we took a Carnival cruise from Miami to Cozumel, Mexico several years before. The ship had stopped in Key West for about five hours and we walked the island, saw Ernest Hemingway's home and the Southernmost point in the United States. Since that time we had decided we would come back one day and stay for a week.

We taxied the runway and in one swift motion we were up in the air. The land west of Ft Lauderdale was full of trees and swamp as we passed over the Florida Everglades and headed toward the Keys. It was truly beautiful and the sky was blue and it was truly smooth sailing. The flight into Key West was thrilling as we landed at the small island airport. Our luggage arrived with us and we flagged down a taxi to take us to our hotel immediately. This phase of the trip ended and my travel worries and anxieties had left me.

The Pelican Inn was located about two blocks off the beach on the opposite side of the island where the cruise ships dock and away from the commercial downtown area. I thought it was very beautiful. The concierge was extremely nice and treated us both like royalty. It was very nice to be treated like a lady. The inn was magnificent and pristine. Our room was off to the south side, next to the pool. The bougainvillea and other flowers were very colorful in their brilliant orange, red, lavender, and pink, an endless palette of beauty. The trees and shrubs were manicured to perfection. The floor was specked beige and white thick tile. It contained a king size bed, refrigerator, two solid cherry armoires, with a huge bathroom, marble countertops, and ceramic sinks with gold fixtures. The doors had wooden slats opened for fresh air which was very comfortable and especially nice for sleeping. It was around 4:00 p.m. when we finally settled in, changed, and then walked around the neighborhood.

Diane and I found a neighborhood restaurant that specialized in seafood. The criteria for selecting a place to dine, at least for me, was that it must serve alcohol; since this place did, I was ready to drink and eat. The entrance of the restaurant was at the intersection and was cozily situated in a residential area. I was dressed in my lavender Ann Taylor sundress with brown Teva sandals and a matching purse. Diane wore a floral sundress and sandals and looked beautiful. As we entered the restaurant, we were seated next to the window and immediately fell into easy conversation. We talked about our marriage and divorce. The good times we had together and the fun, joy, disappointments, and love we had for the children. We were truly best friends and the only thing that kept us from staying married was that she needed a man in her life; I certainly did not like it but totally understood. We cherished the evening and enjoyed each other's company as we walked along the streets of Key West enjoying the comfortable 70's temperature and we breathed the clean, fresh ocean air while we smoked our Marlboros.

We arrived back at the inn and prepared for the remainder of the evening. We both put on our gowns and read a while before going to bed. Diane and I were best friends, no longer married, we both slept in the king size bed together but we agreed that there would be no expectation of sex. We cuddled and fell asleep, safe in each other's arms. It was that way for the next six days, best friends, soul mates on vacation together. It was a blessing to have such a wonderful friend who stood by me and loved me as a person. Sadly, it was a feeling I took for granted at the time. I was still wrapped up in the feelings of being rejected by my family and feeling they had abandoned me.

The morning came quickly, as we both rested very well that night. We put on our capri's, tank tops, me with my bra and silicone breast forms, and we were off to the lobby for a continental breakfast. We had noticed the night before there were bicycles for rent about a block away. After breakfast we walked down to the office and rented two bikes for the day.

We rode into the commercial district, locked our bikes in a public rack and visited the stores along the way. We were in and out of the stores, shopped for knick-knacks, and I purchased a pair of Birkenstock sandals. I spotted Margaritaville and had to go inside and get a beer or three. Diane enjoyed a margarita, her only drink all week, and I busied myself losing count of the number of beers I had consumed. We biked around the city and looked at all the old houses and returned to the marker at the southernmost point of the United States as we had done several years before. Key West is just the most beautiful place, and has something for everyone: old Victorian homes, gorgeous sunsets, tourist spots, arts, key lime pie, alcohol and beaches. On the way back to the inn we stopped in the middle of a residential block and went into a small sandwich shop and I had a Cuban sandwich for the first time. It was delicious, I felt life was wonderful and I felt as great as a girl could ever feel in such a beautiful place. There was no anxiety or fear, only joy for myself and Diane on this fabulous vacation.

We dined that evening at another neighborhood restaurant we had stumbled upon, and made plans to rent bikes the next day and ride to the beach. We also discussed my trip to Scottsdale to meet with Dr. Meltzer.

I explained, "He is the doctor I have selected to perform my sex reassignment surgery."

We also discussed the cost and recovery time and she had a hard time understanding the great expense for this procedure. My insurance would not cover the operation and the money had to come out of my 401K.

I further explained that all surgeries of this nature are "cash in advance." At the time in 2007 sex reassignment surgery was $25000 plus all expenses of recovery and travel. Dr. Meltzer was known in the transgendered community to be the best surgeon in the United States.

I believed Diane was disappointed because she had consistently asked the question, "Why can't you just stay the way you are without doing all the surgery?" And she always added statements like: "You know your family is going to have a lot of problems with it. You will not be allowed to come around them again and you will probably lose everything you have. Philip Morris is not going to be kind to you."

I explained, "It is the only right thing for me to do, in order to live a fulfilled and happy life;" and being the true woman that I was on the inside.

After a while, Diane said, "I do not want to talk about it anymore and wanted to focus on something else."

In the morning, I put on my hot pink, one-piece Calvin Klein bathing suit, with a short matching skirt. I was nervous again because I had never been to the beach as my female self. My legs and arms were smooth and the breast forms fit nicely and did not reveal they were not "natural". Although the hormones I had been taking had started to affect my breast development, I felt they were not ready for display without plenty of help! My breasts had just started to show, much like a like a teenage girl who noticed that her breasts were developing and to that point where she may ask her mother about that certain tingle. However, my anxiety returned as we walked down the street to retrieve the bicycles. My mind started with what would happen if a bunch of guys tried to pick us up on the beach, or suppose my little skirt flew up and someone thought they saw a small bulge and confronted me with the issue. Would someone become angry and want to hurt me? My biggest fear had always been the prospect of getting beat up by some guy who was threatened and not open–minded or tolerant of me and my situation. A person who was looking to make a name for himself. There were plenty of stories around that demonstrated this behavior in the world. Regardless of the world's bullies, I was bound and determined to ride my bicycle twenty blocks down Southard Street to Fort Taylor beach and to enjoy the exhilaration of simply being a girl, who was riding her bicycle to the beach! Diane and I peddled the blocks, entered the state park, and paid our money to use the public beach. We rode our bikes down to the beach and I picked a spot that was only moderately full of people. We laid down our towels and blanket and put on suntan lotion and settled in for a day at the beach. I started out lying on my stomach because of my insecurity and so that I could check out my surroundings. This was the first time that I had worn my bathing suit out in the world and I was happy and scared at the same time. I found enough nerve to roll over on my back to tan the front side of my body. Diane and I talked, read our magazines and books, and slowly my nervousness and negative thoughts started to subside. After an hour had passed, I got up and went into the ocean and enjoyed every moment. After I finished playing in the ocean, I got out and "carefully" ensured everything was in place, and walked back to join Diane, who was still lying in the sun. It was a monumental step for me to participate in life as my true self. Each new experience was a release for a moment from the bondage of self.

We rode our bicycles back to the inn and went swimming in the pool right beside the room. It was another beautiful sunny April afternoon in Key West. The remainder of the week we discussed my transition on the job with Philip Morris and Diane repeatedly expressed her opinion that she did not think it would be successful. I, however, explained that "I was so tired of constantly hiding myself; I knew it was the only way for me to live a healthy and happy life."

Diane and I sashayed around the city in our sundresses, shorts, and tank tops as though we hadn't a care in the world! I loved visiting the city and neighborhoods clad in my short skirts and skimpy tops, I truly felt like a woman. It was one of the fastest weeks I have ever experienced. While it was a great deal of fun, and filled with happiness and joy, there was also the anxiety. Oh, that monster called anxiety! It's a killer. I often wondered why it was so important for society to proclaim who I must be and even more important why it had taken so long to understand how to be true to myself? I think for me, I wanted to believe that my nightmare couldn't possibly be true. Then when I realized it was true I reached a crossroads of "to be" or "not to be". Fortunately, for me, "not to be" only came deadly close but did not happen.

Our trip rapidly came to its conclusion as we awoke on the final morning of our stay in Key West. Another glorious sunny day, with warm temperatures in the 80's and a light, bone warming, breeze filled my body. The week had blazed by so quickly. We ate the inn's continental breakfast and had the concierge call for a taxi to take us to the airport. I wore my beige colored jeans and a nice silk puller over top with platform heels and carried a matching sweater as the driver pulled up in front. He drove us around the island and along the coastline for our final tour, on the way to the airport.

Key West International was very small and we were able to check in right away. We went through a short TSA area, and found their attitude, and all the people with whom we came into contact in Key West, were very genteel, kind, and understanding. It was different for me to experience a place where I felt that people look generally for good in one another without being critical. It was very nice to experience this type of kindness. However, my thoughts again focused on my fears and I had to reel them back in and not worry about what anyone might think. The gate for our flight was outside under a tent and we waited a short while and boarded our flight back to Fort Lauderdale.

As the flight lifted off to Fort Lauderdale, I made the sign of the cross and prayed for a safe trip. The two gentlemen behind me noticed that I had some flight anxiety and started talking loudly about the Everglades below us. They discussed how full of alligators, snakes, and other creatures and if our plane were to have a problem and go down, we'd be gobbled up by alligators in a matter of minutes! I just had to laugh it off and pretend not to hear them so they would stop torturing me with their conversation. It was rather amusing and it had kept my mind off going back home to reality, which was the continued planning of my transition and all the events that must transpire to align my body and spirit together. We landed in Ft. Lauderdale without a hitch and proceeded into the terminal only to find out that our flight to Charlotte had been cancelled, which meant more people to encounter with my female appearance and my male voice.

At the US Air customer service desk I explained our situation and we were booked on a United flight from Palm Beach to Charlotte. Surprisingly, US Air paid for our limo ride from Ft.

Lauderdale to Palm Beach which is a good 40 miles away. Diane and I, along with another man, rode with us and we made small talk, as I watched the geography of the land which has always been an interest of mine. Every part of the United States is different and carries its own unique beauty. It is enjoyable just to sit and take in the sites.

We waited a couple of hours in Palm Beach and a man came through the terminal and just stared at me as he walked past. I knew that I had been read as a male and I felt the tension and negative energy. I sat down next to Diane and told her what happened and disappeared in my seat. We made our way back to Charlotte and found our luggage at the US Air baggage claim area. I found my Camry in the long term parking and drove over to Diane's house in Concord. I was exhausted and went to bed, looking forward to getting home and seeing Zeb.

My drive back to Richmond was quiet and full of thought. The memories of the past week were ever so present as I relived them in my mind. The thoughts of going back to work and the process of discussing my transition with my employer weighed heavily on my mind. I truly felt like it was not going to be pleasant and that I probably would lose my job. Although I believed this was really the only right thing for me to do, I also knew that all I could do was try my best to live through the outcome, whatever it was going to be. I really could not find any help with the method of approaching Philip Morris, so I began to think logically through the process and decided to create my own path.

The 250 mile drive from Concord, NC to Richmond, VA went really fast because my mind was so preoccupied with my future plans. I knew in my heart that I could not continue to live as a male at work and rushed right home and become my female true self for much longer. It was crazy to live each day as two different genders but for now it was the only way I knew in order to survive. Until I could plan for the total transition which was going to take place very soon, it frightened me but it was the only way.

Chapter 10 – IFGE

Monday morning always came fast and as I walked up the steps of the BL Plant, I paused, and looked around at my surroundings, concentrated on the sights, and stored it all in my memory. I looked at the beautiful flowers that were carefully kept out front at the facility and marveled at the cleanliness of the parking lot across the street. As I opened the doors and walked into the lobby, I took it all in and slowly walked methodically down the corridor to my office. I unlocked my solid cherry framed glass door and slowly entered my domain. I sat and thought how much I really enjoyed my job and the company. I envisioned being able to attend work as myself, a woman, and then to being ostracized and outcast. Back and forth, my mind raced with ugly images of things that may, or may not, happen. The minutes spent in turmoiled thought turned into a half-hour before I opened my laptop and started to work on my continuous improvement projects. My life continued on like this for the next two weeks.

Two months prior to this, in a James River Transgendered Society meeting, my friend Robyn announced that at the end of April there was an IFGE (International Federation of Gender Education) convention in Philadelphia. The convention was to be in 4 days - Thursday afternoon through noon Sunday. This four-day convention would provide a significant amount of information for the transgendered community. With that information, Teresa, Danielle, and I signed up for the conference immediately. Robyn, who was affiliated with the organization, was already registered. Teresa and Danielle drove from Richmond to Philadelphia on Thursday.

I drove up Friday and met Teresa early in the afternoon at the Philadelphia Airport Hilton, where we planned to share a room. Teresa showed me to our room, I registered for the event and received my badge. I walked through the hallway which was reserved on one side of the hotel and looked at the books, schedule, and met other transgendered women. The IFGE event was made up of people in many different stages of transitioning. The group was comprised of pre- and post-operation transsexuals, cross-dressers, and those interested in understanding the transgendered world; psychiatrics, clergy, and doctors.

We went back to our room to rest for a while and freshen up for the dinner, which began at 6:00 p.m. We arrived outside the banquet room, met up with Danielle, and waited our turn in line to be seated. The hall was large, I'd heard that 650 people were in attendance for the event and the majority was at the banquet. The three of us found places at the dinner table and conversed with others there. The table seated eight and we met a group from Ohio. We talked about the environment in Ohio and Virginia. The women we sat with were primarily cross dressers, out for the week enjoying their female side with thoughts of possibly transitioning, but in all probability, were not likely to do so.

The dinner and conversations were enlightening. It was amazing to me that, not so very long ago, I thought that I was the only one on the planet with gender identity issues. Now I was enjoying dinner and conversation with hundreds of people like me. During dessert the President of IFGE approached the platform and spoke about the events that had taken place during the day. She recognized those who led and facilitated work and breakout sessions. She announced the two events for the evening were either to join everyone in the bar or take a chartered bus into downtown Philadelphia to one of the night clubs. I opted for the party bus and as soon as the party girl stepped off that bus and yelled for us to "come on" in her high-spirited, cheerleader voice, I was ready and very excited because I was used to staying out all night on the weekends at Doll's.

The new leather smell in the bus mingled with the various ladies perfumes. I found an empty seat about five rows back and sat down and introduced myself to a lady named Kerry from Trenton, NJ. She told me this was her very first time going out in public as a female and that she only dressed at home when no one was around. She said she was married and had two small children and her wife was at home with the kids while she attended the conference. I shared some of my experience and told her to stick with me and to try and feel comfortable. We talked as we went over the bridge from the hotel into downtown Philly. I could see tall skyscrapers and the narrow streets as we approached the very old section of the city where most of the night clubs reigned. There were old cobblestone streets and one lane roads; it was all so beautiful and I enjoyed the wonderful tour, as we were guided to the bars recommended for us to visit. It was obvious that the outing was well planned. We went inside a gay, lesbian, and transgendered bar and I quickly ordered a beer and headed to the dance floor with Kerry. She and I danced. I wanted her to enjoy the experience. We danced, drank, and I chatted with almost everyone there about anything that enter my head and it flew right out of my mouth. I was in rare form, full of confidence and grandiosity.

The night club was packed when it was time to leave and we walked down the one lane cobblestone road where the bus would pick us up. We arrived at the meeting place fifteen minutes early and so we went into a coffee shop for safety rather than hanging out on the street like two hookers. The bus ride back to the Hilton seemed longer than the trip downtown as we talked about the evening and what an enjoyable experience we had. When the bus dropped us off at the hotel I told Kerry that I was going to bed and would see her tomorrow and I gave her a hug. After that wonderful night, I never saw her again. I do hope everything worked out for her because she was a very nice person.

Saturday morning Teresa and I woke up around 7:00 a.m. and prepared for our day. We went downstairs to the restaurant and had breakfast with some of the ladies at the convention. I asked questions about employment issues and transitioning on the job and really did not hear any stories concerning their experiences. However, one of the ladies told me there was some material in the book selling area that may be helpful.

After breakfast I attended a session with Sister, who was also in attendance, entitled "Catholicism and the Transgendered Individual". I loved seeing Sister at the conference because I had been on two retreats with her in New Orleans and Tucson. I was able to share with the group of approximately 20 about my experience on theses retreats and that I had gained the understanding that God loved all people regardless of gender identity. It was very interesting to hear people talk about how society constantly dictated that we are sinners and have no rights to exist in this world. It has always been a very lonely existence to feel this way, and to feel as though the whole world is against you for something you cannot control or change. During the retreats it was great to examine the truth that lives within and then to understand there are no mistakes in God's world. Hearing it was a great affirmation however; believing had to be practiced because of the great amount of negativity that surrounds this topic on a daily basis.

Dr. Meltzer conducted a session across the hall from Sister and I planned to talk with him after her session. Every now and then I heard Dr. Meltzer's voice as he explained the SRS procedure to another group. I really wanted to attend Sister's session because I felt it was of the utmost importance to right the spirit which lay inside of me. Dr. Meltzer's session finished earlier than Sister's session; he was gone and on his way back to Arizona before I realized it. I was extremely happy to see Sister and we spoke for a while as she was arranging appointments for the remainder of her day. I was disappointed at having missed Dr. Meltzer because two months previously, I had committed in my mind to allow him to perform my surgery. The only thing that prevented me from moving forward was the deposit, the real life test and the two letters from the therapist.

After lunch I attended a seminar facilitated by Dr. Pierre Brassard from Montreal, Canada. After sharing his surgical credentials, he discussed his surgical method and used a slide show to demonstrate his technique. He showed before, during, and after surgery pictures and also discussed his aftercare program in

130

Montréal. It was actually the first time that I had seen such graphic pictures of the procedure and this provided me with a greater understanding of the process that I was going to undergo. He was extremely thorough and even took the time to answer participant's questions before he flew back to Canada. It was very educational and everyone there appreciated his time.

After the seminar, I stopped by a vendor stand and purchased a small 32-page paper bound book entitled, "The Employer's Guide to Gender Transition", by Dianna Cicotello. The book was published by IFGE at the request of several companies and business leaders. It was a short guide, but extremely informative, and explained the potential issues employers may experience with transitioning employees. The book provided an explanation of the problems, concerns, feelings of employees and offered suggestions for resolutions to most situations that could occur.

I stopped by the bar to have a beer and conversations with a few of the women who were there as well. I sat down and discussed the conference, asked where people were from, and told my story and my plans for the future. The ladies at the table were a group from the mid-west who travelled together to conferences throughout the United States. They were having a great time and stated they probably would not have the surgery, although it often crossed their minds. But surgery for them just didn't seem to be the right fit.

After several hours I went back to the room to freshen up for dinner. It was a banquet style dinner again with salad, a choice of chicken or beef and vegetables, and a yummy desert. We listened to the speakers. They recognized the conference committee members for their efforts and their extraordinary leadership, which was a very special touch. There was music and a dance afterwards, celebrating the success of the conference. I felt the conference was over before I could bat an eye; it simply flew by so very fast! I hung around, danced for about an hour, listened to the music, and met a lady from New York City who proceeded to invite me up to her room. When I entered her room, I immediately notice that it appeared to be more like a cave than a room, it was a wreck! She offered me a beer, which I accepted, and then she pulled out a huge bag of weed, which I declined. Suddenly a very uncomfortable feeling came over me and I decided it was time for bed. I thanked her for the beer, walked out the door with her mouth agape, up the elevator I went and off to bed for a good night's sleep. In hindsight, I think I escaped a potential train wreck!

Sunday morning we packed for our return to Richmond, checked out, and loaded the Camry before breakfast in the hotel restaurant. To my amazement Sister was in line to get into the restaurant and we asked her to join us for breakfast. She is wonderful, I cannot say enough about her and her ministry, which was instrumental in empowering me to change the way I think. Danielle, Teresa, and I listened to her as she discussed her ministry and the transgendered retreat she conducted for both male and female individuals which was now located in Tucson. She had a very peaceful and loving disposition and has been a huge influence on those in the transgendered community that have sought her help.

Sister soon said good-bye and left for to the airport. Teresa excused herself from the table to attend a previously scheduled interview with Dr. McGinn, a new gender reassignment surgeon in the Philadelphia area. I asked Teresa to pass on to Dr. McGinn that I wanted to speak with her if her schedule permitted. Teresa agreed and I waited anxiously for Teresa's appointment to conclude. Danielle and I spoke for 40 minutes about the conference, JRTS business, and other matters and finally Teresa returned from her appointment and told me that Dr. McGinn would see me. I immediately excused myself and I went to see the doctor, so very glad she made time for me.

I met Dr. McGinn for the first time and found her to be highly intelligent and a very personable; not to mentions she was a beautiful blonde knockout! We briefly discussed our backgrounds and I told her about my experience in Scottsdale with Dr. Meltzer. I explained that I while I wanted to meet her, I felt

132

committed to Dr. Meltzer for the surgery. I discussed where I was with regards to the requirements for surgery and she explained to me what was necessary for surgery with her, which was no different than Dr. Meltzer. The visit was short but she had made a lasting impression on me as we parted. I said my goodbyes to Danielle, Teresa, and Robyn as I listened in on Robyn's conversation with the IFGE President.

I left the Philadelphia Airport Hilton and started my four and a half hour drive south back to Richmond down I-95. I enjoyed the sites as I left Pennsylvania and drove through Wilmington, DE. It is a beautiful part of the country with the big oak, birch, and pine trees, flowing rivers, and the Chesapeake Bay. My mind wondered as I drove and looked forward to getting back to my dog, Zeb. I thought about work, the projects I was working on, JRTS and the group, the bills that needed to be paid, and how I would successfully transition at work with Philip Morris. I continued my drive through the tunnel and Baltimore and into Washington, DC and contemplated ideas for my future. Finally, I passed Fredericksburg, VA and onto Richmond the Fan District, at last I was home.

Zeb was ecstatic to see me when I walked in the door! He immediately ran to get his tennis ball and we went to the back yard. With a beer in one hand, I threw the ball far into the yard for Zeb to retrieve. Wow, what a wonderful trip, I learned a great deal in such a short period of time and met some of the greatest and most loving people in the world. I played in the yard with Zeb for a while and told him all about my trip...

Chapter 11- Confronting the Boss

It had been eighteen months since I had the one-on-one conversation with each of my siblings concerning my feelings about who I felt I really was and my need to transition. It had been about fifteen months since I had this same conversation with my parents. I knew it was time for me to take the next step with my employer, Phillip Morris, and finally put an end to the frustrations I felt that came from living two separate lives each day. I was constantly in fear of additional rejection because of the unwillingness of my family to try and understand. This caused me to drink more, which I thought would help to ease and erase my pain. The pain of not being loved by my family and the total rejection led to self-pity and incomprehensible demoralization. Early in my life, I drank over the confusion as to who I was. I had a genetic background of alcoholism in the family that only further assisted me with my self-medication. Although I was working with a therapist concerning transition, I felt I was educating him more than he was helping me. The mental day to day anguish had started to take its effect on me in that I drank more and more. I lived in fear and prepared myself for the unknown, possible rejection by my employer. There had been many hours spent over my lifetime, where I just sat and looked out a window and thought about why was I born this way and how could I deal with my life and fix it. I absolutely could not help it. I honestly felt sorry that it was me and how it had affected so many people, dead and alive.

On Monday morning, sadly, I returned to work as "John". Since Thanksgiving, I had made the decision to start allowing my hair to grow and had earned the nickname "Ringo" around the office. The guys gave me that nickname as they came to the conclusion that I looked like Ringo Starr from The Beatles with my hair the length that it was grown. Of course no one knew that I had allowed my hair to grow out because of the public transition that was about to take place! My hair grew fast and it was to the point that I no longer had to wear a wig when I finished work and carefully rushed back into the house and change to Kaitlin. My Victorian house was adjoining another as most were, being built in 1915. I talked to my neighbor Nancy about being transgendered so that she would not think she was seeing things. Nancy had lived in her Fan District house for about 40 years so I was sure she has seen just about everything. The Fan District was known for being LGBT friendly and progressive thinking. The next neighbor down was Mike and I told him and then there was my good friend Jennifer who cared for Zeb when I was away. She was a professor at a large University and had a PhD in Anthropology. Actually, the entire community for several blocks around knew me as Kaitlin and understood that I was still physically male at the time. The word was getting around.

As April turned into May, I followed the same routine: work, home, change, drink beer, play and walk with Zeb. I knew the time had come. I had thought about how to approach my job for the prior six months and decided the best avenue was to schedule an appointment with the highest ranking person in Human Resources who I knew and who knew me as well. Throughout the years with Philip Morris, I attended many seminars and team building exercises with all the senior management teams and had interactions with one HR Manager in particular. I didn't consider it a tremendous amount of exposure, but enough that we had developed enough of a professional relationship to speak to one another at these seminars. His name was Scott; he was the Director of Human Resources for Manufacturing, Technology, and Research and Development. He held the number two position in the Human Resources department at Philip Morris, and reported to and worked very closely with the Senior Vice President of Human Resources. I called his office and spoke with his assistant and arranged a time convenient to meet him. She asked if it was medical, personal, etc. and replied that it was both. The date was set for the following week on a Thursday morning in May 2007.

As the weekend came, I went out and drank and danced at Doll's from 6:00 p.m. to 2:00 a.m., then home to take Zeb out before I went to Fielding's to play pool and drink some more until six in the morning. I slept from 7:00 a.m. to 1:00 p.m. and got up and walked and played with Zeb, as I continued drinking. I started the whole cycle all over again at 6:00 p.m. the next day. Sunday I got up late and drank until it was time for bed at 10:00 p.m. I went to bed at that time so that I would be able to go to work. I knew that I drank so that I would not have to think about the all-encompassing pain I felt. The "drink" made me feel so much better.

It was a long and agonizing eight days as I waited to see Scott in HR. The thoughts I had each day went from 8, 7, and 6, down to one as I counted the number of days that I felt were left of being employed with the company. So I would work really hard and then drink profusely after work until bedtime. During that time I would take my beer to bed with me! The reason I had decided to talk with Scott instead of the factory HR Representative was because I knew that he would not have a clue as to what to do and would only have to run it up the chain of command, probably adding or deleting information as he went along. I also knew each time information is passed along, different words are spoken or even left out and oftentimes the story takes on a whole different meaning and the entire subject is interpreted differently. When the story finally got to the right person it is completely distorted. I decided I was not going to take a chance of that happening especially when I felt like my entire future was on the line.

When I attended the IFGE conference in Philadelphia, I had a conversation with a lady who was in the process of transitioning with General Motors in Wisconsin. She approached her boss and discussed her situation and was permitted to transition on the job from male to female but was not allowed to use the women's bathroom. She told me the guys in the plant made fun of her. No one would sit with her at lunch anymore or assist her with her work; basically she was ostracized. Her story weighed heavily on my mind as I anticipated the meeting with the HR director. I also experienced a deepened feeling of anxiety, guilt, and even the old, ugly feeling of shame had crept back in to my psyche.

Thursday morning finally arrived and I woke up at 6:00 a.m. on the dot! I immediately felt a sense of foreboding and my anxiety level was at an all-time high as I anticipated my meeting with Scott. I followed my normal routine and thought about how to approach the issue and decided just to be straight up and as truthful as possible. After I walked Zeb through the park, I headed over to the Operations Center and arrived about 20 minutes early for my appointment. I sat very quietly with my thoughts and was happy that this step in my transition was about to happen.

Scott arrived on time at 8:15 a.m. I stood up, took a deep breath, and walked into his office. We greeted with a handshake and I sat down at a small side table next to his desk. We exchanged pleasantries for a moment while he was putting away the items he carried, into his desk. He got up from his desk and joined me at the small round table.

He asked, "How is the job going with the implementation training and team building throughout the company?" Typical questions from an HR person.

I explained that "things were progressing and moving in the right direction and the training was beginning to take hold and that we could see and measure team's moving toward self-sufficiency."

"That is great and I know Greg, (VP of Manufacturing) will be happy to hear that."

After a short pause, he asked "why do you need to see me?" The words were soft coming from his mouth but they were monumental in my mind. The long waited moment of truth for me.

"I don't know how to say this, so I am just going to say it."

Without hesitation I blurted out: "I am a male-to-female transgendered person and I need to live my life as a female in order to be whole. I know that you may fire me but this is something that I really need to do, transition from male to female on the job".

I brought you and handed him three books *True Self* by Mildred L. Brown and Chloe Ann Rounsley, *The Employer's Guide to Gender Transition* by Dianna Cicotello, and *Working with a Transsexual: A Guide for Coworkers* by Janis Walworth.

Scott shared that in all his years as a Human Resources Manager and now Director, "I have never experienced the process of an individual transitioning on the job. However I believe that Kevin (VP of Human Resources) has had the experience." He said, "You will not lose your job."

I was immediately relieved from this huge burden and I was quite sure he could see that all over my face but then I gave him a smile from a submissive viewpoint, kind of shameful, not looking him in the eye any longer because I had to do this.

He explained, "I need to sit down with Kevin and discuss the proper method of performing this task from an HR perspective. It may take a little time."

"I understand".

He gave me his card and personal cell phone number.

Scott said, "I will get back with you in a couple of weeks."

The meeting was over in a mere eighteen minutes! I thanked him so very much and repeated one last time that this was something "I needed to do in order to live my life as I was truly born to be."

"Ok, I will talk with you soon."

I walked out of the Operations Center and drove to my office at the BL Plant and all I heard repeated in my mind was the glorious fact that I would not lose my job, Halleluiah!!! I accidently went through a red light on the way. It made me very happy to have walked through that meeting only to come to the realization that the anticipation was so much worse than the event. It was a very warm feeling to have told my employer something that momentous, something I had been carrying with me my entire career, and not have it negatively impact me, today.

Back in my office I spent time daydreaming about how it would be when everything was changed from John to Kaitlin: name plate, stationary, business cards, answering machine, etc. I had to force myself to concentrate on my work but it sure felt, well, harmonious, to finally begin being me 100% of the time. During the next six weeks I was scheduled to assess the progress of the Business Unit Teams that I had helped develop as part of a team. We were to visit at least 25% of all the Teams in each facility and access their progress on becoming self-managed and self-sufficient. It was my job to train and work with the Production Teams at the BL Plant and help them to utilize the proper tools for making decisions and problem solving. We worked on elimination of waste and standardization of work so that they would become part of a sustainable process. It was a great job and I loved it and I met so many people in the company and I was very proud that I assisted so many. I was very well known throughout the organization because I had worked at both the Manufacturing Center and the Cabarrus Manufacturing Center for many years in Production and now the Blended Leaf Plant, Leaf Processing Facility, Williamsburg Smokeless Plant, and Park 500. I knew at least 2000 employees easy and more knew me because of my high profile and exposure. They all knew me as John; this was going to be very interesting, to say the least!

The Friday before Memorial Day, I asked Jennifer if she would go down to the John Marshall Court Building in downtown Richmond. I explained that I was going to petition the court to change my name legally. She accepted my invitation and we drove down together, parked on the street, and walked up the long stairs to the courthouse. We went to the civil division area and asked the clerk for an "Order for Change of Name" document. When she returned with the form, I immediately filled out my current name and filed that it be changed to my female name, Kaitlin. I changed my name completely including my last name because I did not want to embarrass my family by using my birth last name. I did this out of respect for my parents. I returned the completed form to the clerk and remitted the

$35 fee. The clerk checked my identification and birth certificate, and informed me that the form would be forwarded to the court and if they needed me the court would contact me. On the following Tuesday, the Civil Court Judge signed the order and it was sent in the mail. It was official and legal ... from John to Kaitlin. It was much easier than I anticipated.

I had met with Scott in Human Resources in May 2007. At that time he had conveyed to me that he would "get back to me within two weeks". It had turned into June and I had not heard anything back from Scott. I had been in Concord, NC assessing teams at the Cabarrus Manufacturing Center. I had become very anxious about the company's internal thoughts and plans that would affect my future. I did not stay in a hotel for this trip but had stayed with Diane at her house so that we could talk. I told her about the meeting and she expressed surprise that the company would work with me. She told me that it would not be easy but at the same time had encouraged me and stated she was happy for me. It had been over three weeks since my meeting and I called Scott from Diane's house on Wednesday evening and asked him if there had been any progress on my situation. He told me that he had met with Kevin and reassured me that everything would be fine and explained where they were at the moment. He asked me to be patient because there were a couple of things to work out. He did not elaborate and I took him for his word. He seemed to be a good man.

I went about my life and business as John with Philip Morris, and knew the days were numbered. I thought and thought about my past career and wondered or at least tried to visualize how the future would unfold. I knew it was going to be different for me and all my coworkers. I worried about the reaction of others and understood there would be a period of adjustment for everyone. I prayed every day that the transition would go smoothly and there would not be any sort of retaliation. Philip Morris was a very conservative environment and I knew this certainly could get difficult at best. However I felt the company, which prided itself in thinking outside the box, also had the tools to handle this creatively and respectfully. The company's harassment policy was strict and I had seen it enforced stringently over the years. I pondered this as I drove from Concord back to Richmond on Friday afternoon. I met Jennifer with Zeb as I parked my car on the street and proceeded with my normal weekend plans. Finally, it was Kaitlin time which was directly related to beer time!

With the weekend over all too soon, eternity had settled in and I was forced to put my "John" on yet again and head in to work. I hoped this would be the week of some movement on my transition on the job. During the week, I received and email and phone call from Scott's assistant stating that he would like for me to schedule some time with him next week and that he had assigned a lady named Gail to my situation. Gail replaced the current Human Resource Representative for the Processing Plants and came to Philip Morris by way of Kraft Foods which was until recently was a former subsidiary. I scheduled my time with Scott and arranged to meet Gail at the Park 500 Plant.

As it turned out, Gail was a very kind and understanding person as if I had known her from the beginning. I felt I could trust and talk with her about anything. She greeted me and we discussed my transition and she showed me the books that I had given Scott. Gail said she had been reading the books and found them quite helpful to her in this situation. She told me that if I needed anything for me to call her and because she would be personally involved in my transition.

Behind the scenes that entire week, Scott, Gail and the Vice-President of Human Resources discussed the situation with the Vice-President's of Manufacturing and Technology, the Director of the Processing Plants, BL Plant Manager, and my boss, the Manager of Continuous Improvement. I was not involved with these meetings at this time and was at the Manufacturing Center and in the Williamsburg Smokeless Plant completing the team assessments.

The following week, I reported to Scott's office and found Gail, true to her word, in attendance as well. We sat down at the conference table in his office and began a discussion concerning the meeting they had with the Vice-President and Managers. I had known Greg, the Vice President, for eighteen years and had worked with him at the Cabarrus Manufacturing Center in North Carolina when he was the Plant Superintendent on third shift. I had been the Group Supervisor of Production in Primary Processing and was his direct report. He had rehired me when I left the company in the 90's; he was a wonderful person and friend. Because we had a long history, I was concerned, so I asked Scott how Greg seemed to be handling my news and Scott replied, "He does not understand it but he is ok". Those words made me feel better. The reason I felt better was I thought that I was letting people down who believed in me, promoted me, and knew me. I did not want the people to think that I was some kind of a freak that they really did not know. That in reality was the furthest from the truth as it is hard to explain something that I myself don't fully understand. The real problem is that I knew I could not come out and tell people that I was confused about my gender. I had to work through it outside of the workplace.

Scott asked me how I wanted to approach the actual transition. I told him I had done my research and thought the best approach would be for me to take my vacation time and return to work in full transition, as Kaitlin. He thought my approach was very good and I discussed that I needed to finish the report for Greg and his staff and then I immediately take my vacation. We reviewed the calendar and scheduled my vacation and the day of my return. Both Gail and Scott thought the dates we selected would work and we orchestrated a plan where they would meet with the employees in my office the first week I was on vacation. They were the Safety, Quality, Production, Maintenance, Engineering and Cost Managers to discuss the issue with them. I felt that this was a really good plan.

I discussed the bathroom issue, which I knew was the number one issue in companies with others who have transitioned on the job. It was written in the book which I had provided and the issue needed to be resolved before the transition. At the BL

142

Plant I normally use a one stall bathroom in the lobby area that is unisex, but that was the only one in the plant. We talked about this issue and they thought it would be fine to use the women's bathroom; however, the one I used would be good if I needed to minimize any issue.

I completed the week, which was a long couple of days, and went on vacation. I stayed around my house and neighborhood, visited with Julie, a friend I met in the Fan District through my son John, Jennifer, and my friends from JRTS and discussed my transition with them. They encouraged me and were very supportive. During the second week of my vacation, on Tuesday, I received a phone call from one of my peers from work. She told me she had attended a meeting that morning and the topic of discussion was ME and my transition from male to female on the job. She sounded very encouraging on the phone and actually wished me well. At that time, that phone call meant the world to me and I really felt my transition was finally becoming real. I thought it might also be a good idea for the group to meet "Kaitlin" in my home, in a more personal setting, prior to going back to work now that they knew, so it would be less of a shock and maybe it would also help ease everyone's apprehension. With that in mind, I powered up my company laptop, went to Microsoft Outlook, and scheduled a meeting with my peers, managers, and director to come meet Kaitlin at 4:00 p.m. in my home on Friday afternoon. By the end of the following day, about 40 % of this group responded that they would attend. I also had let Gail know that I had extended this invitation, just to keep her in the loop.

Julie helped me prepare my home and even purchased refreshments for the gathering. Friday morning came and at 1:00 p.m. I dressed for the party. I wore a beautiful Ann Taylor floral sundress that fit perfectly and selected matching flat shoes. I took a lot of time with my makeup and made sure that the foundation, eye color, and liner were flawless. I had washed and fixed my hair earlier that morning. My home was spotless and Julie came over at 3:00 p.m. with two small red rose bushes for the table centerpiece, and afterwards, for me to plant in the yard at a later time. We set up the table and I ensured that the beer, wine, and sodas were all cold. I had three cases of beer, four bottles of wine and a 12 pack of soda, vegetable and fruit trays, chips and dip, and small ham sandwiches for 12 people. I felt as prepared as any hostess could be.

At 4:00 p.m. the doorbell rang and Zeb barked profusely until I opened the door for my neighbor, Jennifer. Zeb did not like the doorbell or the mail when it comes through the slot. I had to order a new debit card because he chomped down on the original one as it came through the slot! Anyway, the doorbell rang a couple of times until the five of my coworkers who responded had arrived. I introduced myself as Kaitlin and welcomed each one to my home and we gathered in the adjoining parlors. We had wonderful conversation about work and I was asked many questions about being a male to female transgendered woman. The most experience that anyone in the group had was some exposure to a documentary on lifetime television. The questions I encountered ranged from: when did you know, how did you know, what are the feelings, why now, do you take hormones, etc? I felt the questions came from loving hearts that were genuinely interested in what I had been and continue to be going through as a transgendered woman. Their words were encouraging and were like, "you are beautiful" and "it takes a lot of courage to be this honest with yourself". I have to admit, it really was great for my ego to hear these kind words and to feel the understanding spirit these individual possessed. To know these individuals, these friends, these co-workers cared for me and wanted nothing but the best for me meant more than they could ever know. The celebration lasted until 6:00 p.m. Afterwards I invited them all to walk down the street to Joe's for drinks and a later dinner. All but two people stayed and as the group started to leave, I asked them to join me in my bar room which was adjacent to the parlor. This room had a full wet bar with a mirror the length of the bar which was made from solid oak wood. Next to the bar was a working antique phone booth with a phone

144

which you could use for ten cents to make a call. I asked each one of my guests to sign the inside of the phone booth. I wanted to remember this day and the people that had joined me in this new beginning.

Julie and Dave, my former Plant Manager, took me up on the offer and we hung around on the front porch with Zeb. After I walked and fed Zeb the three of us proceeded to the bar and stayed until 11:00 p.m. It was a great day for me, a new beginning. I shared a life-long secret with people with whom I work. For the first time in ages, I slept very peacefully through the night.

The following day, Saturday, after she had completed all her hair appointments, Julie came over for the day and we sat out on the front porch. We watched the people walk and the cars go by as we languished away the afternoon. There were normally many people around on the weekend at the Berry Café and other small businesses that lined the south side of the 400 block of Strawberry Street. We decided it would be a good time to plant the two small rose bushes she had given me so I went through the house and into the back yard and retrieved a shovel from the shed. I told her as the roses grew, so would I in my transition and it would be a great reminder of the gathering with my co-workers. The ground was hard but we took turns as we dug. I looked up and from across the street a gentleman approached and introduced himself as Barry. I had no idea where he came from or who he was but he said he would be happy to finish digging the holes because it was not a job for two pretty ladies. Barry dug the holes and Teresa and I planted the roses. When we finished, Berry declined our offer of a drink at Joe's Inn, but did accept my offer of a cool glass of sweet iced tea. When he finished, Barry went his own way and Julie and I went on our way to Joe's Inn.

It was July 10th and Teresa was having her first official gender reassignment surgery in Doylestown, PA, with Dr. McGinn. I made a day trip up to see Teresa five days after surgery and she explained her experience and showed me the results. Teresa described the peace she felt with herself and praised the work of Dr. McGinn. She talked me through the dilation process and showed me how it was done. We had an absolutely wonderful visit. It was quite an education for me to see the results and to understand the process for maintaining after surgery.

While I remained out of work on my second week of vacation, and completely unknown to me, the company held a Plant Wide Meeting on all shifts to discuss my situation with each employee. Gail, my Human Resource Representative, was present while my peers conducted the meeting. They informed the Area Leaders, Production Supervisors, and hourly employees about my transition from male to female and reviewed the Philip Morris Harassment Policy. They were told point blank that there would be no harassment of any kind tolerated within this company.

Because I frequent the Park 500 Plant in Chester, VA, several times a week for meetings and to see my boss, Gail met with the women in the Plant and discussed the bathroom issue. For some odd reason, during this week all the stalls in the women's bathroom had locks placed on the doors throughout the entire facility.

The environment was set up by the Company to the best of their ability. It had been two months since I first sat down with Scott and I am so happy that I was patient enough to wait for the Company to wrap their thinking around the transition and then to execute my transition with such care. The two months seemed like a very long time but in reality it helped me to prepare myself to be mentally strong to face this stage of my life with strength, dignity and pride.

Chapter 12 – On the Job Transition

I was a nervous wreck on Monday morning as I shaved, readying myself for work and the unknown. I had been going through the painful process of electrolysis for about 18 months, two times a week, on my face but still had hair that needed to be permanently removed. I also had been taking estrogen and spirolactone over a year. Spirolactone is a testosterone blocker and had to be taken with a baby aspirin each day. This was used so the estrogen levels would rise and testosterone levels would be lowered, which allowed for breast development and brought about greater female emotions like crying. Nevertheless, I still had to shave to ensure my face was smooth.

I wore a nice pair of Ann Taylor beige dress slacks and a floral pullover top that was very appropriate for work and was very similar to the manner of dress of all the women in the office. My breast forms were a size D and looked well proportioned on my 5'9"body frame and weighing 165 pounds. I had a pair of brown loafers which had a one inch block heel. My hair was dark brown and had grown to the point that I had it styled in a feminine manner, hanging down to the top of my shoulders. I washed my hair the night before and wet it only to blow dry it to style for the workday. I wore light makeup using a Mary Kay summer tint as a foundation and plum colored eye shade that looks good with my bright blue eyes. I wore a pair of small silver dangly earrings and my twenty-year service award gold, diamond, and ruby ring on my left ring finger. The ruby was the color of and represented the Marlboro Red. It had taken me an hour to get ready. I made sure I looked my professional best because I realized that all eyes would be on me the second I stepped out of my car in the parking lot!

I ate my breakfast of two boiled eggs, two cups of coffee, looked through the morning newspaper, walked in the park with Zeb, and finally walked out my front door to head to work. As I drove over to the Operations Center, I thought, "Wow, what a

147

way to start my introduction to the company: A meeting was with the Senior Vice President of Manufacturing and Technology, his entire staff, assistances, and invited guests"! It felt as though the fifteen minute drive took only one minute as I was there almost before I could blink my eyes. I stopped at the security gate and quickly flashed my identification badge at the security guard. At this point it still had my male picture and name and I hoped he would not stop me and question or harass me right at the start. He gave me a big smile and I passed through the gate onto the property without incident. I parked my car, pulled down my visor, looked in the mirror and noticed I had forgotten to put on my eye liner so I dug in my purse for it and artistically applied it. I sat in the car and smoked a cigarette and when I was finished, I said out loud "it's now or never, time to show the world my true self"! I took a deep breath, gathered my strength, opened the door and walked down the 75 yards of sidewalk to the front door. As I strode down that sidewalk, the tune of the great Diana Ross's, "I'm Coming Out" seemed to be blaring in my head. ... heck, who said disco was dead?! My bravado was short lived however. I felt like there were eyes in every window of the building and boring holes through me with every step I took. I felt very scared. For whatever reason, I remembered back to when I was 15 years old and said out loud," no one would ever beat me like that again." I prayed that everything would go well. My heart raced unbelievably fast. It took every ounce of my courage to walk through the front doors.

I arrived about 25 minutes early and waited down in the lobby for the rest of the team to arrive as we had planned. The people that were to attend the meeting were the Continuous Improvement Company Manager, Processing Plants CI Manager, and my entire peer group from all the factories. There were eight people with whom I worked closely for years that had not seen me as myself, who would be in attendance at the meeting. As everyone arrived they checked me out up and down and even sideways. Veronica and Jill sat next to me and told me I looked great. We discussed the presentation which I had loaded on my computer and was ready to present it however, my boss had assigned the task to Tim from the Manufacturing Center because as he said Tim was new and "needed the exposure".

After our short meeting, we went upstairs to the waiting area just outside the Marlboro Room and waited to be called in to give our semi-annual update on the progress of the Philip Morris Production System Teams which was modeled after the Toyota Production System. The Marlboro Room was centrally located in the Operation Center. It can be described as a large "Great Room" and was decorated in Philip Morris memorabilia and had a big screen television in one corner with an overhead projection system pointed to the far end of the room with a about 10' X 8' screen. The Vice President had two floor monitors which enabled him to view a presentation. There were oak tables placed in a u-shape completely around the room. The Vice President was seated in the middle at the head of the room, surrounded by his staff.

I sat in the upstairs waiting area trying to be very calm and collected, but my insides were racing at the speed of light as I tried in vain to focus on the presentation. However my concentration was broken with horrifying thoughts of what might happen once inside. As the call came, we stood up and walked into the room single file. Kaitlin has arrived and I felt the eyes of every person on me and it felt as though they were burning holes right through me. I normally sit at the table but today the table was full so I quietly sat at the closest and first available seat on the side. Tim plugged in his laptop and the presentation began. I felt very uncomfortable and tried to imagine what they were thinking of me but as we went along, halfway through the hour presentation I started to feel a little more at ease. It seemed that in many cases, presentations of this nature are somewhat sugar coated so at the end Greg asked penetrating questions that got to the heart of the matter. The presentation showed a great deal of progress with the Teams throughout the company. Greg asked a question that implied what is really happening and no one said a word for a moment. So I spoke up and told him what I thought and he said, "That is what I thought, too". A short while later during the conversation, I looked up and it seemed as though one of the women on his staff was glaring at me and it made me feel uncomfortable.

I had a fear that some people would think that I was making a mockery of the company or of gender related issue. All I knew at the time was to be myself and be professional as I had been for my entire career. It was a very strange and hurtful feeling. The meeting came to an end and I walked out with my group and we held a short debrief in the waiting area. We told each other to have a great day and I walked alone down the steps, through the lobby, and out the front door without incident.

By the time I reached my car back in the parking lot, I was shaking and dazed. I had to go to my office at the BL Plant and felt very apprehensive about meeting yet another group of people as my real self, Kaitlin. Normally I would rush from one plant and even racing through the yellow lights. However, this time I only drove the speed limit, stopped when the caution light appeared and slowly tried to calm my nerves. I arrived in ten minutes and noticed it was mid-morning as security opened the gate and waved me through. At that moment, I made a mental note to go to Human Resources and have my ID and other credentials changed to Kaitlin. It bothered me a great deal to have my old Id badge with "John" on it; and I had to repeatedly use it to gain entry into the Plant.

I parked my car in the BL Plant parking lot, checked my makeup, took a deep breath and walked toward the front. I couldn't help but giggle slightly to myself as Miss Ross started singing "Coming Out" in my head again! As I purposefully walked into the front door of the plant, I admit I was a bit relieved to see that there was no one in the lobby or hallway that led to my office. My counterparts were not in their offices either. I was pleasantly surprised to find the twelve brass name plate on my office door had been changed to read Kaitlin Riordan. I unlocked the door to my office and placed my laptop in its holder and powered it up. While it booted up I walked through the lobby and up the steps as I always did to get a cup of coffee and informed Fran and Tonya the Plant Manager that I had arrived. I got my coffee, said good morning to them and retreated quickly back to my office. I closed my wood framed glass door to the point where it was open one inch and sat down at the desk and began business as usual.

My computer was powered up and I went to my Outlook to read my email and found my full male name still present on everything. What the heck? I was extremely disappointed and called Gail to obtain her assistance with this issue. Gail immediately contacted the IS Department to have the problem rectified as quickly as possible for me. In the meantime, all the email that I needed to send out still showed that it came from "John" which also annoyed me. After the struggle I had endured and finally coming out, the last thing I needed was a reminder that I had not completely left John behind! The hallway in front of my office was extremely quiet which usually had people who passed through or stopped by my office for advice. Ken who was one of my peers and was responsible for the Production Department for the Plant had briefly stuck his head in and said good morning. The remainder of the day was very, very quiet in my hallway and there was no activity at all, which again, was quite unusual.

I concentrated on my work as best I could and only left my office twice the entire day to use the ladies room. Even then I waited until I *really* needed to go; I was completely on edge and did not even have lunch. I recall that when 4:00 p.m. finally inched its way around the clock, I gathered my things, walked to my car and went home to drink and see Zeb.

My feelings were somewhat bittersweet when I got home. On one hand, I felt very happy that I had started this transition on the job but sadden by the fact that I felt ostracized, before when I had left for my vacation there had always been plenty of business noise and activity around my office. I had known it would not be easy and I knew I had to be extremely professional; basically I had to continue being the person I had always been. Nothing had changed as far as my performance, knowledge, or work ethic. The only thing that had changed was I let the world know my truth. Nevertheless, I needed to be very vigilant in work and to ensure that the decisions I made were based solely on fact. I realized it was difficult for the people I had worked so closely with to deal with the "new me" because they had known and worked with "John" for 20+ years! I knew this was probably a shock to most, if not all of them and I would need to be patient and understanding with my expectations. As Tuesday and Wednesday crept by, so did a monster named loneliness. I fought it off with all my might as the days remained quiet and the email issue went on unresolved. As I recall this first week, it was one of the times that I had to really dig deep down inside to remain strong in order to not break down.

Thursday was not a great deal different from the other days of the week, but at least it did bring me closer to Friday. I continued to struggle with the IS department to fix my email account. It absolutely baffled me as to why this was such an issue; a simple name change! I remembered thinking how many women had married in the twenty years of my employ and subsequently changed their last names, and never did they encounter such issues with a freakin' name change. Suffice it to say; because all this issue was supposed to have been remedied prior to my return from vacation, I was beginning to get very annoyed! When I called yet again, they claimed they had been working on it and finally called in for more assistance. By mid-afternoon IS had worked on it to the point that my outgoing email finally read that it was from Kaitlin Riordan, finally. That was a really good feeling and it made me more willing to send out more work on a timely basis versus waiting until the name issue was resolved. Sometimes, it is the little things that matter: an email from "John" who was in an office dressed as a woman could possibly antagonize someone who might have been struggling with the situation. However, an email from "Kaitlin" seemed very normal and may just set the recipient more at ease.

With the email issue resolved and work caught up, I had decided it was time for me to get back to normal and get out into the factory. Around 10:30 a.m. I opened the door to the Production Facility and walked down the main thoroughfare towards the back of the factory. I immediately saw Frank, a Maintenance Supervisor who everyday would stop by my office to discuss production and equipment issues but had not done so in the past three and a half days. I was smiling and going to say hello to him but when he looked up and saw me he immediately went the other way. I knew immediately where his thoughts were and it was not good. I proceeded through the plant and could see the eyes popping out the dark forest like in a cartoon. "Boing," as the eyes popped out of their heads and popped back in! They watched my every move, looked, watched, waited, but no one said a word. I really did not encounter anyone, so I just watched the tobacco flow from one department to another. I walked back to my office worked on more team development training material and felt very proud of myself for taking the tour through the plant. It was one more step in the transition and I thought again: I must continue to be true to myself.

On Friday morning I attended a production meeting where I provided an update on both the Teams and plans for the coming months. I noticed that I listened more than usual and really did not comment on the issues that were presented like I normally would have done as "John". For whatever reason, I felt it useless to express my professional opinion at that particular time. In essence, I thought that people had had enough of me for one week and really were not interested in what I had to say on any topic, even if it were work related. Heck, 98% of the people could not even look me in the eye! After the meeting had concluded I returned to my office and to my utter disgust I found the email situation had reversed itself back to "John"! Now I was pissed off! How simple was it to change a freakin' name and IS couldn't or wouldn't get the task completed correctly in three weeks?! After I composed myself, I notified IS about the problem and firmly requested this issue be resolved ASAP. The IS guru stated they had problems when they tried to convert all my history and correspondence over to my new name. Unfortunately it stayed fouled up for the remainder of the day and I have to admit, I was never convinced that the IS department did not do it purposefully in an attempt to embarrass me or hurt me somehow. All I knew was I was glad it was Friday because I felt very rejected and unfortunately, I had allowed it to play with my mind.

The weekend brought about a great need to be around people who accepted me and it also increased my need to drink in order to ease my pain. When I drank, it helped me forget my constant struggle of being me and how I was treated like a second class citizen. I thought this was a form of discrimination that I could not do anything about and tried to convince myself that I needed to be patient with others because it had only been my first week. During that first weekend after the "Kaitlin First Week", I simply walked Zeb, hung out at Joe's Inn, Doll's, and another tavern. As I walked home drunk, I tripped over flower bed boarders, fell down on the sidewalk, and ended up with skinned knees and arms, and scraped biceps. When I arrived home, I was grateful to find my ever faithful Zeb waiting for me. Zeb was my saving grace because I always sat and talked with him and he listened attentively and he looked at me with great love and compassion. But most importantly, my buddy Zeb never once judged me. Nope, not once. He loved me unconditionally, as John and even more so, as Kaitlin. I love my Zeb ...

My opinion of Monday mornings differed from most as I was always ready and prepared for work regardless of how I felt because I have firmly believed that one must work hard if one wanted to play hard. At that time in my life, I was playing very hard. For the next several weeks, I stayed to myself, did my job and attended scheduled meetings. I did not offer my opinion to anyone unless it was totally work related and absolutely necessary. As time progressed, I began to field some questions from some of my peers which concerned being transgendered. All were very courteous towards me and empathetic. I found out who my friends really were and was quite surprised as to the friends that I had gained and the "friends" that I had lost.

154

The majority of the people who spoke with me at that time were women, and a spattering of men, who I only knew from work meetings. They stopped and spoke with me about the courage and strength I had in transitioning on the job. They told me they admired me and I really appreciated their kind words. I told them some of my story and explained how important it was for everyone to be able to be themselves. I found friends that I never really even knew existed. Also, there were people who dropped off the face of the earth who in the past, actually stood by me in my projects and decisions. I immediately understood that it was about the association with me for financial gain or promotion versus being truly helpful and genuine. There were people willing to work with me and helped me out. Conversely, there were also those whose hidden agenda was ultimately to bring me down. They saw it as a greater opportunity to possibly gain a promotion, and thought it would be easy to push me aside. I heard things like I was "damaged goods" and I would not "move forward in this company" and things of that nature. These things came from peers who were in conversations with me and stated they had my best interests at heart. I questioned myself on the validity of those remarks and wondered if they were really trying to get to me mentally. I was not sure but there were all different types of seeds that had been planted. This type of discrimination and harassment was one I had to suck up and take because I could not prove it nor was it wise for me to run to Human Resources over every little comment. At least that was how I chose to handle this particular problem. I looked at the comments as insight into what I thought was really happening and applied it to my integrity, trust, and professional work ethic.

For the past several weeks, I had worked with the Production Teams. I provided direction on how to become self-sufficient working with the teams and the team leaders. I made recommendations for improvement, provided training, and commented on their progress. It was all business and each meeting started and ended on time as necessary and the grouped typically stayed right on topic. I attended my Plant Leadership Team meeting during the past several weeks and become more comfortable with opening up more and more especially with maintenance and production issues, as well as with team updates and training.

The following week was time for me to work with the Maintenance Teams and Team Leaders. The first meeting I had with this group was to perform this exact same direction and training. The meeting was one sided as I did the majority of the speaking, which is not the way I facilitate meetings. To enhance participation, I decided to ask questions. The maintenance group was made up of about 95% men. They were attentive and even answered questions. My last question before the end of the hour was, "What else can I do to help you". A "gentleman" in the far back corner raised his hand and said, "You can stay out of our shop, we do not want you there". A hush fell over the room and all eyes were on me, waiting to see if I would back down. I remember I felt furious, shocked at the gall of this jerk! Well I straightened my spine, walked several steps toward the back of the room and looked him dead in the eye as if only the two of us were in the room and said, "As you know, I am a member of the Plant Leadership Team. I have the responsibility and the right to go anywhere in this Plant as I see fit and I will do so. And for the record, you are subordinate to me, you would be wise to remember that"! I held his shocked stare until he looked away and then I slowly eyed everyone in that room. I swear it was like one of those "When E.F. Hutton talks" commercials! Little did they know I was shaking under my camisole! But they all got the message: Don't mess with Kaitlin!

They all quietly left the Team Meeting Room and I thought about that nasty comment for a few minutes and decided to walk upstairs to the Plant Manger's office. I knocked on her door, walked in and explained what happened, but also stated I felt no need to take action right now, I simply wanted to make sure they understood the comment and wanted it noted for the record. I was assured that I still had full reign of the facility, regardless of any one employee's unprofessional comment.

156

During the next three days, I made it a point to walk through the maintenance shop and inspect the equipment. I stopped and spoke with two maintenance employees about their projects and provided feedback and encouragement before I continued with my business.

The following Tuesday, I looked out my office window and saw Gail and another HR Representative. They both walked in the direction of the Maintenance Shop. I thought to myself, hmmmm, I bet I know what that's about. And I immediately thought that I probably needed to be very careful with what I tell as well. I certainly did not want to create a perceived hostile work environment or an environment where I couldn't get along with others. My interpersonal relationship skills were one of my greatest assets and I certainly didn't want that to be skewed by this issue.

Anyway, a meeting had been conducted with the employee and the next three levels up in the maintenance group. Since I was not part of the meeting, I was told by one of the three that Gail confronted the employee and he claimed he did not mean what he said the way it sounded. He claimed he was only trying to say they were good for now and did not need help. Gail, in no uncertain terms, told the employee that if it happened again he would be terminated. It was wonderful that the company stood up for me, but at the same time I felt like I had lost and employee. He literally ran the other way when he saw me in the Plant. He would have leapt over a forklift and taken off like a scalded dog to get out of my way and I did not want this to happen. It defeated my purpose but reinforced company rules and I knew that rules must be enforced, I certainly had enforced many. I had always worked one on one through conflict with others and thought that I needed to continue that practice before taking things to the next level with at least an attempt to understand or offer the employee the opportunity to agree to disagree but still work together towards the same goal. I made this my practice and it worked much better. It took about nine months before this

guy even looked in my direction but he finally did....he looked.
He transferred to another facility about a week later.

Chapter 13 – "Friends"

On a Saturday afternoon in the middle of August, Teresa and I were invited by Marti and Ivan to Kathy's house for her birthday. I packed a cooler full of beer and met the four of them at her house in Brandermill, a very nice subdivision in South Richmond, half-million dollar homes. The area is considered quite prestigious.

It had been a little over a month since I transitioned on the job with Philip Morris and we sat around the pool and discussed the events of my transitioning and talked with Teresa about her surgery. She was sitting on a tire shaped blow up cushion which is necessary for a couple of months after gender reassignment surgery. She talked about the peace that she had felt, the aftercare of all the nurses in the Doylestown Hospital and the friendships that she had established with some of the nurses. Teresa was Dr. McGinn's first official patient and was referred to as, "the first lady of Doylestown." Teresa told us about her Amtrak trip home in a private room on the car and dilating as she watched the traffic in Delaware.

I drank my beer, noticing that I was the only one drinking. We jumped into the pool and lay on floats for a while before we lit up the grill to cook hamburgers and hot dogs. Kathy's father cooked while we set up the table on the patio and then sat down to eat. The talk at the table was continued from earlier conversations. Once we finished and cleaned up, we walked through the back yard and along the lake watching people in their boats.

We made our way back though the backyard and Kathy asked me to come over to the entrance to her ground level basement apartment. I had just opened a beer and she asked for a sip of it. I handed her the bottle and she drank down the entire beer. Kathy was confined to the property by her parents for some reason and she told me she was not supposed to be drinking. I did not understand why so when she asked for another one I brought us each one. About 15 minutes later her boyfriend / fiancé came over for a few minutes and left after meeting us all and having a short conversation with her. Then, she invited me into her basement apartment telling me to not make any noise, which seemed odd to me, but I agreed. I watched as she checked to see where her parents were and once satisfied they were settled in somewhere else she opened up a bag. It was cocaine. She grabbed a cutting board and then laid out two lines of cocaine and handed me a straw. She snorted the first line and then I took the second. This was only the second time in my life that I had done the stuff. She laid out two more, one much longer than the other. She snorted the long line and I hit the short one. I really don't know why I did this because I really did not like using drugs. But I was a people pleaser and just wanted friends that accepted me as I was, transition and all. Cocaine really did not do anything for me but made me more awake for a short while. I was much more satisfied with my beer but I did think the drug enhanced the alcohol. It was starting to get dark and I wanted to go and check on Zeb before heading out to Doll's to drink, dance, and play pool. Kathy asked me to come back soon and I gave her my phone number and told her to give me a call.

I thought while driving home about using the cocaine and wondered why I had done it. I remembered being the PTA President and supporting the DARE program and how I counseled my children on the danger of drugs. Although, in college, we did smoke weed and sometimes we used speed to stay up all night to study, but I really never considered myself a drug user, only a drinker who would fall down sometimes and had gotten only one DUI on New Year's Day, which translated for me: someone without a problem. Every drinker might have one DUI on January 1st, since everyone drank on that day. That was the way I thought about it, although, technically, the DUI was on January 2nd, 1999. I had no idea I was filling a void inside me and was allowing confusion to continue to build.

The initial shock of my transition had begun to subside a bit after the first six weeks at work and I felt a little more comfortable and thought maybe everyone else might be more comfortable with me as well. I believed that the employees had changed their erroneous thoughts about their associations with me in their own minds. During this period two "hourly employees" came to my office. One gentleman spoke with me about how he accepted everyone and he went on to explain that he did not have a problem with me whatsoever. I found it very sweet of him to come forward the way he did, but unfortunately I had to terminate him about two months later for excessive violation of the attendance policy.

Another employee, this time a female, came to my office in support of me and said, "I do not care what everyone else says about you, I think it is great that you get to be yourself". I told her that I appreciated her support. Once she left, I thought, I wonder what she meant by "what everyone else is saying"! Unfortunately I took this as rejection from the majority of the employees, and that was a personal set back at the time. I know she meant well so I had to take her words with a grain of salt and move forward. It was also interesting to me that these two employees had an extensive disciplinary action rap sheet.

For the next several months I went about my business as usual and actually spent more time away from my office and in meetings at the Operations Center and Park 500. I still worked with the teams, refined behaviors, and conducted elimination of waste exercises, taught problem solving techniques using PDCA, and implemented 5S throughout the factory. I really loved working for Philip Morris because the job gave me a great sense of accomplishment and I could be creative as I learned to use the latest technology which kept my work challenging.

As the fall of the year came, I always found it so beautiful as the leaves on the trees changed to orange, gold, and red and then floated through the air finding a resting place on the earth. The nights were cool, the days were warm and there were many people out and about because of the nice days. Activities picked up as school was in session and kids were all riding the buses or walking to school. From my house, I could hear the children on the playground screaming and laughing. One block directly behind my house on the other side of the park and street was a school and it was always full of life. I really enjoyed living in the inner city the historic district of Richmond. But with the good came the bad as I also saw the people who were living on the street and also the wealthy without a seeming care in the world. People from throughout the state visited the historic city seeing all the wealth and poverty mixed in one place. The environment was a mixture of open-minded and creative thinking and the area seemed considerably ahead of it time, a pocket of liberal minded individuals in a very conservative city.

I worked hard every day and never missed a day due to illness. If I felt bad I would chalk it up to excessive drinking and simply drive on, knowing it would pass soon. Normally, by the time I got to work I would feel better and besides, I immediately grabbed that cup of coffee after I unlocked my office door and fired up my computer. That first cup of coffee usually cured everything. Some days I had to come back to work at 11:00 p.m. and work with the third shift, but I was free to arrange my schedule provided I was assisted all the people over the three shifts. I found this not only fun but very rewarding. I had a great life for the most part, if only I could feel the love from my family that I wanted so badly. This poor me routine led me to feeling sorry for myself and to become a victim of my own pity-party, which led to poor me, poor me, pour me another drink!

At home when I was sat on the front porch with Zeb, we just watched people and cars. Barry would come by every now and then and sit and have a beer with me. By this time he had my phone number and once he asked me if "I did" anything other than beer and I told him absolutely not. Kathy had started calling me and invited me over to her parent's house to "swim". She knew that I would bring at least a 12 pack of beer, and I was happy to oblige because it was *only* beer. I thought about it, and realized I actually enjoyed being around her. I knew that she was confined to her house for some reason and only guessed that it was because of drugs and alcohol. I later learned that she was under house arrest because her parents prosecuted her because she "borrowed" the car and bought drugs. However, I decided that was none of my business. I liked her and gave her a couple of beers. We would swim and then go to her room as she guzzled down a beer in three seconds flat and then reappeared outside as if she had always been there enjoying the sun.

One night it had grown dark as I had stayed over until about 9:00 p.m. and Kathy wanted to go out on the town. She devised a plan where I would drive off as if I had left, she would tell her parents she was going to bed, and then she'd slip out the basement door, through the wooded vacant lot next door and then ride with me. She said she would get a cab home once she had finished in town. I waited one block away and in about 15 minutes Kathy came walking down the street in her blue jeans and long sleeve top and purse. I drove her to the Fan District where I lived and dropped her off on Main Street. She was 40 years old so I was not concerned and felt like she knew what she was doing. I called her the next day and all was well. She had gone out to see some friends and told me all her friends were calling her "GG" as she walked down Cary Street. I knew this was a drug dealing area and I knew what she was doing. She did get a cab ride home, sneaked back into the house and no one knew about this except the two of us.

It had now been about three months since my transition on the job and since some of the people were not as tense around me, I felt the tension within me had begun to ease. I was still very cautious and had a couple of girlfriends there that I could talk to who treated me as if there was never a change. Tammy and Evelyn were cool and upper management had to act as if they understood, which I think the majority accepted from a work relation standpoint. I thought the environment at work had become better and I would talk to a few of the employees on the production floor. These employees I learned, through trial and error, never had a problem with me. I knew who accepted and who didn't or at least I figured it out when I engaged in conversations and watched the body language. I got my message out with those who were willing to listen and could apply peer pressure to others.

Meanwhile, Barry had begun to stop in a little more and I found out that he lived with someone about a block over on Hanover Street and that he also rented a garage behind the house directly across the street from me. I thought this was odd and he told me that he deals in metals and resale's used equipment. I was leery of him because his story sounded a little shady. Nevertheless, he was very kind to me and as long as I was not involved in his business then I felt fine with his visits. After a few beers he told me he had to stay in his garage for the next three days because the person he was living with did not want him in the house when he was away on trips. I felt sorry for him but not sorry enough to allow him to stay with me because the whole situation somehow seemed like trouble. Although I felt all alone, too many warning signal sounded with this one and I just did not want trouble.

Around Labor Day, I went to Philadelphia with Teresa for an appointment with Doctor McGinn to discuss my options with surgery. She walked me through the surgery, discussed the Harry Benjamin real life test, the two psychologist letters, and that she preferred that her patients have electrolysis performed in the genital area prior to surgery. We set a tentative surgery date for August 7, 2008, which was one year and a month after my transition on the job with Philip Morris. The fee was "Cash in Advance" and I needed to cover my transportation and stay in Philadelphia for about 10 days once I was released from the hospital, which would be after about five days. I was very excited and was looking forward to the surgery in just eleven more months!

On a Thursday night in October at 9:30 p.m., my doorbell rang and to my great surprise it was Kathy. I asked her what she was doing here and she said simply stated she had come for a visit. I offered her a beer and told her I was going to bed in about an hour because I had to work in the morning. She said she was fine with that and was going to walk down the street and asked if I would stay up until she got back, and I agreed. I waited about thirty minutes, she rang the doorbell, Zeb went wild, she came in and closed double sliding doors to my parlor and pulled out three small balls wrapped in aluminum foil. She asked me if I had a pipe and when I told her no, she went into the kitchen and pulled out an empty Coke can she had discarded when she was there earlier.

I allowed her to use one of my candles, a spoon, a knife, and watched her dimple one end of the Coke can and poke a hole in the top. She unraveled the foil and filled the spoon with water from my wet bar and sat on the hard wood floor just below the bar. I watched as she placed a white rock in the water and lit the underside of the spoon. The rock separated with some floating on the top and some went to the bottom. She explained that the stuff on top is the good stuff and therefore the stuff you want, while the stuff that floats to the bottom is cut, and not good. She told me this was crack cocaine and it had a fair amount of cut with it. "Crack"! I shrieked, and then, "that shit is addictive"! Oh, Lord have mercy! What had I gotten myself into and was that all I could REALLY think to say? Not maybe something like, oh, let's see: "Get out of my house with that shit Bitch!" Oh no, I just stood there frozen and watched, horrified, yet mesmerized at the same time. She allowed the top piece to get hard again and then she placed it over the hole on the coke can and lit it with her lighter and inhaled through the top where you normally drink the soda. Then next thing you know she broke a small piece off and served me, and I thought, "I might as well try it once just this once, it's just a little bitty piece of rock. I won't get addicted to crack. Oh no, not ME!" So I inhaled and it really did not do much for me other than wake me up as if I had plenty of rest. Kathy finished the remainder over the course of the next hour and we sat on the floor in the bar and drank a beer.

We talked about her being able to leave her parent's house one day and possibly renting a room from me especially since I really could have used the extra cash to pay for my house and the renovations. Although, my income was six figures there never seemed to be enough money. I talked with my banker about shortage of funds and she looked at my account and said that I did not need to buy everyone drinks when I was at Doll's. I did not have the heart to tell her that it was **my** bar bill and not the whole bar! It averaged about $70 which included an $8 sandwich. Although, once in a blue moon, I bought someone a cherry bomb: cherry vodka in a shooter dropped into a glass full of red bull.

It was midnight, Kathy asked me to drop her off on Cary Street so she could score more crack. I agreed and waited for her at the gas station on Main Street. Since I was still wide awake I drove her down six blocks and waited. I was parked at the gas station and the wait was eternal. Ten minutes had gone by and I felt extremely nervous about this situation. I thought how it might look to a cop: a pre-op transsexual sitting in a gas station at one in the morning, with an open container of beer, after having had a hit of crack. I could imagine the cop would probably not look at it as a good thing. I felt very paranoid and thought the police were probably ready to show up any minute and just as I was about to go over the edge, my cell phone rang and it was Kathy. She said she was on her way and just around the corner but some guy was following her. I spotted her coming around the corner of a house and she ran up to the car and this guy was with her. She hopped into the car and the guy kept saying he wanted to party as we took off. She told me that she bought crack from him. I thought that this was absolutely crazy and very dangerous. It was only a couple of minutes from my house. We went in, Kathy got the stuff ready, I took one more hit from the coke can and she smoked for the next couple of hours. By this time it was 5:30 a.m., I told her I had to get ready for work and it was time for her to leave. She called a cab and I walked over to the café with her as the cab driver pulled up. She explained that she had the cab company pick her up at the café so her exact destination would be unknown. Kathy told me that if anyone asked to tell them I had not seen her. I thought it odd, but agreed. I went to work and was horribly exhausted during the afternoon. When I got home I went to bed early and prom-

166

ised myself not to do any more partying overnight on a work night every again.

I really did not want to get involved with Kathy and the drug use so I did not see her again for the remainder of the year. I focused on my work as the founder and president of JRTS and continued to work with the women in the group. We, the committee,, Teresa, Danielle, Bethany, and Melissa, conducted monthly planning meetings at my home to schedule speakers and events for the group. By this time the group was over a year old and we had 25 people who were interested in transitioning who would show up for the meeting. Danielle and Teresa had gender reassignment surgery with Dr. McGinn and they had their experiences to share. Teresa arranged for Dr. McGinn to come and speak with our group and we had Electrolysis, Endocrinologists, Mary Kay representatives, Lady Ellen from NJ, and others to speak to us at our monthly meetings concerning transitioning to female. Also, some of the monthly meetings were to simply go around the room and allow the members to share their feelings and experiences. JRTS is a very informative group and still ongoing under the direction of Melissa, Teresa, Danielle, and Bethany and her mother. However, there are a few very promising lady's ready to take over the helm.

I also focused on my work at Philip Morris. It was that time of year again, time for the Team assessors to go back into all the facilities for the semi-annual audit. We were to begin in late October and for me, this time around, would be much different. I would be out as my true self, Kaitlin, a female to every organization that touched Manufacturing. It would be a true test of my most inner strength and I knew that I had to reach down and grab every ounce of courage inside of me to complete this daunting task!

At the onset of my transition in July, Diane called me and told me that the employees at the Cabarrus Manufacturing Center had talked about me walking through the plants in Richmond wearing a dress and had made jokes about it. This was one time that I had to call Gail and let her know what was told to me. In middle of November, I was scheduled to assess teams at the Cabarrus Manufacturing Center in Concord, NC. I was transferred there in 1983 as part of the management start up team and I had deep roots with that plant. Concord, North Carolina, was the town where my children were raised and where Rebecca was born. John and Mark were three and one year old when I moved there with Kathleen. Diane still worked and lived there, so I had deep emotions about going back to the plant that I had helped start. I only hoped that things would go well and I really was concerned about the mindset of the people in the Heart of Dixie. I knew there were still small pockets of hate groups in NC. I feared in 2007 these people would show up at my hotel or heaven forbid, I would have a problem on the highway. Nevertheless, it was the right thing for me to do in order to live a truthful life.

Now nearing the end of October 2007, it was time to assess the teams and my group of peers, Mary, Veronica, and I scheduled and communicated to the teams that we were coming. Reggie and Tim accompanied us as alternates and backups. Mary was going to retire at the end of the year and my boss was preparing Reggie to possibly replace me on the team for next year's assessment. So, the five of us set off to assess teams at the two facilities in Richmond, one in Chester, and the smokeless plant in Williamsburg. The Cabarrus Manufacturing Center was our last stop on the list.

Admittedly it was different for me this time around. Because of the transition I was very much aware I wanted people to really like me as they had when I appeared male. So I took a more kind and gentle approach while I went about my business and tried to be very helpful. My peers got after me concerning the way I lead the teams during the assessment. Since this assessment was directly related to the plants performance and pay, it was very important to get to the real truth and not focus so much on other issues. I also felt that all eyes were on me and actually they were since the entire company had heard about my transition and this was the first time everyone was seeing me! In the plants that I assessed there was a tremendous amount of people who greeted me with open arms and an equal amount of people who would not speak. Granted I was more reserved and cautious, but this was certainly how it was as I used to speak with everyone. There was more whispering behind my back than I have ever heard in my entire career. I felt it and sensed it, it was palpable. It was especially obvious when I entered a room full of people and then immediately quieted down. Nothing was wrong with that, but my thoughts behind it were of the total focus on me as people were beginning to see me for the first time. People that I once had good rapport with and had respected were now a little quiet and disconnected.

The main issue about the fact that my position was "high exposure" within the company and the environment was that people who supported me would come up and talk, and that was great. Those who did not would stay away or politely say hello and move on. I thought that everyone understood the harassment policy and just did not want to get caught up in making a mistake that would stifle their career which was smart on their part. Nevertheless, I found it awkward to find out who my friends were and it was a relief to really know who my friends and colleagues were and who I could trust and count on. I felt alone even though most people were kind, courteous, and treated me with respect, they still kept a distance. It was this distance that really bothered me; they acted as though I had some sort of disease, a communicable disease!

It was time to drive east to Williamsburg about 52 miles from my house to assess teams. I felt comfortable as I drove around through Richmond and the metropolitan area in the back of my mind I was concerned about leaving the city and driving in the country off the Interstate. My driver's license name had been changed to Kaitlin Sine Riordan but the sex column stated M. I worried about ramifications of being stopped by the state police and the whole license issue would ensue. Who knew what some yahoo rookie local deputy sheriff, who wanted to be a hero and prove some point would do. I left my home in plenty of time so

I would not have the urge to speed and observe the traffic laws primarily because I did not want any trouble or to have to go through all the questions and have to explain myself to that rookie deputy sheriff.

I got nervous when I went into a different facility for the first time since transitioning because I really did not know how people would react. Although the company had specific guidelines on behavior, in the back of my mind I still had that sense of uneasiness and felt that something could go wrong. Dealing with people, I just never knew when someone was going to go off. I had the "waiting for the shoe to drop" mentality. But, I believed that it was very helpful to me to have worked through my fear in the beginning at the Operations Center when I sat in the same room as the Vice President and then walked out without incident.

I made my presentation to the Plant Management Team in Williamsburg and it went very well, just like old times. We toured the factory and looked at the new equipment, improvements to the process, and assessed the teams. It was a very good day and the smokeless facility had made great strides toward a self-sufficient and self-managed workforce. The employees on each team had great records regarding safety, quality and production and problem solving techniques as implementation of their solutions were making a difference in the efficiency and operating costs of the plant. It was a very good day for me. As I drove back into Richmond, I felt comfortable and better about myself and my job. I started to feel like I belonged again. Still there I felt a twinge of uneasiness and I wondered, was it me or was it them that created this feeling? I thought about it as I continued to drive and realized there was no reason for this uneasiness, this feeling of foreboding, and I decided to let it pass for the moment and relish the victory I had enjoyed at the plant.

The drive to North Carolina was as always, very scenic. I had traveled it for the past twenty-five years, going back and forth from Richmond to Charlotte. I had traveled this road many times dressed as a female for the past two years. I always got concerned when I drove through Dinwiddie and Spotsylvania counties in Virginia and Davidson County in North Carolina. Davidson County had the infamous pink jail cells and I imagined being humiliated in that place. These three counties always had deputy sheriffs patrolling the Interstate. They were "good ole boys" and in the south that always meant danger. I had no basis for my claim it was just one of those "feelings", call it women's intuition. If I got stopped I wanted it to be a State Trooper; I thought they had at least a little more knowledge about transgendered individuals as they were employees of the State. I figured I had a better chance with them if something happened.

I often thought how horrible it was to travel around in fear simply because of the lack of understanding, tolerance, and knowledge of other people. I knew that being transgendered was something that the average person didn't understand and because of this, it caused fear. That fear of people like me perhaps, in turn, caused anger because they might have felt "fooled" by a transgendered person. This anger often, if not always, could lead to rage and then to violence. That was why I tried to practice the truth so I'd never catch anyone off guard which would activate their rage. This truth lasted for a while until the real test came five months later.

I met Mary Ellen in the parking lot of the Manufacturing Center in Richmond and we followed each other to the Marriott Hotel in Concord, NC. It was a beautiful sunny Monday morning in the middle of fall, during the time when it was warm in the afternoons and cold at night. I checked in using my Virginia Driver's License with the "M" on it without a hitch. I proceeded to the fourth floor of this beautiful hotel and as I looked down into the lobby and bar area before opening my door, it reminded me of a cruise ship. If nothing else was right, at least the accommodations were gorgeous!

Once I set up the room, Mary Ellen and I met in the lobby to drive over to the Cabarrus Manufacturing Center to meet Veronica (Reggie and Tom did not make this trip) for the opening meeting. In each plant that we visited we had an opening meeting to introduce ourselves and lay out the agenda and schedule for the week. It was really simple and it gave the Plant employees an opportunity to ask questions. Also, when the assessment was finished we conducted a summary meeting to identify high level issues and general accomplishments with the teams. The General Manager and all the Department Heads were present, and a host of employees who represented their teams made up of safety, quality, production, maintenance, and engineering. I felt relatively comfortable as I walked through the main entrance and down to the auditorium and stood in front of the stage to give the presentation. There were no issues or problems and it was very basic and simple. The room filled and emptied quickly and soon we were up the elevator to the Continuous Improvement Managers of Manufacturing office for a visit. DeNorris was my boss when he was at the BL Plant and we had a tremendous amount of coaching sessions discussing, Providing Direction for the Teams and this was no different. I had learned a great deal from him at the BL Plant, painfully at times but a tremendous amount of good stuff which ended up being the truth.

After a short organizational meeting we went back to the hotel and prepared for dinner at a local steak house. I took the opportunity while I waited for everyone to leave, to stop by the bar and have my two complimentary drinks. Off to the steak house and a couple of beers and a steak with the Continuous Improvement Department from the Plant and then back to bed.

We were scheduled to be in the plant for the week and return to Richmond on Friday. We met with the teams on all three shifts some at midnight, others at 7:00 a.m., and still others during afternoons and evenings. It was a tough schedule to assess 25% of the teams on a random basis over the course of the week, and it kept us very busy.

One of the teams we assessed was in the tobacco delivery area of the plant to the making machines that were located upstairs. This is the area that I transferred to from Richmond some 23 years earlier and had led the team start up while I worked with mechanical and electrical contractors which installed equipment and programs. Also from this area came the joking that Diane told me about and the supervisor of this area specifically was mentioned to me as being the instigator. However, it was obvious to me that from the time I called Gail to this visit there had to have been some communication with the employees in the Plant because there was no harassment from the employees in this area or from the Supervisor, even though previously the supervisor of the Team we were assessing had acted and showed signs of disapproval and disgust with me. This time he simply reminded me of the safety rules and watched to make sure my hair was up and within the guidelines of the Safety Policy as we left the conference area and back onto the Production floor. It was this kind of thing that bothered me as the company was wonderful to me but there were those who could operate within the letter of the law and make me feel very uncomfortable without violating the harassment policy. I had to develop thick skin and not allow this type of behavior to bother me and just go about my business as if everything was good. I was sure there was more going on with this individual because he was hired as a Supervisor 20 years ago and was still a Supervisor and had never been promoted. I had been promoted three times over the course of the years and actually left the company for six years before returning in 1999. I did not allow his insecurity to affect the way I conducted my business but I was aware of his unspoken thoughts and did not show any discomfort I may have felt. Although I do recall I thought something like, "Screw you Buddy, I am here and you cannot do anything about it!"

I was still very much in the people pleasing phase of my life and wanted everyone to like me, so I tried really hard to ensure that I was liked and this is where my fear developed. I was afraid people would not like me anymore and so I approached everything cautiously. There were two other teams I assessed that I walked into with a low comfort level. One was at midnight where my former next door neighbor worked and another area where Diane worked. Although Diane worked on the third shift and I assessed the second shift, it was nerve racking to go into the meeting, knowing very well all the people in the room who had worked for me at one time and were good friends with Diane. Once the meeting and assessment were over everything was fine. The employees treated me with respect, asked how I was doing and even privately complained about Management with me and discussed the way things were being done. I spoke with them and helped ease their minds as I had in years past without a problem. It was good; it probably was me that had the fear and feeling uncomfortable especially because of the previous day in tobacco storage.

In the cafeteria, my former boss came over and sat down beside me. We had a nice lunch together and talked in general about the teams and how things were going and life in Cabarrus County. One of my really good friends, a graduate of University of Tennessee, who I used to hang out with, was sitting three tables over. He and I used to take our wives to dinner together, and we watched the Notre Dame versus Tennessee football game each year while our children played together. As I got up to put my dishes away and return to the assessment, all I got out of him was a barely perceptible nod of the head. He did not even make direct eye contact with me. I was disappointed, but thought it was a shame, a waste actually, and went on with my professional business at hand. I grew to accept that everyone was not with me and I had to stay with those that were kind and tolerant. Furthermore, it was important for me to do my job and walk through every situation without showing any fear and ensuring my professionalism was beyond reproach. I was a leader and made sure everyone saw me as such, regardless of my manner of dress or gender.

On Friday morning the close out meeting was held with the VP and General Manager of the Cabarrus Manufacturing Facility. The high level synopses of our findings were provided at that time. I answered everyone's questions and explained the results would be provided within the three weeks after Thanksgiving and the score would go on the Plant's scorecard for their pay for performance bonus. All in attendance seemed satisfied with the contents of the meeting and the meeting came to a close without any awkward questions or ill feelings.

After the meeting, I stayed in the auditorium with the team members until everyone had left and answered individual questions, which took an additional 20 minutes or so. Afterwards we departed through the front door and since I had already checked out of the hotel, I proceeded to my car to drive home. Veronica, who worked at Cabarrus, was going to Richmond so she rode with Mary Ellen and we stopped for brunch in Mebane, NC. We discussed our parts in the upcoming reporting process and divided everything up and worked off the same spreadsheets and power point presentations.

I was anxious to get back home and thought about the visit and assessment in Concord, NC. I was truly emotional as it was a growth experience for me to have visited all the facilities in the United States as my true self, a female. It was very satisfying and a bit disappointing at the same time. I really did not like the fact that some of my old "friends" were not tolerant. As I drove into Virginia, I thought about the meetings that had obviously taken place before my arrival, i.e. the big jokes at my expense just three months ago. It was not my purpose to be disruptive or waste the company's time, but it was a goal for me to be the best employee possible and I needed to be myself and eliminate that personal distraction. I had to admit, I felt very lonely at that time.

Julie and Jennifer had been dog sitting Zeb for me and I could not wait to get home to see him. As I approached Richmond I thought about Zeb and how happy I knew he would be to see me. I wished deep down that other people in my life would be like him and feel the same way. After I squeezed into a parallel parking spot, I rushed into the house and gave Zeb a big hug and a kiss before I opened the refrigerator, grabbed a beer, outside he and I went for a good long walk.

Chapter 14 – The Turkey Died on Thanksgiving Day

I sat on the back porch steps, looked over the fence into the park, drank my beer, threw the ball to Zeb, and thought about the 60+ teams our group had just finished assessing. The overall movement of the teams to become self-sufficient was a major Strategic Initiative of the company to develop the Philip Morris Production Systems and build quality Business Units. It was working and the organization was making huge strides toward accountability of each employee to eliminate waste and operate efficiently. It felt great personally to be part of such a wonderful organization. I thought about the day I believed the company would fire me for being transgendered. My only wish was that my family would soon allow me to see them and that some of the people at work would be a little friendlier. Unfortunately I dwelled on the negativity of my parents, family, and coworkers, which led to an increase in my unhappiness and more beer consumption. When I drank, I thought it was a great way to sit in self-pity and relieve my pain. I allowed this negativity to enter my spirit and I fed it continued negative thoughts.

It was a week before Thanksgiving 2007 and since I had five weeks of vacation I normally take that week off, and this year was no exception. On Friday at 4:00 p.m., I locked my office door, headed home to see Zeb, and to let the good times roll by drinking. I went over to Doll's after I spent time with Zeb, had a sandwich, a few beers until 2:00 a.m. and left with a bar bill of $70. I drank, played pool, danced all night and about 2:15 a.m. decided it was time to take my drunk self home to walk and check on Zeb. While I drove, I looked for a place to park by my house and spotted a place across the street in the opposite direction I was traveling so I turned left on Addison and backed up really quick and to my utter surprise I had bumped into a VCU student driving her VW. I jumped out of my car and told her how sorry I was and immediately looked at her fender on the left front side. It was not bad and told her it would probably cost about $200 to repair, which I felt was true because this was not the first time this had happened to me and it had cost $200. I begged her to not call the police because I had been drinking and offered her $1000 on the spot to forget all about it. I told her that I lived only seven houses up and wrote her a check for $1000 on the spot and she accepted it. That check, or perhaps I should call it what it was, "hush money", cleared my bank in two days! I dodge another huge bullet, again. As I walked inside to see Zeb, I decided I had enough for one night, and changed into more suitable clothes and Zeb and I went for a nice sobering walk and retired for the evening.

I thought I was pretty smart; I had outrun the police a year earlier and paid off people just to cover up my drinking and driving episodes. My excessive drinking had really started to worsen as my loneliness set in and the feeling of rejection of my family worsened as well. Teresa told me she thought I drank a little too much and I told her I would slow down. Unfortunately I started to go into another part of the bar and drink more. I no longer drove to Doll's anymore and started calling a cab instead. I typically walked the 14 blocks at 2:00 a.m. to get home. Many, many times I fell down on the sidewalk and it took great effort to get up on my feet and stagger home. I had become the drunk we have all seen and pitied an despised. Yet, I did not see that myself. Unfortunately this was a normal weekend activity all the way until Christmas.

During the week of Thanksgiving, I went out on a Tuesday night with Julie and we had dinner and did some bar hopping. Once we got back to her house she asked me to watch her dog Magic while she walked down the street. She wanted to go get something and so I watched the dog for about 20 minutes. She returned with one rock of crack cocaine. She gave me a very small piece and showed me how to smoke it in a glass stem and I did. It lasted just a minute or two and I watched her smoke the rest. It felt good, but nothing special and I went home to Zeb and went to bed.

Thanksgiving Day arrived and I was home alone. My friends had plans with their families or significant others. It was just me and Zeb, as we sat in the dining area at 11:00 a.m. I drank beer after beer and thought about my family and the celebration that they all enjoyed together. Just like 2006, I was not invited to participate in the Thanksgiving Dinner at my parent's house. My mother and father always had a huge dinner at 1:00 p.m. with all my siblings and a few close friends. I could almost taste the 25 lb turkey, dressing, casseroles, freshly baked bread, and the pies that my mother worked to prepare for days. I felt totally abandoned by my family and came to the realization that I no longer have a family. It was bitterly sad, I cried and cried. I walked Zeb around the city, crying all the way, took him home and drank some more.

At 2:00 p.m., I walked a block and a half over to Joe's Inn, sat at the bar directly in front of the beer on tap and ordered a pitcher of beer and a barbecue sandwich and watched the football game on the wall television in the corner. I drank the whole pitcher while I watched the game talking with the barkeep and anyone who would listen. I finally walked back home at 5:30 p.m. to feed Zeb and take him for a walk. I sat down at the dining room table and felt so very lonely and sorry for myself. Naturally I drank some more beer. I thought about my family and wondered how they were doing and knew they were having a great time. I felt sadder as the day moved to dusk and decided to take Zeb for another walk around the neighborhood.

Zeb and I walked out the front door and down the steps as it was just starting to get dark and the clouds had gathered. It looked and smelled like it may rain. I always carry my cell phone with me when I walk Zeb in the city for security reasons and in my drunken wisdom decided to call my parents and wish them a Happy Thanksgiving. It was about 7:45 p.m. and I dialed my parent's number and my mother answered and said "Oh it's you".

I said, "Happy Thanksgiving Mom, I hope you had a great dinner".

My mother said, "We did."

I asked, "How's Dad doing?"

I then heard her hand him the phone and she said it was John, as I was starting to walk through the alley behind my house with Zeb.

My father said, "Hello?"

I ecstatically said, "Hey Dad, how are you?"

My father said, "I want you to know, you are the worst experience of my entire life!"

I said, "All I wanted to do was wish you Happy Thanksgiving and tell you I love you." The phone went dead as he hung up.

I fell to the ground and laid on the gravel and tar in the dark alley, rain drops pelted me in the face as I sobbed after hearing those hurtful words. After 22 months without any contact with my father whatsoever, his last words to me were, "You are the worst experience of my entire life". His words were devastating and shivered through my bones each and every day for the next couple of years. I totally understood that I was no longer a person in the eyes of my family and it led me down an even more destructive path. When my father said this to me it totally changed the way I looked at everything. I was totally alone and I felt that there was no such thing as unconditional love in the world. When my own flesh and blood would disown me, I rationalized that love only came with certain conditions. My condition was not one of them. It became easier to focus on my work, and my transition, as I drank to ease the pain. It was the ultimate rejection. I felt worthless. I tried hard to stay away from these feelings as much as possible in order to continue on with life. I was born this way and that was the truth regardless of the pain it was taking to make things right. It was a life or death situation for me. The thing about Zeb was that he was always there for me no matter what, and I had something living to hold on to and a few friends and the JRTS group. I still maintained the thought that I loved my family even though they did not understand or love me. It was a feeling of being dead, and cremated, with the ashes thrown to the wind, but still having feelings.

Chapter 15 – A Different Lesson

I awoke Friday morning with an all-consuming, unbearable lone-liness that tore at the very fiber of my being. I was still in shock from my horrific Thanksgiving Day telephone call yesterday and was not thankful for anything at the moment. I drank coffee, read the paper, and threw ball to Zeb and after I finished an en-tire pot of coffee, I walked Zeb around the neighborhood. Upon our return, I switched my beverage of choice from coffee to beer and sat alone in the dining room, slammed back beer after beer and thought about my family. The more I thought about my family, the more I drank. Since I was on vacation, I could con-tinue my destructive behavior if I desired because I had nowhere to go and no responsibilities. I was in the throes of a full blown "Pity Party", it was poor me that I was no longer a member of my own family, poor me that I was all alone, poor me that I drank too much, poor me, poor me, pour me another drink! I stayed there until the late afternoon when the mail came and Zeb chomped down on the letters as they came through the slot. It was a moment of laughter as he always seemed to know how and when I needed cheering up. After I put the mail away, I finally decided to get off my butt and get myself fixed up and dressed for the day. I felt there was no need to call anyone. I felt like it was me and Zeb against the world. Zeb and I went for another long walk about seven blocks down. I talked with him and he would stop from time to time, cock his head and look at me as if he understood. After we walked about seven blocks in a differ-ent direction other than our norm, I played a game with Zeb and told him to take me home. I did not lead him, I just allowed him to take me back to see if he could do it. Every time he led me back to the house no matter how far we had gone and he would even take a different route back. He was truly a wonderful gift for me and helped me to maintain my dwindling sanity and brought me great joy, then and now.

I went down to the Inn and had a pitcher of beer and a cheeseburger and promptly returned home to sit on the front porch with Zeb. I could see down Strawberry Street toward Monument and Barry appeared from around the corner of the alley halfway between Park and Monument. He saw me and I'm sure he already knew I was there and came up and had a beer. I was talking to him about the events from the day before and he told me that he was an orphan and had lived his childhood in the orphanage in the city down just on Board Street. I thought, "Oh great now both of us do not have a family so we can be miserable together". As we drank a couple more beers, I asked him if he ever did cocaine and he told me he used crack. I asked if he had any and said, "I thought that you said you do not do drugs". I told him that I don't, but if he had some I might try some. He went about his business, whatever that was, and I remained on the porch and talked with people as they walked by and watched the craziness at the intersection with people, cars, and people with dogs and people with their children in strollers, as they tried to make their way in different directions. I just sat around with Zeb, and whiled away the afternoon.

At 8:00 p.m. the telephone rang and I heard Barry at the other end. He said he wanted to come over because he had something for me that would make me feel better and he asked if I would go get a 12 pack of beer. I told him I would and walked across the street and bought the beer. He came rolling up Strawberry Street in this old blue truck that I had never seen before and lumbered up to the front porch where I was sitting. We went into the living room and I offered him a beer and he took it and went upstairs to my television room which had an enclosed porch surrounded by glass and a stained glass door that opened onto the porch. The room had a window that looked directly through the window of the vacant four story home next door and about three feet separated the two houses with a narrow walkway in between. Barry asked for a comforter, covered the stained glass door, tightly closed the Venetian blinds on the window and turned on one small lamp. He pulled about 5-6 white rocks and two copper pipes out of his pocket. He inserted a troy, a metal mesh ball used for scrubbing, into the tops of each and lighted the ends to burn off the residue from the troy which acted as filters. He asked for a small wet rage and loaded up one end of the copper pipe with crack cocaine, fired it up, and held the rag around the pipe so it would not burn his fingers. As he inhaled I could hear a crackling sound and watched his face turn red as he held it in as long as possible before exhaling.

Barry handed me the second pipe and broke off a piece of crack cocaine and I put it into one end just like I watched him do it. He told me to be careful that a part of a rock would be enough for now. So I fired it up, inhaled, held it in for as long as I could before exhaling and immediately my "Thanksgiving Day experience" and feeling of rejection was gone. I felt no pain whatsoever! In fact, I felt carefree, alive and quite frankly, it was the best feeling in the world. Suddenly I had no problem at all and I finally felt great, just like the alcohol used to make me feel, many years ago when it took away my pain and confusion. At that moment, I was not aware that the crack highway was a road that led to nowhere to the point that it would cause me to completely lose my spirit.

We smoked and drank until about 2:00 a.m., until the crack was gone. Barry asked to borrow my car and went out for some more. He said he would be only 15 minutes and so I agreed. Barry was very paranoid as he looked outside, checked the blinds multiple times to see if anyone was watching and hustled out the front door to my car parked directly in front of my house. Zeb and I sat on the front porch in the dark at 2:15 a.m. as Barry pulled back up. He told me to get in the house and not to come outside again when he was gone on a run. We smoked and drank until about 5:00 a.m. and all I can remember is that I gave about a two and half hour lecture on supply and demand, I imagine from my days studying Economics at the University of Richmond. I just remember that it was fun and I was actually talking to no one. I finally got in the bed around 5:30 a.m. after I played ball and walked Zeb and told Barry he had to go and although not too happy, he left without incident.

After I woke up Saturday around 1:00 p.m., I felt horrible and made a pot of coffee. I picked up the newspaper off the dining room table, and while I had no memory of it, I had obliviously brought it in early that morning. After I consumed the entire pot of coffee and read the paper, I sat on the back steps and played with Zeb and switched over to beer for the remainder of the day. My entire afternoon was spent drinking beer, walking Zeb, and playing with him in the yard while intermittently watching NCAA football on television. As the sky darkened, which was around 5:30 p.m. this time of year, I went upstairs and prepared to go over to Doll's for the usual Saturday night ritual of dinner, dancing, drinking, and playing pool with the lesbians and transgendered girls. My close calls with the law had made me smarter, because I had called a taxi to pick me up and take me there. I was being proactive in my thinking: I was not going to drive and get a DUI tonight or hit anyone or out run the police. After I spent six hours at Doll's and closed the place down, I asked one of the bartenders to call me a taxi and at a little past 2:00 a.m., I paid my bill and waited outside. I waited maybe five minutes and lost my patience and decided to walk the 14 blocks home. As I crossed Cary and the Boulevard, I stumbled closer to home, I heard the sound of a gun shot off in the distance, which at the time did not faze me, but I hurried home as fast as possible which was a chore considering I was drunk and in heels. I learned the next day that someone was shot in Byrd Park, which was only two blocks from where I had been stumbling alone, earlier that morning!

I slept again until about one in the afternoon and did the usual coffee, paper, Zeb routine. It was Sunday, so I turned the TV on and watched two NFL games while drinking beer and took it easy because my vacation was over and I had to get back to work on Monday. I stayed home the entire day and thought about the craziness that I had created from Thanksgiving until this point. I did not want Barry over again and I did not want

any more drugs. I went to bed around 9:00 p.m. and set my
clock for 6:00 a.m.

Chapter 16 – Holidays 2007

I had a rule that if you play hard you must work hard. Monday morning was no different. I knew that since I had played all week it was time to work really hard this week and get to the weekend. I woke up and worked on my face. Although I disliked shaving immensely, it was a chore I was forced to undergo on a daily basis because the electrolysis and hormones had not rectified the problem. Typically I kept a razor in my purse to touch up any spots that I noticed during the day, but usually the hair issue was kept at bay until the next morning. After years of practice and serving as a Mary Kay representative, I was really good with makeup. I learned to lightly apply makeup and looked as natural as possible. I actually helped a lot of girls in JRTS with their application of makeup.

After such a wild week and weekend, I was actually ready for work and buried myself in the presentation for the Vice President on team development and progress. Once the presentation was complete and we three assessors where on the same page, our bosses were notified that we were ready so that a review could be done prior to their perspective plants receiving the information so that they would know what was coming down the pike. Furthermore, I had to provide a report to my boss, detailing each of the team scores and discuss in writing the basis for the score, by line item. The overall continuous manager was not in agreement with this and there was some conflict between me, my boss, and the company manager. However, I had to do what my boss told me to do and it was very tedious. None of the other facilities had to follow this procedure, in fact, they chose rather to work with the teams face to face and provide them direction. My issue was teams in the Process Plant group that did not fare well. My boss came down on me as if I was responsible for not standing up for them. I resented the fact that the assessment team treated everyone the same and there was some implication that I could sway the number more in favor of the teams my boss represented, which was a wider range than in my control. There-fore, I felt a bit of behavior change between my boss and I and I could not help to think it was related to my transition. The pos-sibility existed that I had imagined it, but then again, I had been around a very long time.

I walked into the Marlboro Room and said a few words to Greg, who was the Senior Vice President. He and I had known each other for 20+ years and after we exchanged a few words, we both took our seats. We gave the presentation to the Greg and his staff and we discussed the overall movement of the teams from an organizational level. My role in the actual presen-tation was to simply sit with the team of assessors and be availa-ble for any questions which were somewhat minimal; in other words, to sit and look pretty. After the presentation and Q & A, Greg thanked us for our work and we were dismissed. As I left the room, my former boss from the BL Plant Manager who named me as her successor ignored me totally and acted as if I was not even there. That really hurt me because we had worked so closely together in resolving plant issues a few years ago. I decided she needed to at least give the "greeting of the day" to Miss Kaitlin and made a point of speaking to her directly and a bit on the well, loud side. I simply cleared my throat with a cough that would make a whooping crane proud, and when eve-ryone stared in my direction I ever so innocently said, "Why hel-lo Beth, so good to see you! I didn't see you ducking, oh I mean bending down over there! What a darling blouse you're wearing! We'll have to catch up someday soon, bye now! I turned on my heel and left, but before I could get completely out the door, I did hear a nice chuckle out of Greg and a very faint, "Oh, uhm, hiuh, bubye Kaitlin" out of 'ol Beth! Her bright, crimson red face certainly told me she wasn't feeling quite contrary that mo-ment ... Ignore me after all these years? Ha!

Over two weeks had passed since I had seen or heard any-thing from Barry. I came home from work on a Tuesday night and had a strange crack craving. Without a thought I called Bar-ry, just to see what he was doing of course.

Ring, ring. "Hey Barry, whacha doing?"

"Nothin' much, what's up?"

"Welllll, I'm kinda in the mood for a beer or two, you?"

"I'll be right over. Get at least a twelve pack."

I immediately went to the store and picked up the beer and started frying some chicken breasts in olive oil and said out loud, "What in God's name are you doing Girl, this is so crazy, getting involved with the crack and Barry, let alone on a work night, Lord Have Mercy!" I shook my head and had just finished cooking the chicken as the knock came on the front door. I covered the chicken, removed it from the stove and let in Barry. He immediately went upstairs and performed the same paranoid routine of covering the windows and looking all around to see if anyone was watching. Satisfied that all was covered and no prying eyes could see what we were about to spend the next few hours doing, he pulled out 5-6 more rocks and fired it up. I gave him a beer and he handed me the cooper pipe again and a bigger piece of a rock than I had two weeks ago for my first hit. I thought it was just as fantastic as it was two weeks ago and all the pain, rejection, work issues, I had been carrying were all suddenly gone. During the entire crack attack, I never abandoned Zeb. I took him out periodically, but I never took care of myself. The chicken stayed on the counter all night, as I drank and smoked crack cocaine. I went to bed about 3:00 a.m. and got up three hours later and got ready for work. Barry was asleep on the sofa, but I woke him and told he had to leave because I had to go to work. He was angry when I woke him up but got up and left nonetheless.

Although I felt horrible, I followed my own rule: play hard, work hard regardless of how I felt. I knew I had to pay the devil for being foolish the previous night. I had to go to work and not only do a good job, but excel! I had a very tough day but I willed my way through it and made progress on my work. I vowed to never party like that again on a weeknight and meant it.

For the past ten years I had come home from work and drank beer, it had progressed from a couple to almost a 12 pack a day on many occasions. I never really felt it in the mornings but I did notice a change in the way I felt once I started hormones. I could not drink as much before feeling the effects and in the mornings I felt very bad for a few hours. Now that my internal hormones were flipped with more estrogen and less testosterone and I had the same levels as a female, my tolerance level for alcohol had diminished significantly.

Christmas of 2007 had rapidly approached, so I called my brother David and sister Ann and asked them if they would go to dinner or even lunch for a Christmas celebration. David and Ann had begun to accept me and I viewed them as my link to my family. I could check up on everyone through them and I really appreciated that they tried to reach out somewhat. Although my brother and sister would not introduce their children to me, I still considered it a move in the right direction. David, his wife Melanie, and Ann came to my house on the Saturday before Christmas that year and we walked over to the Café for lunch. We visited for about two hours, had lunch, and I gave them a tour of my old, 1915 Victorian home; the time we spent together made my heart feel so much better. It had been at least ten months since I'd seen David. He is a CPA and he was kind enough to do my taxes for me. We had gone to a BBQ restaurant earlier in the year to get that daunting task accomplished. It was so very nice to connect with all of them. I gave them all a Christmas coffee mug as a present, which they all seemed to genuinely like.

Christmas Day had arrived and Zeb and I rushed downstairs like youngsters! We looked at our presents on the sofa, went into the kitchen for coffee, and out the back door for our daily romp. It was very cold outside so we did not stay too long before we came back in and opened our presents. Zeb immediately wanted to play with his new tennis balls; he loved to chew on the new ones and break them in much like a baseball pitcher would rub down a new ball before pitching it. I opened my present from

Zeb. He "got" me a new pair of slippers, jeans, and a top ... he always seemed to know exactly what I wanted! I thought about my family, wished them a Merry Christmas, and hoped they would "feel" my blessings. I thought about how they would all be together at my parents house enjoying each other, exchanging gifts, and sharing the joy of Christmas Day. Normally the family member arrived around 1:00 p.m., had dinner at 2:00 p.m., and exchanged gifts by 3:00 p.m. Afterwards we all sat around and simply visited with each other and started back to their respective homes between 5-6:00 p.m. This was the second year that I had not been invited simply because I was transgendered. At 2:00 p.m., I walked the block and a half to the Inn, ordered a hamburger and a pitcher of beer and wished the few who were there a very Merry Christmas.

I not only had a very difficult time during the holidays, but throughout the year as well, because I could not handle my family's complete rejection. I was still the same person inside and I was only matching my physical appearance with my most inner feelings. I was being true to myself which I honestly felt was a life saving journey. I thought back on the time when I wanted to kill myself and knew it was absolutely the wrong thing to do. Life was too valuable to take it and I <u>knew</u> this and regardless of the circumstances, I knew I could make it through. The lack of understanding or even the willingness to understand was quite simply, a pure shame in my book. I was a woman without an island, nonexistent in the eyes of her family; a family that had a great attraction to appearances and who thought of me as an embarrassment. So they kept me "out of sight", which helped them keep me "out of mind"; at least this was my thought.

Chapter 17 – Crossing the Lines

There was a huge New Year's Eve celebration to bring in 2008 in Carytown for the very first time, modeled after the one in NYC's Time Square. It was a giant street party with bands, beer, food, and entertainment. All the shops and bars were open and the police barricaded the area from vehicle traffic. I arrived at Doll's at 6:00 p.m. and began my normal routine of dining, drinking, dancing, and playing pool. Several members from JRTS were there and we all prepared to bring in the New Year with a blast at least that was my plan. At this stage in my drinking I had become a big shot in a small world. I declared Doll's as "our" house for the evening acting as if I owned the place. And heck, why not, whenever I walked through the front door my beer was waiting on the bar for me without even asking, and when I started to drink it, the second one appeared. I slammed the first one down, picked up the second and headed to my booth. It was my house, my rules, and my people. I even helped kick people out or called them a taxi and told them to go home.

Teresa, Bethany, and I walked out of Doll's around 10:30 p.m. the street which was about five city blocks was absolutely packed with people. We battled and elbowed our way down to the stage where a band was playing surrounded by the police and people. It was a mob and it was fun. The ball was to drop off the old Carytown Theater at midnight and we wanted to see it. I vaguely remember that the ball did drop but I cannot recall seeing it only hearing a roaring countdown to the New Year. My two friends decided it was time to go home but I decided it was time to go back to Doll's. I walked back about three blocks and there was a waiting line of about 75 people. I walked to the front of the line and told the ID Checker I owned the bar, and then I simply opened the door confidently walked right in without skipping a beat. I guess that's what three years of being a regular and spending a couple of thousand annually will get you.

The place was jamming and I danced until we closed the bar down at 2:00 a.m.

I paid my $80 bar tab and walked out the side door onto Cary Street to find that most of the people had gone home. The barricades were gone and the police seemed to have taken their leave as well. I thought about hailing a taxi but decided to walk the 14 blocks home. I was so snookered; I almost stumbled out into the intersection at Cary and Boulevard but managed to get my footing before I staggered down the road. It scared me that my coordination was so impaired and I was thankful that the one car applied its brakes rather than run my drunken butt over! I walked past a house in the middle of the block heard three guys talking about the football game from earlier in the day. I have no idea what possessed me, but I thought it would be a fabulous idea to yell to them that this particular team sucked. When I'm drunk, I get all kinds of dandy ideas like that one! Anyway, I was about two blocks away from the "football" house and just three measly blocks from my house when one of the guys on the porch, got up, ran up behind me and pushed me down, which caused my left hand to split open as I hit the sidewalk. I got up and made it another block, then called the police. The police arrived in three minutes and they asked me why this guy pushed me down. I explained that I wasn't sure, but I thought it was because they thought I was transgendered. The city cops turned on their blue lights and headed down the street as a formality. I finished the walk home, took Zeb out, and told him how terrible that guy had treated me. The New Year had already started off kind of rough for me.

On January 1, 2008, Zeb and I performed our regular routine in the late morning. Later, I sat down at the dining room table and talked to Zeb about the past year. I told him about how I had lived a double life at work and home and how cumbersome and ridiculous I had felt in doing so. I talked to him about our move from the country to the city and my transition on the job and how they were both life altering events. I told Zeb, that although the year started a little rough, I felt it was going to be another year full of change and joy. It was the year that I would finally have gender reassignment surgery and I was so looking forward to August 7, my surgery date! It was going to be the best year ever. We walked through the neighborhood and he led me back home. I went to the Inn for a Greek salad and a pitcher of beer. I watched part of a college bowl game on TV, drank a little more beer, and then walked home. The remainder of the day was spent walking Zeb, drinking beer, and watching football. That evening I went to bed with a beer in my hand, finished it and placed the empty bottle on the nightstand next to the other seven from nights before. What a way to start the New Year ...

I was off work for the next couple of days and sat around and enjoyed the time with Zeb. I took a little bit of a break from going out and stayed home these next few days and prepared myself for getting back to work. The New Year brought about a new set of strategic initiatives at the Plant for which I was accountable. I thought about that and of the execution of these initiatives, watched football, drank beer, and played with Zeb. I was in bed early because I wanted the New Year to start out on a good note, a sober note. During the month of January, I knew there could be some changes at work. My own performance appraisal for 2007 was due and I suspected a different direction and assignment may be on the horizon. I had trained Reggie to assess the teams and I knew that he would be replacing me as an assessor. Although I did not want to give up my position, I felt like it was going to be taken from me by my boss.

The performance appraisal system at Philip Morris was subjective. The numbers speak for themselves but much of the rating came from "how" an employee obtained the results. The company tried everything possible to take the subjectivity out of the system by utilizing input from all the managers, plant managers, and directors into the individual's performance. However, the individual's boss would make a presentation to the group and recommend a rating on their direct reports and the panel would agree or disagree. Basically an employee was at the mercy of their boss. I had seen ratings in the past, because I was on such a panel for the Supervisors and Area Leaders, that for some individuals the rating did change up or down, depending on who made the comments. Often it depended on who followed next and for the most part it was fair, but I had seen some very unfair ratings and I had voiced my opinion. Once my boss told me that I needed to rate a particular employee with poor marks and I disagreed to the point that he moved her to another area in the plant and had her new boss rate her poorly. This sent a message loud and clear to me to make sure I did a better job for my people as I fought this move and did not agree with it.

It was time to get back to my normal work routine. It had been the same for the past six years and it was no different going back to work this day. I unlocked my door at the BL Plant and wished Ken the Plant Superintendent a Happy New Year and he and I briefly discussed the issues he faced when starting the plant back up after the holidays. I knew the equipment and process like the back of my hand and he did too. If there had been any major problems, we would have put together a problem-solving team made up of subject matter experts. It was my job to implement and encourage this type of teamwork to resolve issues efficiently and effectively. The plant was doing well so I went next door to my office and started thinking about my projects and Strategic Initiatives for the year.

In the third week of January 2008, it was time for me to go down to Park 500, and see my boss for my performance evaluation. We were supposed to have a semi-annual review each year but that never happens. I typically wrote my first six months and send it over and I never heard anything until this time the following six months. Therefore, I had to believe that everything was fine. I drove the 20 mile stretch down I-95 and Route 10 over to the Plant. I parked out front which was reserved for Managers and above and proceeded to walk up the four steps and the front landing to the lobby. The lobby was small and had two security guards who were always present to allow permission to either enter the plant through a single door or allowing access to the upstairs administration area. I performed many meetings and worked in the administration area where the director had an office. However, my boss had a very nice office off from the lobby and I entered waving to security and walked into the room.

He had a very nice office with a 10' window that looked over the plush green grass out front which was a little brown this time of year but nevertheless a nice view. He had a solid oak desk, credenza, and bookshelf and was working on his computer when I entered. He said, hello, and finished working on whatever he was doing for a couple of minutes and closed it down and motioned for me to have a seat. I sat at a small oak table which was across from his desk while he pulled up my performance appraisal on his computer and provided me with a hard copy. It was a very different feeling for me this time in his office. We would normally talk and compare notes and he would listen to my ideas and suggestions and confirm that they were really good. However, this time he went right into the appraisal; it was a very uncomfortable feeling. I was very interested by the fact that he discussed document appearance with me, talked about how all the lines needed to match up and the formatting must be perfect. It was kind of surprising and the discussion about the teams at Park 500 and how they needed to come up to snuff with the other teams in the organizations. He claimed that I could have protected the teams better at Park 500 and stood up for them in the assessment process and I thought to myself "you have got to be kidding me". My performance rating ended up being a "GP-" Good Performer which meant I would get the minimum raise and all my profit sharing. There was no development plan for the future. I received my next assignment and that was to work on the brand new sheet product at the BL Plant and establish standardization of work for each operator in the plant on all three shifts.

As I drove back to the BL plant, I wondered out loud, "WTF was going on, something was so not right here in Dixie!" I did not like the fact that I was now being confined to one plant and would be working with the same employee's day in and day out. It was a position that took me away from the complete exposure that I had over the past few years. Deep down I felt the company had a plan to get me off the assessment team, and by doing so, out of the limelight with my transition. But the way it was handled, through this assignment, well, it appeared and felt like I was being demoted. I had no choice but to wonder if my transition had anything to do with this assignment. I knew if I asked that question the answer would have been "no, of course not". I never ran it by Human Resources because I did not want to keep bringing issues that may or may not be just construed by me as real. I did not want to be labeled as a troublemaker. My new job in the standardization of work area with a brand new product was an important one, so I shocked them all: I never said a word, just moved on and counted my blessing that I still had a job.

I reported to the BL plant and went upstairs to speak with the Plant Manager about working with the employees to standardize the work. It entailed each operator and support person in the Plant and it was a very detailed description with a step by step set of documents. Also, my normal job of problem solving and working with the teams was intact, as was the 5S program. I had a lot of work to do over the course of the next 6-8 months. The BL Plant had to move its operations to Park 500 and one of the three lines had been taken apart over the Thanksgiving to Christmas timeframe. In the meantime, the old LPF Plant was starting a new smokeless product line and the production personnel were being transferred in from North Carolina to assist Research and Development with the trials, tunes, and tests. The plant received its own Director and teams had to be developed as part of the implementation process. I had worked in the Continuous Improvement Department with Lisa, who was the Director of this new process. At this time, I had no involvement with this highly restricted access process and security was tight.

I had a scheduled appointment with Dr. McGinn in Doylestown, PA in a couple of weeks and I was looking forward to seeing her. My appointment was sort of a "pre", pre-op sort of thing. I was basically going there to confirm my surgery date of

August 7, 2008, discuss my progress with the Harry Benjamin standards of care and to discuss my therapy. Dr. McGinn recommended that I have electrolysis performed in the surgical area prior to gender reassignment surgery and her office would perform the electrolysis. I called her office and arranged for Carol to dedicate time for the hair removal. It was at least a four hour appointment.

I continued with my work, took care of Zeb, drank at night after work, and entertained Barry once every two weeks. I began to understand that Barry needed a safe place to smoke his crack and I provided that place, and for doing this for him, he would share the drug with me. The only problem I saw with the whole arrangement was that it had started to become a regular event every other week in February, and that probably wasn't such a good thing.

The day before my appointment with Dr. McGinn, Teresa and I drove up from Richmond, VA, to Doylestown, PA. We left at 11:00 a.m. and arrived at the hotel in Doylestown, PA about 5pm. Teresa, who was the first lady of Doylestown, had gotten to know several people in the area and had visited with on some frequency since her surgery in July 2007. She knew where some of the best restaurants were but I always insisted on going to The Barn for dinner because they had a large selection of beer. It was the only place I knew that served "Bemish" and I loved that beer, besides it was brewed in County Cork, Ireland where my roots had been traced to, I referred to it as my local beer.

We woke up around 6:30 a.m. on Saturday morning, packed our bags, checked out of the hotel and started our journey to Dr. McGinn's office. I had a 9:00 a.m. appointment and Teresa wanted the Doctor to examine her progress on her gender reassignment surgery that had been performed in July. We stopped for breakfast and had bacon, eggs, toast, and coffee before we made our way down Main Street to her office. We arrived at 8:45 a.m. and Carol was there and had my file up and ready to go. She told me Dr. McGinn would be there in just a few minutes and in the meantime, we could both sit down and relax and be seated. Her office was located in an old historic building also the headquartered the National Democratic Presidential Campaign. Dr. McGinn's office had a calming effect for me which I found very important, particularly as I considered the next stage of my transition. As I sat and looked around, I wondered if Dr. McGinn's choice of pictures and replicas of butterflies that decorated the waiting area was merely a coincidence or a conscious choice as this beautiful creature represented the change from one stage of life to another.

Dr. McGinn walked into the office just slightly before 9:00 a.m. and invited me into her office. We exchanged greetings and immediately began discussing where I was with my transition. At that time I only had one therapist, so Dr. McGinn reminded me that I needed a letter from two psychiatrists of which she approved. She discussed the step-by-step process of the surgery and emphasized her discussion with pictures of the process and the results. She showed me the results from her earlier surgeries and we both agreed on August 7, 2008 as the date, my "birth date". She took me into the examination room and looked at the surgical area and described the process and discussed the depth she estimated she would be able to obtain for my vagina. She further explained how all my existing parts would be used for creation in surgery and that the sensitive skin inside would be used for my interior vaginal wall. She explained that I would need to send her a chest x-ray, stress test, c-scan results and have a mammogram prior to surgery. Further, I would need to have my endocrinologist forward the results of my hormone levels and blood work. I agreed to these conditions of the surgery.

We returned to her office where I completed consent forms and she quoted me the price of the surgery which included the anesthesiologists and the five days in the hospital. She explained that I would be required to quit smoking at least one month prior to surgery or she would not perform the operation and a nicotine blood test would be included with the work given to me the day before the surgery. Dr. McGinn told me I needed to stay in the Philadelphia area an additional 8 – 10 days after being released from the hospital to recover and to attend consultations. That actually suited me fine because it would significantly reduce my costs since this type of surgery was considered "elective" and was not covered by my Cigna Insurance Plan. On page 33 of the benefit plan it specifically stated the insurance did not cover sex reassignment surgery in any form. Imagine correction of a major birth defect NOT covered by one's insurance plan! This was a cash in advance procedure and the cost was enough for a brand new luxury car. Other expenses would be travel, food, medicine, and 10 days in the hotel. I gave her my deposit to secure the date, and was told the location would be determined later. Dr. McGinn was not sure if the Doylestown Hospital would allow her to continue to perform this surgery in their hospital when my date arrived, but I would be informed well before then so arrangements could be made in plenty of time.

I had chosen Dr. McGinn because of the conversation we had at the IFGE convention, the work on Teresa that I had seen firsthand, and my conversations with Danielle, Dr. McGinn who had been an Air Force Fighter Pilot and astronaut. Dr. McGinn herself was transgendered and had had the surgery in Wisconsin several years prior to attending medical school. She studied under the guidance of Dr. Bowers in Trinidad, Colorado. My feeling and overall opinion of her was that she had a very amiable personality and demeanor, led a very healthy lifestyle, was physically fit, served as a pilot in the US Air Force, and had a very steady hand from what I was able to ascertain. Her work was amazing and she along with Teresa and Danielle had changed my mind to allow her to perform her miracle on me.

Dr. McGinn sent me back into the examination room so that I could be set up for the four-hour electrolysis procedure in the genital area. I had a choice between the painful method and the non-painful method. Since I was not a pain person I opted for the painless route which was still quite painful. The painless route consisted of approximately thirty shots in the genital region just to make the area numb. The needle was easily 12" long and it hurt more than any pain that I had experienced in my entire life! It took about five minutes to complete the series of shots and it seemed like eternity. Once the numbness took effect, Carol returned to the room with the doctor and with the use of a magic marker, pointed out the surgical area and instructed Carol to remove the hair inside those lines. Electrolysis was a procedure where electricity was shot into the root of the hair and pulled out, one at a time. I lay on my back and tried to distract myself by watching music videos while she worked. Every now and then, I felt the electricity as she interjected and pulled at the most sensitive area of my body. Once I got over the initial shock and pain of the shots then it was relatively a painless procedure.

After 4+ hours, Dr. McGinn came in for the third time and took a look at Carol's handiwork and deemed my torture session completed for the day. I got up, dressed, and proceeded to reception to remit payment for the treatment. Teresa had just returned from shopping and walking through downtown Doylestown and was ready to go as I finished my business at the counter. We both said our goodbyes and before we could even get out of Doylestown the numbness had begun to wear off and my "area" was very uncomfortable. In fact, it hurt so badly I wasn't sure how I would make it back home! We stopped for gas in north Maryland and stopped again just south of Baltimore for dinner. I had a sandwich and six beers in 30 minutes in hopes of relieving the pain. I had to go to the bathroom before we left and as used the facilities, I looked down and it was a train wreck! My penis was swollen, bent, and almost L shaped in the middle. You can only image what I screamed when I saw it; which was not pretty. It hurt as though someone had dug out each hair one by one with a jack hammer! I thought, "Good Lord, if this was the "painless route", I'd sure hate to have taken the alternative".

We finally made it back to Richmond and Teresa dropped me and my burning crotch off at my house. Despite my excruciating pain, I walked next door and thanked Jennifer for watching Zeb for the past two days. I then took Zeb out for his walk and he took it easy on me as I walked bowlegged through the park with him. When we returned I gave him some fresh water, pulled out two Vicodin I had in the kitchen cabinet that were about a year old and went straight to bed. I woke up about eight hours later on Sunday morning and to my surprise the pain was not as intense. It was painful mind you, but nothing like the night before; I still had to handle it with care. It took about three days before the swelling went down and for things to straightened back up and return to what was normal for me. I was back into my work routine, stayed close to my office and worked with the employees in the plant on a one-on-one basis.

I decided to take on projects to help fill in my idle time rather than go to the Inn and drink whenever I was bored or felt sorry for myself for being transgendered or the lives that I had affected. I still could not understand why my family and society had such a problem with the entire issue. It seemed perfectly normal to me that I was born one way, was remorseful that it took so long to work my way through these feelings and to begin to be honest with myself, and finally to be brave enough to do something about it. Anyway, the project I chose was to paint the columns and front porch railing of my home and return it to as close to its most original look since it first was built in 1915. I went down to the local home improvement store and purchased a gallon of mold inhibitor base primer, brushes, and appropriate containers. I had a ladder from my previous four story home in the country and started at the top and the plan was to work my way down. As soon as I started to work on my porch, the four story house next door which had been empty for over a year suddenly filled with contractors. It was a group of guys, four of them from Turkey, who were hired to renovate this house and restore it back to livable apartments.

I worked on my porch from time to time, drank beer and watched those guys bring out torn wall board and take in new wall board. For the next eight weeks, they hammered, repaired and built everything in sight. I could physically see an upstairs kitchen being renovated from my upstairs porch, complete with new counter tops, walls, and flooring. The houses were only three feet apart and I could look straight into this room.

One morning after my Zeb work routine, I opened my front door to head off to work and I found a vase full of flowers. I looked over to the house next door and saw one of the gentlemen from the group who had been working on the house. He was sitting on the porch and he smiled really wide and said, "Good Morning" in broken English. I waved, smiled back, proceeded to my car and went off to work. These flowers continued for the next week and a half and he smiled every day and told me to have a great day. On a Saturday morning, after a night out at Doll's, Zeb woke me up with a loud bark and looked toward the front door. When I got up and picked up my newspaper I found my flower guy outside painting my porch. I asked him what he was doing and he said painting your porch. I said ok and returned to the house for coffee and to throw ball to Zeb in the back yard. Periodically I checked on my admirer only to find him hard at it, still painting my porch. I went through the back gate with Zeb and we had our nice little walk. After I returned home, I pulled out two beers from the refrigerator and headed for the front porch. I handed my new friend a beer and thought to myself, "This guy really did not understand what he had gotten himself into when he started this project". At this point, I was pre-op and I knew extreme caution was necessary. I knew being a pre-op transgendered female was a very dangerous place when a gentleman caller was involved. I started to tell him but never got up my nerve. This was an area that many transgendered individuals often got physically hurt or even killed over when the person found out that the person they had been pursuing did not have the usual body parts. It was extremely dangerous and admittedly, quite deceptive. Nevertheless, my need for love and respect was high at this point in my life and I played along which in itself was frightening and misleading but exciting at the same time.

This led to him coming over after work every day and to paint my porch. The flowers continued to be left for me on my

202

front porch each day as well. They were beautiful, thoughtful and I knew exactly what this guy wanted, yet I continued to lead him on. Not only had he painted my porch, left flowers, but now he brought over twelve packs of beer so he could sit on the porch and drink with me in the evenings. Separately, Barry was not out the picture either, he still called and came over more frequently and brought his bag of goodies. It was about every 8-10 days and if he did not call me, I called him because my craving for crack cocaine had intensified from once a month to twice a month, to every 14 days, to every 8 days. It was literally being given to me for the use of my car to go buy more and my house was used as a safe haven. It became beer and dinner with my Turkish friend and beer and crack with Barry.

After about three weeks my Turkish friend had started to hit on me and tried to love on me too. He grabbed me from behind, turned me around, started kiss on me, and felt my boobs. I had been taking hormones and my boobs were growing but they were still an A cup so I still wore silicone breast forms over the top of my breasts, inside my bra. He played with them to the point that my bra came unstrapped and I had to hold up my breast forms in so they would not fall out. Once I had to quickly run into the bathroom and put myself back together again; thank goodness he never suspected!

He wanted me to have sex with him and I refused telling him that I needed surgery down there and unable to right now. He did not like my refusal and continued to try to get in my panties, over and over again. I continued to refuse his advances, and again cited my need for surgery and further explained that sex at this juncture would hurt really bad and be quite unpleasant. I had to dodge that bullet with him on several occasions, but I was successful.

He wanted a place to live and asked if he could live with me and I told him that at some point I may consider renting him a room. However, when I gave it more serious thought, it really scared me. I needed the money, but made no decision one way or the other at that time. Several weeks later, I invited him to live in a room in my basement. I knew I could lock the door that came up to the kitchen and he would have his own entrance from the back alley through the basement door. He immediately accepted the terms of my rent. He brought over two of his friends from Turkey who were in there twenties and we would sit around in the dining room and drink beer and he taught me Turkish words and I taught him English. I purchased a Turkish to English translator dictionary so that we could communicate better. He spoke with me about his twelve year old son and his former wife who both resided in Istanbul. We would go on the Internet and look at the place where he was born. He seemed to enjoy these activities and we both enjoyed each other's company, or at least I thought so.

After "Mr. Turkey" had lived in my basement about two months, I went down to collect my rent and found he and all of his things were gone. I think his friends had either figured out that I was transgendered or as they explained to me, he was going back to Turkey because his son was sick. Or another theory was that I had been spending time with Barry upstairs in my home and had allowed two other people to rent the upstairs bedrooms. I had become more and more addicted to crack during this timeframe and had allowed the drug to begin taking over my life. Anyway, they drove Mr. Turkey to the Deli and asked me to come outside. He was passed out drunk and would wake up and cry, then pass out again. His friends returned my keys to the basement door and back gate. I felt real sorry for him, leaned into the car, gave him a little kiss on the cheek and said goodbye; and his friends just laughed hysterically. This basically confirmed my suspicions that the guys figured it out and lucky for me there were no repercussions for my lack of integrity. He had stayed in my house during the months of April and May.

During these two months, Barry was coming over once a week with the crack and I would walk over to the Deli and purchase the twelve pack of beer. I knew he used my house as a safe place to use drugs and his payoff to me was a portion of the crack what did I care? What was important to me at that time was that I found something that obliterated my pain of rejection. He borrowed my car when we ran out of crack, which was around midnight, so he could go get more. I learned the reason he used my vehicle was so the same car wouldn't be seen each time. At first I thought that was Barry's paranoia kicking in, but then I thought what good "crack" sense that made. He would call in advance to whomever and run out for 15-30 minutes and return; he was always punctual with his crack runs.

Eventually I was curious and wanted to go along for the ride to see where he was getting our crack. One night in April he let me go with him to an apartment community to buy some crack. Although I did not see exactly which unit he went into or even meet the person he dealt with, it was exciting for me to tag along and I actually felt a rush just to be out in what I thought was an exciting situation, like mafia activity. I had always enjoyed mafia movies, books, and stories and had watched them early on in my life. It was intriguing to me to follow their storylines. Out in the street like a mafia thug and buying crack no less, seemed to bring the sort of excitement I had read about in books and seen on TV and in movies to me. Good grief, I think I was seriously losing it!

Barry was coming over frequently he began to really badger me to rent him a room. It had gotten to the point where we were drinking and cracking until the wee hours of the morning (2:00 and 3:00 a.m.) and then I tried to sleep a few hours, get up, get ready for work, then kick good 'ol Barry out at 7:00 a.m. because I had to leave for work; oh trust and believe, he was never happy about that wakeup call either! In the meantime, I was in contact with Kathy and she was just about ready to leave her parents home, because she had nearly completed the house arrest sentence. She had tentatively plans to move about eight blocks away from, with her boyfriend and family. However, she really wanted to move in with me and I gave it some serious consideration. I started meeting her at the Inn to drink and she would buy crack for us. Now I started buying crack from Kathy, because she really did not have a job or money, or at least this was how I rationalized this endeavor. Her parents gave her a little bit of money for food but money went directly to alcohol and drugs. She was well known in Richmond's drug world and went by the street name of "GG".

I would drive her to make deals and she introduced me to some of the most influential drug dealers on the north, south, and west side of town. There were five different dealers that we would visit and all had really good crack. These guys knew that she demanded the good stuff and did not try to sell her a cut down version. Kathy was way into the drama and lifestyle of the underworld and she absolutely loved it. Since I was with her and met all these people, I came to be known as "Momma K" on the streets. "GG" spent more time at my house than she was anywhere else. She was always asking me to rent her a room in my home because she did not like her boyfriend keeping tabs on her all the time. He knew she had a drug problem and did not want her to get back into that lifestyle. He constantly called and drove by to check on her and eventually she would go back and stay with him and his family for a few days, primarily to sleep and reenergize her after being out all night and gone for days. Finally, she convinced me when we were smoking crack one night to think about renting her a room in my home. She would make arrangements with her father to send me a check at the beginning of each month to pay her rent.

I introduced Kathy to Barry in May and it often became the three of us in my home drinking and cracking. Since I was purchasing my own crack through Kathy or going out to get it myself from the connections she had introduced me to, Barry was not as generous with his own crack. He would give me very little but by this time it had an expectation that he always had a place to go smoke and it was safe for him. His logic was that I was an educated executive with a major company, I lived in an historic house, I really never did drugs before, no one really suspected, therefore a safe haven. Kathy finally convinced me to allow her to rent a room during one of my weak moments while doing crack. I have since learned that this drug takes away your ability to think logically and actually takes away good decision making skills all together. All you wanted to do was go get some more drugs. Once Kathy moved in Barry wanted to know why he could not since I let her in, so I acquiesced and allowed him in as well. I knew I could use the money because I was getting behind on all bills and house payments and really did not understand how this was happening. Then the real insanity started in late May Kathy and Barry all lived in my house. Zeb and I got up each morning and did our work routine at the same time regardless of the time I went to bed. Some nights I would go to bed at 10:00 p.m. while others it was 5:00 a.m., but I always made sure that I was up at 6:00 a.m. regardless of how I felt and got myself ready for work. One day, I went to work and Barry told me when I arrived home that Kathy had one of the drug dealers over all day long. When I approached her about it she told me that he does not know what it is like to get away from the streets and come to a place where he could relax and watch television for a while. I told her that it is not a good idea to bring the dealers into my house. She told me how appreciative he was just to relax. I knew that this could bring about tremendous trouble and asked her not to do it again. I knew that this guy was a big time drug dealer and very dangerous and although we purchased from him and helped him we did not need to get so close.

A week later, Kathy and I went to see "A", the dealer who spent the afternoon in my home, to purchase some crack, so I thought. However, when we arrived at his house he got into my car as prearranged by Kathy and he handed us a pile of rocks for taking him up to The Hotel on Jefferson-Davis Boulevard which was about 10 blocks from his house. This hotel was notorious for shootings and other drug related incidents as I had read on some frequency in the newspaper. But heck, for a hand full of crack and now because I was addicted to it, I would have done almost anything, especially while under the influence. As we drove, "A" pulled out at .45 caliber pistol and said, I just wanted you to know that I had this in the car and since I had been all cracked up it was not a problem, we were like gangsters. We pulled up to the hotel, he got out and went to the door with his gun hidden and this Jamaican man opened it up for him.

I wasn't sure what was going on, but only suspected he was either there to sell or buy a large quantity of drugs. The dealer wore real baggy clothes, probably to conceal a weapon or maybe to haul thousands of dollars of drugs. He could have easily hidden a couple of bricks of crack and I never would have suspected it. Finally, he came out of the room about 15 minutes later and when we dropped him off at his house he remarked that it was easy getting a couple hundred dollars worth of crack. "A" had plenty of helpers and he represented the South Side gang. He said, "We need to do this more often" and laughed a sort of sinister laugh. I was still shaking in my heels and thought, "Hell no, well maybe if I can't get my crack any other way..."

Then there was "B" who was the big, tall black man that would sit on his front porch and motion us to the back to meet him under a big tree. He had four "soldiers" working for him and we could buy cocaine behind his house across the street in the other alley or a couple of doors down in the alley behind his house. There was always someone out after school let out around 3:00 p.m. until dawn the next day. "Popcorn" was one of his soldiers and he always commented on how nice my car was and even asked if he could use it at some point for a fee. I told him I'd think about it, and hoped it never came up again. These guys were the North Side gang of drug dealers.

"Blue" and "Caboose" represented the West End gang of drug dealers. I would often take them over to the east side of town where he purchased his quantity of crack for distribution. Not only did I now use on a more frequent basis, but I now drove these guys to pick up their stash for re-distribution in their neighborhoods. I believe I was doing this because crack was so highly addictive and these people accepted me for my transgendered self. I needed the attention because of all the rejection from family, work "family" and "friends". I thought I had made new friends when in reality they were after my money and everything else of material value they could get their hands on that could benefit from themselves.

There was "D" and an offshoot of A, and "Skip-a-Long", who was a 16 year old kid who was a couple of blocks over from Blue and Caboose who feed off Blue, and the Lincoln Continental that rode through the hood playing very loud rap-gangster music which I was sure was a signal which indicated the shipment was in town. The ice cream trucks and vendors that supplied the cones to the children also distributed crack to their parent's right out of the same truck! Although not formally educated, these dealers were the best of the best on the street and they would just as soon kill you as to look at you if you tried to fuck them over. As long as you had the money they were your friends. If you crossed them or if they thought you crossed them then they were out in force to take you out without a blink of the eye. They were judge, jury, and executioner, period. This was a lifestyle I worked myself into in a very short period of time. I was introduced to all these people through Kathy. The drugs held me hostage in this underworld as I deepened my imprisonment through my addiction.

Chapter 18 – The Dark Side

I tried to stay away from drugs because I did not want to be involved with this element, I knew that my behavior could cause me to lose everything I had worked so hard for; I could not continue if I was to have my life saving surgery as scheduled. I started working on the tests that Dr. McGinn required for surgery. I went to my Primary Care doctor for an examination and told him about the tests that were necessary for surgery. He made the arrangements and scheduled all the appointments for me, some with other doctors and another at the Henrico Doctor's Hospital.

I first went to have the required chest x-rays performed at a local radiology clinic in Richmond and everything was in order. Next, over to the hospital for a stress test where the doctor injected die into my body before I had to run on the treadmill and then through a C-scan, all of which turned out normal. Finally, I had to go have a mammogram and bone density test completed.

I walked into the doctor's office and found it was so packed with women that there was not one open seat available. I went to the window and completed the compulsory paper work and immediately froze. There was an insidious block staring up at me, demanding that I disclose my "legal" sex. My hand literally shook as I forced myself to check the "male" box, which obviously was a big fat lie; damn these government forms to hell! Once I was done, I moved away from the counter and stood as inconspicuously as possible against the wall. Finally the nursed called a patient back and that seat came available. I jumped in it like white on rice but as I sat down, it felt as though all the eyes in that room were on me and they definitely did not approve. I felt very uncomfortable, but minded my own business and my anxiety soon subsided.

After an interminable thirty minute wait the nurse called me back and had me put on that ill-fitting robe, opened to the front, so the test could begin. She asked me to place my breast into a metal clamp while she asked me questions.

She immediately asked, "How many children do you have?

Now I had no idea what on earth her question had to do with my breasts but I thought maybe she was attempting to put me at ease a bit; I stood up a little taller and proudly answered, "Well I have three beautiful children and thank you so much for asking."

Her next question however threw me for a loop, "How old where you when you first started your period?"

I definitely gave her the hairy eyeball and answered as innocently as possible. "Well let me think that one over. Hmmmm, well I can report that I have never had my period, yet, nope, not yet, sure haven't!"

The poor, poor thing! Her jaw hit the ground and she turned shades of red I don't even think Mr. Crayola had invented yet! The Q&A session was over and my breasts were put through the Jaws of Life in one fell swoop! I swear she gave them an extra squeeze because she was embarrassed over the darn period thing. Oh well, after the "Melon Masher", I was sent to the bone density technician for my next set of tests.

While my bone density exam was in full swing, the female technician who performed the bone density test explained that she had to report my results from a male perspective rather than a female. I said that was fine, to do whatever was necessary to have the results forwarded to Doctor McGinn so that I could have gender reassignment surgery. Quite frankly, I had no idea if it would have any bearing one way or the other; I figured I'd leave all that up to Dr. McGinn to decipher.

I had an appointment with Dr. McGinn and Carol for round two of the electrolysis for hair removal prior to surgery. I told Kathy about this appointment and she wanted to tag along with me to Doylestown. I had stopped using crack a week prior to this appointment and only drank moderately because surgery was very important to me and I did not want to mess it up. So we executed the plan to drive up from Richmond at 5:00 a.m., and drive back to Richmond late that afternoon a few hours after the electrolysis procedure. Upon arrival, Dr. McGinn was ready for me and took me back into the examining room. I disrobed, hopped on the table and immediately was injected with 30 shots using a 12" needle for "pain free" electrolysis; which again, hurt like hell! After the four hour process, I confirmed with Dr. McGinn, my August 7, 2008 surgery date. The results were the same as the previous visit in February and it was a very long drive home. Somehow, as I drove along feeling as though someone had driven 1000 red hot ice picks into my crotch, I made a wrong turn off the interstate and ended up in Dover, DE which made for a long ride over to Route 301 into Maryland and down through Virginia. Once home, I found Zeb, walked him as quickly as I could, then went straight to bed. Unfortunately the pain lasted about three days and I had nothing to take it away. I was however, feeling good that my life long journey of being physically matched up to my internal self was only two months away.

It had only been a few short days after my appointment and unfortunately, I had picked up my wretched alcohol and drugs use, right back where I had left off. I was now roaming the streets with a 9mm pistol stuffed down the waistline of my panty-girdle as I traveled alone in the hood. Kathy and Barry had started hanging out together during the day and that soon turned into the two of them sleeping together in one of my bed-rooms. I went out on my own for the next four to six weeks and left them to their own devices. I was a corporate executive during the day and a gangster crack addict at night and had now begun to live a double life. Before my "double life" was male at work and female everywhere else so the confusion continued only in a different form, but the root cause was still the same, based on oppression and rejection from my existence on this earth in the wrong body. My "bondage of self" was continuing.

People do not realize the affect they can have on another when they reject others based on things they did not understand, like one being transgendered. Rejection of any kind, whether it is violent, passive, aggressive, or simply the "silent treatment" can cause such irreparable damage to a person's psyche and it can send the rejected one down a path of self-destruction, self-loathing, and feelings of worthlessness. I really did not want to use drugs but I was very weak and all it took was one time in a moment of despair after I had been rejected over and over again. I tried something I knew I should never have tried. All the stories you hear about crack are true, it is a very powerfully addictive drug and takes a very good person and blocks all good decision making and "right thinking" skills all because one cannot cope with whatever pain they are feeling and they need some sort of relief. This drug can be used by anyone, on anyone, so the initiator can, take everything from the addict, physically, mentally, spiritually, materially, including their dignity, over a very short period of time. I had a very deep-rooted resentment against Barry and Kathy because they knew exactly what they were doing and why they were doing it. I was very upset with myself because I allowed this to happen and really did not know how to get out of it. I was addicted and I had to continue with my addictive drug use instead of fighting for my life.

I continued to work with the employees at the BL Plant on the step-by-step process of the new blend formula and production which kept me very busy as the timeline at the Plant was moved up to "as soon as possible". Lisa, who was the director at the smokeless plant, had discussed the possibility of me assisting her develop and implement a process for the employees to work as a team and solve problems. I was very happy to accommodate her because it got me out of the office and out working with others. She had contacted Greg, the VP of Manufacturing, and told him that she requested me and he thought that it was a good idea. My boss did not like the idea because he wanted me to work solely on the new brand. I explained that Greg was aware of Lisa's request and was onboard with the idea. I felt that my reference about Greg angered my boss because he wanted to know exactly what I was doing all the time and wanted to place others in that area and he called Lisa and told her he would allocate someone to her plant but she refused to budge. Clearly there was a conflict and I felt this was going to be a big issue.

I noticed my boss's behavior grow more negative towards me and my work seemed to be under more scrutiny now than at any other time in my career. My intuition told me I was being set up for failure by my boss because I was transgendered and chose to transition on the job. Right or wrong, every single way he acted made my suppositions seem all too real and true. This did not make me feel very comfortable in my work although I had learned two new processes and had a tremendous amount of knowledge in the tobacco processing business. I had written my performance appraisal for the first half of 2008 and had submitted it, but there was no word as to anything being of consequence. As a matter of fact there was no mid-year review. Therefore with the increased responsibility, it was my assumption that everything was going well and even in my insanity I made sure that I completed my work to the very best of my ability. I never, ever jeopardized my career and drank or used drugs while on the job. I at least kept that much sense in tact!

In June I began to separate myself a little more from Barry and Kathy. I would frequent the Inn for dinner and beer, and I'd talk to whoever would listen. One night as I sat at the bar having a burger and pitcher of beer, I noticed a blonde-haired lady about my age at the other end. She was a little loud, appeared quite drunk, and after a few minutes, she fell off the bar stool right on her ass onto the floor. I watched as two guys picked her up and put her back on the barstool again. I inquired about her to the bartender, who told me her name was Belinda. He explained that she came into the bar some and normally did not leave until she was good and drunk. So I watched Belinda for a while and decided to approach her and find out what was going on with her. Belinda was one of those people who was hard to get rid of once you made initial contact, so once we talked she followed me back to my house and we sat around my place, drank some more, and told each other all about ourselves. She lived exactly two blocks from my house and we soon struck up a drinking re-

214

lationship and she quickly became a pest but I allowed her to come over and talk. My family rejection put me in the mindset to accept any "friends" exactly as they were, faults and all, without judgment.

One day Belinda came over and I had beer and some crack with me and she wanted it. I told her that it was not a good idea to start on this stuff, but she insisted and picked some up anyway and she was off in another world just like me. She wanted to go with me to get more and I absolutely refused. After only a week, I finally conceded and took her along. Belinda was screwing one of the married sheriff's of the City of Richmond. Every Thursday night they met for their "fuckdezvous", and I knew if she opened her mouth it would be lots of trouble, but on the other hand this information gave me ammunition somehow, I just didn't know how I could use it. Anyway, she was mouthy to the drug dealers and on several occasions, I had to tell her to shut up and stay out of my drug deals because she created too much drama. Kathy told me over and over to get rid of her because she was going to get us all in trouble. Barry wanted nothing to do with the police or from anyone he knew that had any association with the police. Both Barry and Kathy constantly told me I was getting in way too deep by roaming the streets in search of crack. I never was one to isolate myself when I drank and smoked crack, possibly because I had used alcohol so long to give me courage to go out dressed as a female. I was accustomed to this type of behavior. My personality type demanded that I be out in the world, in the limelight and in what I thought was control of all situations.

My personality led me to the pool hall near the corner of Staples and Broad Street, in Richmond. Kathy and I had been there three times before because there was a guy who worked behind the bar and wanted to date her. That allowed me to float a check for a couple of day so that I could get some money for alcohol and drugs. On this particular day, I walked into the pool hall alone, sat down at the bar and ordered a beer. I was dressed in my short floral Ann Taylor skirt, baby blue tank top, and white flat sandals. I got up and picked out a pool stick from one of the many racks on the side wall and then perused the hall for a table. This pool hall had at least 50 tables and was divided in half, one side for professionals and the other side for amateurs.

There were six men at each table who all sat around and drank beer while watching the NASCAR race on TV. I looked over the room every now and then and finally one guy asked me how I was doing. I told him I was fine and I asked him if he wanted to play a game of pool. He asked if I was any good and I told him that I could play a little bit but was not really all that good. He wanted to play me and I challenged him to one beer per game. He seemed very eager to take my money in a game of eight ball so we started a game immediately.

He broke and nothing went in so I knocked in all but two of the solids. He shot again and missed and I finished off the two solids and the eight ball and told him I wanted a beer. He walked over to the bar, bought me the beer and racked the table for me to break. I broke and three balls went in and I had my choice of stripes or solids and the solids were more in align so I chose them and put one in and missed the next shot. He proceeded to knock in two and I ran the table again and sent him off for another beer. For some reason he was quite perturbed; although I had no clue why!

He racked, I broke and had another choice again. For some ungodly reason, Kathy walked into the pool hall, and directly over to me and introduced herself to this guy. Then without provocation and completely out of the blue, he threw his cue stick, looked me directly in the eye, and through gritted teeth said, "You are not a girl, Mutha Fucka!" Before I could respond or say "boo" he turned to Kathy and told her he was going across the street and would be back in a few minutes with some friends to "kick his ass". It was one thing to hustle someone at a game of pool, but when the "hustled" figured out the "hustler" is transgendered, e.g. not the sex you appeared to be, well, that is sometimes a huge problem for some people to accept. I watched him storm out the pool hall and Kathy told me I needed to get out of the bar fast so we both left. Three days later, I went back to the pool hall to float another check and the cashier told me that I could never come back in the bar again, ever. He told me the guy I was playing pool with the last time I had been in the bar had left and returned with an army of men about 15 minutes after I left and they were going to kick my ass, just as he had promised. He was a regular customer and the hall did not want any trouble because they were on the lookout for me. That was one of my biggest fears, being beaten up because I was transgendered. I swore to myself that no one would ever beat me like I had experienced when I was 16 years old. I have not been back to that bar since the incident.

I played pool in the gay clubs, lesbian bars, and the clubs where anything goes and I pissed off enough people with my play and arrogance that there were two 18 x 18 chalk boards of names behind mine to get a chance to play and hopefully beat me. My alcohol abuse turned me into a different person to the point that I was in your face, courageous, and felt like I owned everything that I was around. I was special, transgendered, and no one could tell me what to do because I was already doing it. This was my great escape from the reality of a rejecting world and society. I got kicked out of the "anything goes" club because I was told upon entry one night that I had broken a cue stick in half, which I had no recollection of doing and I am sure I must have lost a game if this was in fact true. I was so angry that I told my JRTS group of girls that we were not going there again because the bar closed down and in my arrogance thought, see what happens when you mess with me. I was out of control and did not know it.

It was near the middle of June and I had been seeing Dr. Bears weekly for three years now concerning my transgendered life and the need for surgery. Over the course of these two years he performed psychological evaluations, counseled me, invited my family to attend, which my mother did go see him alone. He counseled me and my two sisters once, and listened to me as I walked through the path in my transition. I believed it was more of an education for him than it was for me. However, I felt comfortable talking with him and it provided me an outlet or a sounding board for my feelings. He agreed that I was in fact a male to female transsexual with gender dysphoria and needed to have gender reassignment surgery. He feared that my family would sue him over this recommendation because of a letter he received from my brother. In this letter, my brother, the attorney, stated that Dr. Bears was not qualified to recommend surgery for me. Instead my brother recommended another doctor in Richmond who was supposedly more qualified. Dr. Bears, I learned afterwards, consulted with this other doctor on numerous occasions and was told that I was the real deal. This upset me because I had spent all this time with this doctor and I knew without a doubt who I was. I felt that I really didn't need a doctor to tell me who I am because of the life-long journey that I had to undertake.

I pressed him for the letter of recommendation to my surgeon because my surgery date was August 7, 2008. So he told me to write the letter and he would read it and sign it. I had read other letters from therapists to surgeons and I followed the same line of reasoning as it was applicable to me. I hand-carried the letter to Dr. Bears and he read it, signed it, and I mailed it. During this same timeframe I had also been seeing another therapist in the west end of Richmond. After only an hour with her, she immediately knew I was an excellent candidate for surgery. She had been a guest speaker months earlier at our JRTS support group meeting and discussed her transgendered studies at a major university in the Midwest. She told me she would write the second letter of recommendation but I needed to follow-up with her because she was not very good with writing letters. So I paid her for her time, for writing the letter, and kept after her three different times to write and send the letter. It was now within one month of the surgery and she had not produced the letter and I was getting worried. I was not going to come all this way in my life to have a therapist just sit on her ass and not write my letter of recommendation, especially after she had been paid in advance for it! However, she still had not written that letter, which added to my anxiety.

It was July of 2008 and everything at work seemed to be moving along nicely. There were no complaints that I was made aware however, I was given a retiree to assist me in writing the standardization of work process for the new product. She had been the former Document Control and ISO Certification Manager. The timeline on the project was repeatedly changed to match the construction on the new BL Plant inside of Park 500, which was escalating. I was also working across the street in the new smokeless facility and had learned that process as well. I completed the task of putting people and teams together. Lisa and Brian were pleased with the progress and direction the group was taken and they wanted to increase my service. The plant shutdown for semi-annual maintenance and I took a much needed week's vacation because I was definitely burning the candle at both ends.

Since May I had been drinking everyday and I was smoking crack every weekend. As hard as it is to admit, sometimes I even smoked once during the week. I did not WANT to smoke this stuff but had become so addicted to it that it had started to control my life. I thought about it almost everyday and my cravings had become stronger and stronger. My uncontrollable need for crack led to increased usage through the months of June and July to the point that I began using crack almost every day. I had two clothes baskets full of unopened mail and had not been paying my bills at all. I was only collecting my rent and then I spent my hard earned money on eating out, drinking, and crack. I spent approximately $700-$1000 a week at bars, restaurants, and with drug dealers in the streets. Slowly I isolated myself from my friends and took up with a crowd that used drugs and drank all the time, just like me. I thought I had chosen this path because this group of people seemingly did not care that I was a pre-op transsexual and accepted me. However I have learned that it was not about me, it was about the escape from reality into the world of alcohol and drugs where you can be comfortable being whoever in your own mind. The nature of the drug was so addictive and the need to be comfortable in my own skin was so overwhelming that it brought me back over and over again.

I found it very exciting to be out on the street sneaking around like a gangster. During June and July, I was the only girl allowed in the backyard of the crack house. Caboose borrowed my car, Barry and Kathy did drugs with me, and when I slept Kathy used my car and debit card. In the morning when I found out they both teamed up against me and said I gave them permission to do so. I told them I never said they could do such a thing, but they insisted that I did. I had no recollection of that and it really got on my nerves and I finally started to get the picture. I had a weekend where Kathy, Belinda, and I were up drinking all day Friday, Saturday, and Sunday until about 9pm Sunday night and all we did was drink and go buy more crack when we ran out. Barry had started to stay away from the house more and more because it was become more open with more people and dealers hanging out, a regular "crack house". I learned that he had two criminal charges pending in two different counties just outside of Richmond and he was at least smart enough to know that a drug charge would put him away for good along with the other issues he was facing. He was a lot more cognizant than I of what was really going on in my house.

This is very difficult for me to write because I am disturbed about the fact that I had allowed myself to get caught up in this world. This is not who I was but once in I did not really know how to stop so it continued longer than I would have wanted. Belinda and I were hanging out more and one night we wanted to go drink and smoke but we did not have any money. Blue from the west end gang had told me that he wanted to have sex with Belinda and would offer some crack for the opportunity. He told me this about 10 days previously and since we were so desperate, I struck up the conversation with Belinda.

"Belinda, you know Blue has some crack, right?"

"Yea Girl, but you we ain't got no money."

220

"I know Belinda, but I also know you have something Blue wants and I happen to know Blue would be willing to trade crack for a little bit of what you got!"

"Whacha talkin' about? Are you talkin' bout my kitty?" Belinda started massaging her thighs sort of suggestively with a glazed look in her eye. This whole persona she had taken on surprised me just a bit.

"Well, yes, Blue is interested in sleeping with you and he said he would be willing to trade for it."

"Sheeeeit, Blue's not talkin' about sleepin' that's for sure," Belinda laughed at her own joke. "He wants to make my kitty purr! Hell I don't have a problem with that, give him a call so we can get this thing hooked up!"

"Wait a minute, wait! You mean to tell me you would do THAT for crack?!!" I asked incredulously.

"Hell yeah, it would only take, what five minutes anyway and we would have enough crack to last an hour. Fuck it, sounds like an easy plan, call him and let's get this deal done!"

So I called Blue and told him that Belinda would have sex with him for some crack.

We drove to the west side, Blue met us on the street corner and I parked my car about three houses from his house. We went through the side gate, down into the basement which was a fully furnished apartment. Since Belinda agreed to have sex with Blue, he handed me a handful of rock and I sat down on the sofa and immediately started smoking it. Belinda and Blue were getting busy on the bed right behind me; they were moaning and groaning so vociferously that I was forced to turn around just for a moment to take a peek at what on earth could cause such ecstatic squeals. When I looked, I saw two huge black guys, one stood at the door and the other off in the corner as though they were a body guard. I continued smoking and I thought nothing of it because I thought they were guarding the stash and watching out for the police. By the time Belinda and Blue and finished doing the "do", I had smoked three rocks. Blue zipped up, walked over to me and gave me another handful from a bowl on the fireplace mantel. Afterwards we were unceremoniously escorted from the house by the two large black guys, with Blue who followed closely behind. Although I was high, I knew this was wrong, but crack allowed me to not care.

It had started to get very dangerous being out on the streets around the dealers so I started packing a 9mm Ruger between my legs when I drove late at night. I had purchased this gun ten years ago when I opened up my own furniture store in Harrisburg, NC; I felt I needed it for protection when I worked alone during evening hours.

I felt like a gangster when I traveled with the gun and it was exciting to a certain degree. I really did not want to use it but kept it for protection only. Several weeks after the Belinda incident with Blue, I called him up and made my crack order from him and he had some available. I got in my car and drove over which was less than five minutes away and of course had my gun at my side. When I arrived at his house he was nowhere to be found, so in my insanity I got out of my car and started to walk down the middle of the street with the gun in my right hand in plain view for all to see. Blue came out within a few minutes and angrily asked what was up with the gun and I told him just as angrily that I wanted my shit now. He and one of his big lieutenants walked me back to my car, shoved me in the driver's side, then got in the passenger's side door and allowed me to make my purchase. He picked up my gun and the big black guy handed me about 10 additional crack rocks for the gun and they walked away. I did not think anything about it at the time because all my focus was on my crack. Even in the throes of my addition, I wanted to stop drinking and using but absolutely could not find a way to stop.

Kathy and I went out one night in early July to buy some drugs and we found Caboose roaming the streets on the west side. He did not have anything available so he got in the car with us as we cruised over to the north side. We drove past the crack house and down the side street to the alley and found B, C and Popcorn out by the big tree. We pulled up and I immediately jumped out of the car; suddenly all three of them pulled out guns and pointed them directly at me, and wanted to know why Caboose was in the car and why we had brought him from the west side over to the north side. Caboose got out of the car and ran like a scalded dog. I thought these guys were going to shoot me dead, right on the very spot I stood instead, then they lowered their guns and told me to get back in the car. Once I was back in the car and they were sure no outsiders were among us, they approached the car and sold Kathy some crack. They told me not to ever bring Caboose into their territory again. We drove away and found Caboose about three blocks, still running his ass off. I slowed down and told him to hop in and we got the hell out of there. I passed on the warning I received about him never going back to the north side. Unfortunately I don't think he heeded my words because three days later, Caboose was in the Medical College of Virginia Hospital due to multiple gunshot wounds. Somehow he survived and hopefully learned a lesson.

One Saturday afternoon about midway through July, Popcorn showed up at my house. I asked him how he knew where I lived and he said he just knew. He came in and asked to rent my car for an hour for $50, I agreed but asked for crack instead. He gave me about $120 street value of the crack and I gave him the key to my car. He was gone with my car in about an hour and when he returned it he gave me more crack. He then asked to borrow my car again to pick up his girlfriend and I agreed. All I remember was that while I was sitting on my back porch, drinking beer, smoking crack, and throwing the ball to Zeb, I heard about three different police car sirens. I briefly wondered to myself if the cops had found my car with Popcorn driving it, but I was in my crack mind and just kept doing what I was doing. I finally went back into the house and sat at my dining room table and finished off my crack. I was feeling no pain when about ten minutes later my doorbell rang and it was a Richmond City Police officer. I collected myself the best I could and was convinced he had no idea I was "stoned to the bone" and did the only thing a good 'ol Southern girl knew to do, I invited him into

223

the parlor. He came right in, glanced around, looked sternly at me and asked if I knew where my car was and without skipping a beat I told him it was parked right out front. He looked at me oddly and explained that he and his fellow officers had stopped a suspicious looking guy who said he had rented your car for $50. With the truth all out on front street like that, I had no choice but to back track so I just tried to play the "dumb blond" role and simply smiled, batted my eyes, and told the officer that he was absolutely right. "Oh my goodness! You see officer, you just caught me napping in the middle of the afternoon and I had not properly collected myself you see. Yes that's right, now I re-member. I did loan, I mean rent my car out to that gentleman earlier today before my nap. I'm so sorry if I've caused a prob-lem to Richmond's finest." He looked at me not at all convinced with my "damsel in distress act", handed me the key and told me my car was parked six blocks away and I needed to go get it or it would be towed. I immediately walked the six blocks and found my car parked cockeyed on the side of the road and drove it home. I vowed to never do something that stupid again, crack or no crack!

I had been back after my vacation a little less than two weeks and decided to take off Friday, July 18 and Monday, July 21. I wanted to make sure that everything was in order for my surgery, check on the letter from the west end therapist, ensure my money was in order so I could pay my surgeon. I was also extremely exhausted from my horrific escapades of staying up late, drinking, drugging, and working hard all day long.

Friday, July 18, 2008, was no different than previous months when I went to Doll's and had a $75 bar bill and found a little crack and smoked while at the bar. Thankfully I treated myself to an "early" evening and got home around 2:30 a.m. and went to bed. Barry and Kathy were no longer there because I told earlier in the week that they could no longer reside with me and they needed to have everything out by August 1st. I did this because I knew I had to stop my illicit behavior prior to surgery and I knew there was no way I could do it with those two in my home. My surgery meant everything to me and I figured if I could get them out I could stop the insanity. Unfortunately, it did not stop on this day.

Chapter 19 – Thunder and Lightning

Saturday, July 19th, I awoke around 10:00 a.m. and I realized I had peed myself and had slept in it all through the night. I had been too drunk and well, just plain fucked up to even notice! I was consumed with shame and emptiness. The feeling completely consumed me. I was looking at myself from above, outside of my body, seeing just a shell. I had no spirit at all; I was just this shell of a body with no purpose and I felt there was absolutely no meaning to life whatsoever. It was the most all-encompassing feeling I had ever felt and it became absolutely crystal clear to me that I had a problem of epic proportions! It was my moment of clarity. I was both shocked and revolted at my realization and as I whispered the eight most hideous words I thought I'd never hear come out of my own mouth: "Kaitlin, you have become a filthy crack head", tears streamed down my face as I sobbed quietly into my hands.

I went downstairs, made a pot of coffee and after I finished the entire pot, I took Zeb out for his morning walk. I was barely able to read the newspaper. so logically, I opened a beer and didn't stop until I had drunk the entire 12 pack. By now it now about 3:00 in the afternoon and I had decided that I was definitely going to stop using crack. I realized it was destroying me and I had to find a way to stop or the drug would kill me. Since I did not know what to do, I picked up my car keys and drove over to St. Paul's Catholic Church. I walked into the church I had grown up in, since grade school. I had sat in the front row with my family every Sunday and on Holy Days. I looked up at the crucifix and cried, and cried, and cried. When I was a child, the statue of the Virgin Mary was placed next to the podium where the gospel was preached but it had now been moved over to the left at a side alter. I cried my way over to the side alter and knelt down.

Now, I have struggled on whether or not to include this part in my book, but it seem appropriate to include it here and now.

What I am about to divulge has been something that I have kept to myself all these years. I have kept this secret inside me because I did not think anyone would ever believe it. However, I know it happened with all my heart and soul. So this is something that happened to me when I was nine years old in that church:

I was sitting on the front row with my family, right in front of the statue of the Virgin Mary on Sunday morning. I was 9 years old, very confused about my gender, badly wanting to understand why I was a boy who a liked to dress as a girl. I sat and thought about how hard and strict life was and how I had to keep this a secret in order to survive. I had no one to talk to about this feeling and as I looked up at the statue of the Virgin Mary, her eyes opened and she said to me, "everything was going to be ok". My eyes filled with tears and immediately I was filled with peace. I have carried and looked back on this experience my entire life.

As I knelt down on that Saturday afternoon, on July 19th, I cried out to the statue of the Virgin Mary for help. I said out loud, "you told me that everything was going to be ok!" I cried for thirty minutes, until I heard someone in the back of the church moving around, apparently preparing for the Saturday evening Mass. I wiped my eyes, walked to the exit and found a book for Mass intentions. It was at least a legal size hard bound book and I wrote in big bold letters across two full blank pages. "Please help me...Kaitlin Riordan."

I took my crack pipe out of my purse and threw it out the car window and it shattered on the pavement. I drove home and walked Zeb about seven blocks around the Fan District. I had him lead me back home and grabbed a bottle of beer and sat on the back steps and threw the ball. I took a cab to Doll's that night and met the girls from JRTS, played pool, danced and then walked home.

Sunday I woke up around 10:00 a.m. and followed my normal routine. I sat down in the dining room and watched the NASCAR race until about 5:00 p.m. I came up with the idea that I would invite my neighbor Jennifer out to dinner because I was celebrating being off of crack. She answered the phone and was hungry and said she would love to go with me.

I met Jennifer at the restaurant about 7:30 p.m. and I ordered a beer and we talked and had a nice dinner. I think I drank at least five more tall glasses of beer and told her all about my experience with crack and explained that I was finally done with it. I told her about the drug dealers and how they wanted me to go to New Jersey and pick up $3000 worth of cocaine bricks and bring them back to Richmond and all the ins and outs of the business. I was so proud of myself for being off of crack and drank to celebrate.

I do not remember how I drove home but my car was parked out front when I took Zeb out for his last walk of the day. I drank bottled beer as we walked along the lighted street and dark alleys. I remember I took him in, gave him his snack and then I went to bed. As I laid down just after midnight, again something came over me. A feeling so overwhelming that made me feel beyond a shadow of a doubt that I could not live my life like this anymore. I immediately called Jennifer and asked her to take me to Tucker Pavilion at Chippenham Hospital. This was the same hospital where I had taken my son when his bouts of mental illness were no longer controlled by medication. I don't know why I wanted to go to the mental ward of the hospital; I only knew that I needed to be there. I felt that my alcoholism and drug addiction had driven me to the point of insanity and I needed help immediately!

Jennifer arrived at my door with her son Larson about ten minutes later and I walked out of my house wearing only a light baby blue slip with no shoes and a bottle of beer in my hand. While she was driving me to the hospital I suddenly changed my mind and I opened the passenger's car door while she was moving at 55 mph. I told her I was getting out and she screamed at me in a voice I barely recognized. I could tell she meant business and thought better about my ridiculous decision to exit her vehicle while she drove the full speed limit. We arrived at the hospital and as I was walked in, a black family with children was walking out. I stepped right in front of them and in my drunken and very belligerent state, asked them if they had any crack! Jennifer was mortified, but that wasn't all. The family, who realized I was an alcoholic and addict, ever so kindly ignored my pathetic ass, stepped aside, and attempted to keep moving. I turned and yelled at their backs, "What the hell is wrong, I KNOW all black people have crack, so fuck you very much!" And with that, I took a big gulp of my beer, walked through the doors, slammed my beer down on the emergency counter and told them that I wanted some help. Jennifer stared on in horror, but she was kind enough to not only contact my sister Ann, but she also waited until she arrived before she went back home. Ann stayed with me in the back room as I told them I had been using crack almost daily, drank daily, and I needed help desperately. They took my blood to determine my alcohol level and it came back 0.32. I was admitted in a lockdown ward and given Phenobarbital for the next three days and was detoxified.

On Tuesday morning I made the dreaded call to my boss and explained that I was in a medical facility for treatment for alcohol abuse. I confessed to having a problem with alcohol but made no mention of my crack addiction. With that chore completed, I spent the remainder of the day the same way I did on Monday, I slept and ate. When Wednesday morning rolled around I felt much better and of course asked the nurses to release me. The nurses looked at me knowingly and told me quite firmly that the doctor would be the one to determine my readiness for discharge, and not me. The doctor made his rounds around 1:00 p.m. on Wednesday afternoon and after he examined me and read my chart, we discussed my release. He agreed to allow me to be discharged that day. I waited about three hours which seemed like eternity and finally I was called to the nurses station and processed for discharged. A taxi had been arranged to drive me home. The driver even supplied me with a much needed cigarette since I had not had one in three days. Of course if I had any sense, this would have been the perfect time to stop smoking, but I was anxious to get home to Zeb and the cigarette helped take the edge off. Jennifer had been feeding and walking Zeb while I was hospitalized and I was so grateful to her for being there for me and Zeb. When I arrived I had to get my key from Jennifer to get in and was so happy to see Zeb; I gave him a very long hug and we went out back to play ball. It was peaceful around the house since Barry and Kathy were no longer there, Zeb and I had our home to ourselves again and we loved it! We came back inside and I opened the refrigerator there was a six pack of beer staring right at me so I took it out and instead of pouring that poison down the sink, I poured it right down my throat while I sat on the front porch and watched the cars and people go by. After that beer I proceeded to polish off the entire six pack that night, and then I ate dinner, and went to bed. Great way to start my sobriety, right?!

On Thursday I went to see Doctor Bears, my therapist, and discussed my issues concerning alcohol and the need for further help. We discussed going away for treatment or getting involved in a 12-step program here in town. I told him that I would be willing to attend a 12-step meeting on Friday and there were three of these meeting all within walking distance of my home. After my therapy appointment I went to the Inn, had dinner and a pitcher of beer, then stopped by the Deli and bought a six pack of beer to go. Gotta love this sobriety thing, right?!

Later that evening, my phone rang and when I answered I found Blue on the other end.

"Hey Momma K dis Blue, you ok Gurl?"

"Yes Blue, I'm ok. You sound funny, what's going on, why are you asking?"

"Look Gurl, you is good people dats why I'm callin'. But you needs to stay in the cut, stay on da down low for a while. You feel me Gurl?"

"Why Blue, what the hell is going on?" I asked as I began visibly shaking, not knowing what to think as I imagined all sort of horrors.

"Look hea, Belinda done called me freakin' talkin' all kinds of crazy about somma dem northside gang bangers had come kicked in her door and had guns. They tore up her digs and beat her down den dey said dey was lookin' for Momma K.

Dey was talkin' shit about you and your car and rattin' out to the po-po. Belinda didn't give you up, but dey be lookin' for you so do as I say and stay on the down low cuz they be trouble. You feel me?!"

"Thanks, Blue!"

Still shaking, I slowly hung up the phone. Oh I "felt" him alright and that scared me to death! I called Belinda's number, her sister answered and screamed at me to never call again and to stay far away from them forever. She also screamed so much flaring filth I couldn't get a word in edgewise; called me everything but a child of God! Zeb and I took our last walk of the night and I felt extremely paranoid while walked the city streets and became ultra-cautious. My imagination went wild as I thought these guys could just shoot me right here on the street and the police would probably think it was a transgendered person shot for not revealing their true gender. Just as my imagination had started to get the better of me, I heard three gun shots way off in the distance. I kicked up my shoes, grabbed Zeb and nearly sprinted the last seven blocks all the way home! I quickly ran to check every door and window in my home to ensure they were locked up and extra secure, especially since I made the stupid choice of trading my gun for crack when I was high …dammit to hell!!! I searched my home and came up with the next best thing I could find, a baseball bat. I put it next to my bed and turned off all the lights and tried to sleep. Where were my Wonder Woman bracelets when I needed them because Lord knows that dang bat wouldn't stop a bullet. Crap!

On Friday I spoke with my therapist again about my treatment options and the need to get a Medical Leave from Philip Morris so that I could seek proper treatment. He told me he would fill out the paperwork for my leave request and would research several treatment facilities and if I thought about drinking that I should call him. I thanked him, continued with my routine, cleaned my house and went to the grocery store for a few things. I purchased another six-pack of beer, came home, drank it all, walked across the street and bought more. I sat on my front porch and after I drank the first of six more, I finally got up off my ass and called Dr. Bears. I told him that I had been drinking again and he asked me how many I had in my house. I told him I had already polished off a six-pack and I had finished the first beer in the second six-pack. Currently there were five more left. He told me to take the remaining beers to the bathroom and poor them down the toilet. He said he wanted to hear me complete this task. So I simply finished the beer I was drinking and very quietly filled the bottle with water and poured the water down the toilet and said, "Ok number one down the toilet bowl". I repeated this five more times and he fell for it, hook, line, and sinker. He told me I did well and to call again if I wanted to drink. I hung up with that moron and I went back to the refrigerator, grabbed another beer, went out to the front porch and drank it. Afterwards I went to Doll's for dinner, drinks, pool, and dancing, then staggered home, walked Zeb and went to bed.

Saturday came and as I sat at my kitchen table drinking my third cup of coffee, I reflected on my life thus far: I had lived full time as a female for over a year, transitioned on the job with the conservative tobacco company in Virginia, started a trans-gendered support group, all of this at the expense of losing my family, but all the while with the knowledge that I had to complete these tasks in order to survive, to be truthful, to be myself completely. I was happy to be my true self, but I was sad and depressed that it seemed that my happiness came at the expense of others. But it was so much better to be ME, than to hide and be John. I drank myself deeper into that depression because of rejection and utter loneliness. By this time I had lost a great deal of weight and my 5'9" body frame was down to only 139 lbs. My skirts were literally falling off my body and I had to purchase size 27 jeans and size 4-6 skirts which was a long ways from the size 12 from two years ago.

That night at 8:30 p.m., I decided to drive over to the Richmond Braves baseball game which was about a mile and a half from my house. I had drunk at least a 12-pack of beer and was definitely feeling it. I drove into the west entrance of the ball park and as I looked around for a parking space, BAM! I had hit a light pole head on with my Camry. I backed up and went around to the other side of the field and parked my car. I got out and checked my car for damages. There was no mistaking what happened to it, it looked exactly like I hit a pole. The hood was crinkled and water had already begun to leak. In my liquored state I decided it would be ok and walked on into "The Diamond". The gates were opened and it was already the 6th inning. I ordered a beer and walked down to the box seats. I was loud and obnoxious to say the least, and the families who were there trying to enjoy the game with their little children, grabbed a hold of their kids and placed their hands over their ears in horror! Once I noticed this I got up for more beer and decided to sit further back away from everyone. It occurred to me, even in my inebriated state that I may look female, but I certainly was not acting very ladylike and did not want any trouble. I yelled for the boy to get a hit, get a steal, score some runs, strike someone out, hell I just yelled for the sake of yelling. It was baseball and I loved beer and baseball. After another inning I got up and went to the concession stand and the workers would not sell me another beer because they said I was drunk and it was against park rules. I thought I could outsmart them so I went four sections over and they would not sell to me either, what nerve! By now I had caught the eye of park security and they were now following me. Big bad beer police were on my tail so I decided it was time to leave the ballpark, post haste. I found out later that my oldest sister was there and saw the whole thing. Hmmm, wonder why she didn't come over and have a beer and watch the ball game with her big Sis?!

I looked at my car again and thought I could get it home to assess the damage. By now a big puddle of water had amassed directly underneath the engine. I headed out the exit and towards what I thought was home, only to realize I was on the wrong side of town and had been driving in the wrong direction, only I just could not understand why. I turned around and headed back towards the ball park and suddenly my car just stopped in the middle of the road. My great idea was to call 911, which I did and I told them I had just been hit by a pickup truck and needed help. The police and rescue squad arrived and within minutes the officer assessed my car and told the ambulance driver to leave, and explained that their services were not needed. The female police officer looked at me and told me to tell her what really happened. Her voice was definitely no nonsense and I realized I had better just fess up and take my licks. So I was honest and told her exactly what happened. She took my license, registration and insurance and I held my breath as I thought here we go, female name with and "M" in the sex block. She asked me to get in the car and show her the pole I hit and we drove a few blocks to the ball park which was now empty. After she examined the pole, the fortunate thing for me, was there was no damage whatsoever to the pole. We went back to my car and I asked her not to ask me to say my ABC's backward because I could not do it sober. She knew that I had been drinking and it seemed that she actually felt sorry for me. We called my friend Teresa who agreed to come and pick me up. Teresa asked her if I had been drinking again and the officer said yes. My car was towed to the city lot and she gave me a ticket for reckless driving and told me I was lucky and need not contest this ticket; I knew I was given a huge break. Teresa took me home without a lecture and dropped me off. I walked Zeb and went straight to bed.

Sunday morning I called my insurance company and was told they would look at my car, get it out of the city pound, and let me know what could be done. They did advise however, it would be Monday before it would be appraised. I was just grateful they were going to help. I stayed at home all day and watched the NASCAR race and played with Zeb and of course, drank more beer. My thoughts late that afternoon had gotten the better of me. I wanted to see my entire family to let them know I was going to have surgery in a little over a week. At the time I felt like I needed them to know and I was trying to force them to love me. I picked up the phone and remembered telling them I wanted them to come over and see me right now. The part that I do not remember but got me in a great deal of trouble was I told them to come over now or I was going to shoot myself. I have been told by my sister that I was quit adamant about that fact.

With no recollection of time, but in a short period, four Richmond police officers, two paramedics, my therapist, interventionist, and my oldest sister were at my house. They handcuffed me, placed me in a rescue squad, took me over to Richmond Community Hospital, and a police officer stayed with me all night and into the next morning. I remembered that one week ago, I had gone to the Catholic Church and cried out for help and asked in the book of intentions to please help me. I do believe that I was receiving the help I was seeking but could not do for myself. It did not seem so at the time but in hindsight it was one more step in the right direction.

I was placed in a private room off from the emergency entrance until there was a bed available. I talked a little with the Richmond police officer who was assigned to me. He was very kind and when I needed to smoke, he would handcuff me, walk me outside, and allow me my smoke time. The whole experience was very humbling. I was still there Monday morning and the nurses were talking with my doctor about not having a bed available and they wanted to send me to Central State Hospital in Petersburg. That made me really scared because when I was a child I heard about Central State and how all the mentally ill people were sent there and they received shock treatment and other horrors went on there. I walked out of the room, picked up a phone and called my sister Ann. She is a lawyer and I told her what was going on and that if I went to Central State I would come out of there in worse condition than I was currently in because I knew the reputation of that place. I know society looks at the transgendered community as mentally ill due to their limited education and lack of understanding but by no means was I mentally ill. I had visions of being locked away forever as my parents constantly threatened me with when I was young when they thought I might have a learning disability. Little did they know that I had a gender issue that was all consuming, not a learning issue which is another reason why I had to bury it and not allow them to know.

Fortunately one of the nurses overheard my conversation with Ann when I expressed my firm stance against being placed at Central State. She told me that she would try to arrange for me to have a room. Since I was pre-op transsexual, I had to have my own private room which was making it difficult to find on the drug and alcohol abuse floor. Eventually late Monday afternoon the nurse had arranged for a room all the way at the end the floor, with one bed. It looked as if it was really not a normal everyday room but maybe one converted over for me. I didn't care; I was just so relieved that she found me a spot here.

On Tuesday, my sisters and brothers all came to the hospital with my therapist Dr. Bears, a Judge and clerk of court. The Judge recommended that I stay in the hospital for five days and I told him that I would do it voluntarily. Then my doctor, brother and sister spoke up and they recommended it be court ordered. I was already willing to stay and told the judge he did not have to do that but he sided with them and it became a court ordered intervention which to me was very upsetting and unnecessary. I did not even know where this came from unless it was from my prayers on Sunday night. I utilized my detox time well and attended all the classes and was released on Friday afternoon. My oldest sister picked me up and I could not wait to see Zeb. Ann and Jennifer had watched him one more time. I played with Zeb, did not drink, went to a 12-step meeting, came home and went to bed.

Saturday I went and met the girls from JRTS at Doll's and we had dinner and I did not drink. It was now six days without a drop and I was beginning to feel very good about myself. After we finished dinner it was still light outside so I decided to walk the 14 blocks home. About halfway there I took my phone out of my purse and called Blue. I asked him to meet me on the way home and to bring me some crack. I met him and purchased one rock and smoked it while I walked home. It really did not do a thing for me, and once home I walked across the street purchased a six-pack. I wanted so badly to just be me without feeling all this pain.

My gender reassignment surgery was only seven days away on Monday morning, I called Dr. McGinn and told her that I needed to go into rehab for alcohol and drug abuse. I knew I had to conquer that problem before I could have surgery. My surgery date was probably the one thing that had given me the thought that I needed to stop this foolishness so that I could get on with my life. I tried but I could not do this myself and I knew I had to find the solution and thought that rehab would be a great beginning. Dr. McGinn was very kind and understanding and told me to get some help and to keep her informed of my progress. I was extremely disappointed and sobbed over the fact that my procedure was going to be delayed, but I knew in my heart that I needed to take care of my addiction because I was way out of control.

I met with Dr. Bears on Monday and we looked for an inpatient rehab facility; all the while I did not drink at all. On Tuesday afternoon, one of my new found friends from the Richmond Community Hospital called me and wanted to come by for a visit Tuesday night. I told her I would cook some burgers on the grill but drinking was out of the question and she agreed. At 5:30 p.m. I was out walking Zeb and I saw her walking up the street towards my house and I yelled over to her. She was on her cell phone and did not hear me so Zeb and I doubled back and met her on the front porch of my home. We chatted for a minute before we went inside, then I started to get out the burgers. She told me she had just come from a 12-step meeting as she pulled a pint of vodka from her purse! My eyes nearly bored a holed right through her as I gave her the meanest look I could muster. In more of a statement rather than a question, I merely said, "I thought we agreed not to drink." She just looked at me like I was speaking a foreign language or that she had no comprehension of what I said whatsoever, so I added that I would most definitely not drink and went outside and cooked the hamburgers on the grill. When I returned, we sat down to eat and she hit the pint of vodka. For no reason whatsoever, I walked over and took a hit myself. I asked her to wait right here and keep the burgers warm and I walked across the street and bought two bottles of wine and 12-pack of beer. We ate out burgers and drank the rest of our dinner and she passed out shortly thereafter. Her phone rang and it was her father so I decided to answer it. I told him she was passed out in my dining room and he needed to come and pick her up. By this time we had polished off all the vodka and the wine and there were only eight beers left. Her father came and we put her in the car and they took off. I went back in and finished off the remaining beer while sitting on the front porch with Zeb. Afterwards I went upstairs to bed; this was August 5, 2008.

Chapter 20 – Clueless in West Virginia

I spoke to my therapist on the 6th of August and agreed on a rehab in Charles Town, WVA called The Crossing Point. We made arrangements for them to pick me up in Richmond, VA. I started to panic about being in rehab and worrying about Zeb, so I began to call all around to find him a place to stay while I went off for help. I thought that Brandon and Stephanie would watch Zeb while I was gone. When I called and asked, Brandon got on the phone told me what a piece of crap I was and that they would not have any part of this and told me not to disrupt his family ever again. I called Ann and she agreed to help. Then my therapist called and told me the folks at the rehab could not come until tomorrow and I did everything I could to keep from drinking; thankfully I did not take a drink. I busied myself with preparing for this journey by cleaning my home, packing my bags, and praying. Instead of alcohol, I had lots of coffee, soda, and water; I never left the house to go get the devil's sauce.

August 7, 2008, was a bittersweet awakening for me because I knew I was going to get help for my alcohol and drug use but conversely, I was so very disappointed because today was the day I supposed to be having my gender reassignment surgery. I reassured myself that all was not lost and my plan to become the real me was still in the works. But in order to have a fulfilled life I needed to take care of my issues and it was of great importance to my health. I desperately wanted to make sure that Zeb would be fine while I was away and my sister Ann reassured me that she would take him into her home and find him a place to stay until I returned. Although not knowing where he was going to be was disheartening for me, I knew in order for me take care of him or even to have a happy and complete life, I had to take care of myself first.

I laid on the floor of the main parlor of my house and held Zeb and cried and told him how much I loved him. I have never seen a dog cry before but Zeb lay there with me and cried too as we shared our tears together. It was one of the most powerful bonding moments that I had ever had in my life. We both cried together for a long time. About 3:00 in the afternoon the phone rang and a man on the other end said he was from the rehab center and would be there to pick me up around 7:00 p.m. I called my sister Ann and begged her to please take good care of Zeb. Ann again had to reassure me he would be fine before I would hang up the phone. Zeb and I stayed side by side until the rehab driver showed up and when he arrived, I called my sister one last time to inform her my ride had showed up and beg her to not leave my faithful friend and companion Zeb alone and to take great care of him. She promised me she would come for my buddy within an hour, told me not to worry, and to just concentrate on my recovery. I cried as I hugged my Zeb one more time and then I looked him in the eye and apologized to him for all I had put him through and for yet one more thing he would have to endure. He was such a great dog and seemed to understand, he rested his big head on my shoulder and raised his paw up to my arm as if to say, "There, there Kaitlin, it's ok, I love you so much and I will be here when you get home and are all better." With his encouragement, I was out the door I went, into the little Ford Escort and headed north to Charles Town, West Virginia.

The drive seemed very long, especially when we were west of Washington, DC in the dark country, the foothills of Virginia, the Appalachian Mountains and the countryside of West Virginia. As we drove into town, we passed some of the town's sites, but I was too lost in thought to really take much notice. I arrived at The Crossing Point in Charles Town at 12:45 a.m. on Friday morning and I was greeted by an orderly who helped me with my luggage and showed me to my room. He took my cell phone, identification, wallet, and told me he would lock my items up in the safe. I had a beautiful room upstairs with a comfortable single bed, dresser, cedar chest, and a closet. The floors were hard wood oak covered with a floral design rug that matched the rose room color. I fell asleep almost immediately and slept until my wakeup call at 7:00 a.m.

The house was located on the corner of Main Street, just two blocks from the downtown strip. The mountains were beautiful, the yard had large oak and maple trees, and the beautiful backyard was lined in flower gardens that needed to be weeded. The property had an iron fence about chest high around the back yard, and the front yard was open from the house to the street. The house was very old but had been renovated and furnished with antiques throughout; it was a nice setting for me to start my work on myself. There was a rolling hill park about three blocks away that we walked through for exercise on Friday afternoon. Charles Town was what I called, "a one horse stable" town. It had no major chain stores, only family owned and operated shops. There were only three patients at the rehab, myself and two guys, one of whom was scheduled to leave in two days, so there were really only the two of us.

I met with Tom the owner and principal counselor at the Crossing Point and we discussed my case, being transgendered, missing the surgery, my alcohol and drug abuse, and my financial situation. He discussed the 12-step program with me and explained that I would need to stay on the property at all times except for the meetings he would drive us to in town. I had a 12-step book with me so he gave me my first assignment, which was to read the first 164 pages, underline the word "recovered" every time I read it, and let him know how many words there were in those pages. He also gave me 175 questions to fill out which was part of my first step. We discussed ego, guilt, shame, fear, pride, envy, and sloth. I did not see what that had to do with anything, but I accepted the assignment without question and started immediately on reading the book. He said we would meet again and discuss what I had learned.

Over the course of the next several days, Tom took us to meetings in the back roads of West Virginia after dinner. We finally arrived at the meeting hall and I walked into the room of about fifteen men and five women, and a sense of not being accepted came over me. The hairs on my arms literally stood up as I sensed hostility in the room as I felt all the eyes staring at me. I told the group my name but dared not speak a word. After the meeting three of the five women cornered me in the women's restroom and handed me a card with their name and phone numbers and I simply said thank you. I thought it would not go well if they discovered I was a pre-op transsexual especially in this part of the country. I was not about to talk about being transgendered with this group because I knew in my heart it spelled trouble with a capitol "T". They were truly all "good 'ol boys and girls" and I was in the wrong place which I think was confirmed a short time later.

On Sunday morning, a minister came in and we read a daily reflection and discussed it between the three of us, I found it very enlightening. Tom arranged for one of his former students, who was now a now part-time counselor, to take me over to the mall which was just outside of Charles Town, about eight miles away. I was actually surprised to see there was a four lane highway in this town because I mistakenly thought not a lot existed here. We went to the mall and she and I went to a shop that was having a "buy one get one" sale. I tried on a top and she purchased one and told me to get the one I tried on since it would be free. It was a nice girls outing for a couple of hours. Later that evening, Tom and I discussed finances and I paid him $2000 for the first week.

On Monday afternoon, Tom told me to get in the van and we drove two blocks into town to a coffee shop and bought me a cup of coffee. He was visiting a female employee there who appeared about 30 years old, because she had gone through his program and volunteered to help out around the house; she was the same female who took me shopping. Tom, who was about 60 years old, confided in me that he liked this girl a lot and for more than just a friend; so while he talked with her I sat alone and read the newspaper. At this point we were all cut off from the outside world, the only exception was an hour or two of television on Sunday afternoon.

We drove through town, all of three minutes of it, over to a car lot where the new Dodge Charger was being displayed, then back to the house. I felt as though he was sizing me up and that was the only purpose that I could think of for the drive. That evening, he called me to his office and we discussed me being transgendered and we worked on an alcohol and drug treatment plan suitable for me. The conversation led to my needing to "work on" being transgendered and while I wasn't quite sure what he was going through, I explained very adamantly that I was positively sure of my need for surgery. I also gently reminded him of why I had come to this facility, and that was to be treated for my alcohol and drug addiction. He said in that case, they would be unable to help me. I sat there incredulous! This place was recommended by my therapist and they supposedly knew that I was transgendered before I even arrived. So, now I'm being told that they won't help me because I am transgendered?! I told him that I needed for them to arrange transportation for me to be taken back to my home in Richmond. I immediately got up from the meeting and I went to my room and sobbed because I honestly wanted help with my alcohol and drug abuse problem. I could not believe I was taken all the way out into the middle of the middle of nowhere, only to be discriminated against and rejected. I finally understood: he paraded me through Charles Town and got input from the town minister and his girlfriend, then took me to a meeting in the sticks, and made his own uneducated assessment that a male to female transsexual was not welcomed in his town. This had always been one of my fears and I thought that since I went and was honest with this group, then the fact that I was transgendered would not be an issue. Before I even left for Charles Town, the group stated that it would not be an issue; however, once I was there in person apparently they could not deal with it. Although, I was passionate about doing the work to stay sober, it was not about them helping me to stay sober, it was more about appearances or some type of social pressure going on in that area. Finally at 5:30pm on Tuesday, we loaded up the van and he picked up his girlfriend, and we drove to Richmond. Disappointed and disillusioned, I unpacked and I went to bed.

Chapter 21 – San Jacinto Mountains

I called Ann early the next morning to ascertain the whereabouts of Zeb. I discussed the events that had taken place in West Virginia and told her I was back home and was looking for another rehab to attend. I wanted to come and get Zeb but she reassured me he was in good hands with Kyle. Kyle lived in the country with his collie and had a large yard for him to run and play. I thought that leaving Zeb there was a good idea. I then called Sister and asked if she knew of a good rehab for me to attend and she told me she would make a few calls and get back with me as soon as she had some information. In the meantime, I stayed away from the bars and the deli. I walked down to a 12-step meeting that night and came home and went to bed. I missed Zeb so much and found it very hard that day not to drink, so I kept myself very busy.

Thursday morning the phone rang and it was Sister. She explained that her friend in Philadelphia was looking into the situation and she might call me. Her friend did indeed call me and left a voice message to call Mario at Michael's House in Palm Springs, California. I listened to the message, called and spoke directly with Mario and he took my information and insurance. He said he would call right back after he checked my insurance and bed availability and he actually did. He told me to go to the Richmond airport the following day at 11:00 a.m., provided me with the flight information, explained that everything was paid for, and they would pick me up in Palm Springs upon my arrival. I did exactly what I was told and found my way out to California, by Charlotte, Phoenix, and then into Palm Springs. When I exited the plane it was hot and dry even at 9:00 p.m. on this August 15th evening. A lady counselor from Michael's House picked me up from the airport at 9:00 p.m. PT and drove me a short distance near downtown to the rehab facility.

Once at Michael's House I was given a drug & alcohol test. I was both surprised and a bit embarrassed to find out that I tested positive for cocaine which I had not indulged in since August 2nd. I had not had a drink since August 5th which meant I had eight days of sobriety upon entry. I was briefly shown the facilities and found the place absolutely beautiful. It was almost like I was on vacation with the pristine meeting rooms, kitchen, pool and grounds loaded with palm trees. I was taken upstairs to my room and where I was introduced to my roommate Denise. She had been asleep as I came in, so she said hello and went back to sleep. I found out later that the counselors there had asked Denise if she had a problem rooming with a male to female, pre-op transsexual and she said she had no problem whatsoever. Michael's House was LGBT friendly and as were the majority of the residents of Palm Springs.

The days at the rehab were structured. I awoke at 6:00 a.m. every morning, glanced through the LA Times for about 15 minutes, read a "thought for today", went for a walk, had breakfast, took a break, and had two classes in the morning. Lunch was served at exactly noon and dinner was at 5:00 p.m. In the afternoon we attended process groups which were made up of 5-6 people with our individual counselor. Yoga, one-on-one counseling and homework made up the remainder of the afternoon. After dinner a 12-step group came in and shared their story with the group, however dependent upon one's level, one could pile into the van and go to town with a resident counselor to an outside 12-step meeting. There was an abundance of food, drinks, and snacks at the rehab facility. In the first week we would sit outside at night and share our "war" stories about our past drinking and drug abuse. After about ten days of this it became boring because it really did not serve me very well so I made it a point to get in bed by 10:00 p.m. It was so nice to not worry, and to sleep a full eight hours. I knew I was in a safe place.

My first assignment was to write about the ten consequences from my abuse of drugs and alcohol. My consequences dealt with missing my surgery date, financial issues, lost relationships with family and friends, inflicting my alcohol, meanness to others, separation from Zeb, and the total loss of my spirit. This was the first time I had ever taken a look at the results of my alcohol abuse. It was the very first look at only the tip of the iceberg of a deeper cleaning that would become a lifetime of work in progress and the peeling away of layer and layer of confusion and rejection. However, I did not realize that at the time. It was my plan to spend 30 to 45 days at the rehab facility and not drink or drug and then get back home to Richmond. Upon my return I planned to return to work and have my gender reassignment surgery. I thought with rehab I could learn to control my drinking and would be able drink like a normal person after I completed the program. I considered what was normal and realized what was normal for me was not necessarily normal for mainstream society.

There were 30 of us in residence at Michael's House and they were from all parts of the United States. I made new friends and talked about the parts of the country each person was from and how life was in each of these areas. I asked each person about the kinds of things to do in their hometowns and also asked about the places of interest. It was interesting to me and it kept my mind occupied. I was actually very interested in everyone and hoped to learn something from each individual's experience. On the 15th day of rehab August 30th, my birthday, a 24 year old man named Luke was admitted and I meet him in the kitchen of Michael's House South on his first day. There was something about him that I found attractive and we struck up a conversation and began what became a special friendship. He was a person with whom I felt very comfortable sharing my life experiences. He slept and had snacks for the first six days he was there but I kept my eye out for him. I really did not know why I felt so protective over him, I just knew I had an unexplained attraction to him and wanted to help him. He was like an older spirit, full of wisdom, in a young body and he was a friend.

The days were the same for the first three weeks and I grew very restless, irritable, and discontent. I was very angry at myself for missing my surgery due to my drug and alcohol addiction. During process group, I told the residents and counselor I

246

was going home after I completed 45 days and my life would be just fine. I planned to stick to my plan of being sober for 53 days and then to return home and simply control my drinking. I was not ever going to use drugs again, because that was what got me in rehab in the first place. In my mind I never thought of myself as a drug addict anyway, but I readily admitted I needed help controlling my alcohol abuse.

After I was in rehab for a little over two weeks, I was upgraded to Level Two which meant that I could attend outside 12-step meetings in Palm Springs in a controlled environment. That meant the Resident Counselors, would load us up in the van after dinner and take us as a group to one of these meetings. I started to hear other stories of those in recovery and the steps that they were taking to live a clean and sober life. The one thing I heard on a regular basis was that I needed to "live my life one day at a time". I understood this meant that I had to learn to live in the present because yesterday was a memory and tomorrow was a vision, so all any of us have is today and we should strive for progress over perfection. I thought I should at least give this philosophy a try and do the best I could just for today. This was preached at the meetings and in the classes at the rehab.

The days in rehab were always the same, but each day brought a different outlook on life. We talked about family relationships, we talked about environmental factors that affected our lives, we had even had classes with medical professionals who come in and explained the physical effects drugs and alcohol had on our brain and body. It was very eye opening to learn how the abuse of drugs and alcohol played a huge role in our thought processes and the physical condition of our bodies. I wasn't aware that cocaine cuts off the decision making function of the brain when using the drug and that therefore one could not differentiate right from wrong until I learned this in rehab. The drug looked for more of the same so the body would not feel any physical or mental anguish. Thus cocaine would make a good person bad and a bad person evil. I certainly did not want to be a bad or evil person, not ever again.

While I was in the 12-step meetings, I listened to people talk about relapse and how difficult it was to go back to the meetings and that their low points in life became even lower than before. I learned in rehab that once off the stuff for a while the brain starts to heal itself and the dopamine tentacles in the brain grow back and become even more numerous than the brain pervious held and that the highs were much higher after being off of the drugs than they were before, and that is what kept people from returning to rehab as they chased this newfound high. Drugs and alcohol had three main roads a person could take and they all met at the same intersection. These highways all led to jails, institutions, or death and while the trip may have been enjoyable, they were all slippery slopes along the way and they did eventually come together at one low point. Personally, I was so very fortunate that mine led to an institution because jail and death were just over the horizon. Today, I believe my life was spared to enable me to be of service to those who have taken the wrong path, thinking drugs and alcohol are the road to cure their pain.

The stories of those who relapsed really caught my attention. These people shared that they had been in rehab before and their next round of abuse lead to incomprehensible demoralization. Most found themselves waking up in a jail cell on the cold hard cement floor wondering what had happened. The counselors discussed several cases concerning people who had completed a couple of years of sobriety and decided they could control their alcohol use only to use and end up dead. One of my girlfriends, who maintained 18 months of sobriety, said she was doing great, was packing to go visit her family for Thanksgiving, died that same night with a needle in her arm. This was after she spoke about how well she was doing in the program. She was only 23 years old and had a wonderful, bright future ahead of her; but she just had to stick that needle in her arm one more time. It was these real life experiences and stories that I held onto when I became negative and thought that I had all the answers. I also kept my own story in the forefront of my mind and remembered and used my own lows and rock bottom points. I knew there was very little room left at the bottom. I knew that if I went back to my old way of life my next stop would be death.

I spent my time learning as much as possible, working on myself, and discussing sobriety with my friends Josh, Denise, JoAnne, Kayla, Lori and Luke. Mike, my therapist, gave me the advice to stay in rehab as long as possible and not to return to Richmond. I was determined to return until about day 38 when a light went off in my head and I realized I was not ready to be on my own. I requested to stay another 45 days and my insurance through Philip Morris approved my request. This was so very important and helped me tremendously. Josh and Denise, my roommate, were released from treatment and JoAnne became my new roommate.

I had a court date in late September for the reckless driving ticket I had received prior to coming to rehab. Thankfully Michael's House intervened and wrote to the court and I was granted a continuance. I was elected peer leader of the group of 30 residents', based on the fact that I had maintained my weekly chores and had perfect attendance at all classes and outside meetings. During the first week of my assignment as peer leader, the renovations on Michael's House North were completed and JoAnne, Luke, and I were given an option to move into the new complex. The three of us readily accepted the option and moved into the new facility. I was elected peer leader at this house for the next five weeks.

Michael's House North was more enclosed than the South house. I preferred the South house because of the huge open lawn, meditation, and beautiful seating area, and it was right up against the San Jacinto Mountains. The North house was located away from the mountains but close enough to the mountains to provide the most breathtaking view! Inside the courtyard was a coffin shaped pool and on the back side of the rooms was a large patio and with a large sitting area upstairs from the offices where all the smokers would congregate. There was a large eating area and kitchen where the chef would prepare the meals for both houses and next to the kitchen was a large classroom that would easily seat 75 residents. This is where both houses held their two morning classes each day. There was a huge wall mounted flat screen television just outside the classroom where we could watch television on Saturday and Sunday afternoons only. The group had to agree on the program we would watch; typically we split the time between football and movies.

By this time Luke and I were on Level 3, which meant we could go into town on our own from 1:00 p.m. – 5:00 p.m. on Saturday and Sunday if approved by our therapist. Luke, Jo-Anne, and I were always approved and we would ride the bus to the mall in Rancho Mirage or Palm Desert. Later, Bev and Allison joined our little group and we would cut up and act silly. Our inner child came out which felt very good. Luke and I "hoo-la-hooped" in front of the coffee shop on Palm Canyon Drive in Palm Springs and laughed until we cried. One Saturday afternoon in October Luke and Allison watched as I picked up a turkey baster in the drug store and went around and asked people for samples! It was hilarious and for the first time I realized that you could have fun without drinking or drugging.

I found myself in a good, solid routine and was actually having fun in rehab. I shared my own story and listened to others as they shared theirs as well. I quickly found a sponsor as required by the program. Serena would pick me up once a week and we would discuss working the 12 steps. In rehab I read from two different 12-step books and studied the 12-steps and traditions of each group. One of the public buildings in Palm Springs rented a room to a 12-step group and it was there that I picked up my 30 and 60 day sobriety chips and was working steadily towards 90 days, but continued to remember the motto, "one day at a time". Although I often got into my own head and thought I was still a victim of my family, friends, and coworkers, I tried hard to be more positive. The negative thoughts continued to return and I knew I had to work harder because those thoughts only made me feel bad. During the times when I allowed the negativity to sink in, I thought about quitting and running back home to Zeb and my booze. On the weekend we could use the telephone for 10 minutes. I'd use that time to call my sister Ann and if she wasn't available, I'd call Kyle's phone and leave Zeb a very long message. These were my two phone calls, although I did call my boss a couple of times to let him know I was still in rehab. Rehab was not conducive to us going very deep into the world outside. The philosophy was that we needed to work on ourselves and forget about the outside world until we were better able to handle things without drugs and alcohol.

Sierra, my sponsor of approximately three weeks, was hired by Michael's House as a counselor. Due to the House regulations, she could not be my sponsor, nor could she have any association with me for the next two years. While I understood the rules, I still found it absolutely ridiculous because she was a great sponsor for me. Thankfully Sierra introduced me to her sponsor, a lady named Marcie, and she readily agreed to become my sponsor.

Mike, who had been my original counselor, left the House before the end of September, which necessitated a change in therapists for me. Tina, who was the Clinical Director of both houses, became my therapist. We had several very long discussions about my feelings toward my family, especially my father. We also discussed in depth, issues concerning my being transgendered; she absolutely knew without a doubt and accepted that I was a male to female transsexual person. In one of the therapy group sessions, Tina had me look at one of the male counselors and pretend he was my father. I had to use him as a surrogate and tell him everything that I had thought over the years and my tears just poured out. I asked my "surrogate father" many questions, beginning with why he did not love me, why he did not accept me, why did he beat me so badly when I was a young boy, and why was he so hard on me, just to name a few of my questions. I thought of myself as a victim and allowed the outside world to control my world within. Because I allowed others to affect the way I felt about myself I felt that was one of the root causes of my drug and alcohol abuse. In the program I had heard people talk of acceptance but had never grasped the concept. I needed to find the root cause of my issues but realized I still continued to blame others and it continued to have my "pity party": poor me ... at least now however, it was no longer "pour me"!

During a session with Tina in October, I asked her if she would write a letter to Dr. McGinn and update her on my progress in rehab. I asked her if she felt comfortable recommending me for my surgery, and if so, would she please include that in the letter. Tina reminded me of the day the Michael's House group went on a field trip to a beach just south of Newport Beach, CA. Her conversation was centered on the fact that I wrote my name in the sand and the letters were approximately 20' tall and just as wide. I had filled each letter with sea weed so my name would stand out and the world would know that I had arrived! I remember when she asked me what I was doing that day and I told her I wanted the entire world to know who I was and that person has a name: Kaitlin. Tina wrote that letter to Dr. McGinn and she recommended surgery as soon as possible. It was one of the most beautiful letters about me and my progress that I had ever read. Tina knew my thoughts, mental, physical and psychological conditions because all of these were evaluated while I was in treatment.

During my last few weeks of treatment at the rehab facility, my days were filled with scheduled activities, peer leader duties, and my own activities required to continue my sobriety. There were many different people who had come to the facility and only stayed for 30-45 days. As they left, I wondered if they would make it, or would they become a statistic and relapse or worse, end up dead. Allison, who had joined my circle of friends, had begun hanging out with Luke and I. My roommate JoAnne had completed her treatment program and returned home to her girlfriend and son. JoAnne was a wonderful lady in her early thirties, who was full of life and joy. She had always been very helpful and inspirational to me while in treatment. I thought of her as a good friend.

Allison had been in a lock-down treatment center in New Jersey for one year prior to coming to Michael's House. When she arrived, she and I became good friends. We found ourselves holding hands while walking down Palm Canyon Drive one Saturday afternoon and that was the beginning of a six month friendship and developed into a romantic relationship.

Luke and I were scheduled to complete treatment within a couple of weeks of each other and we decided we wanted to get some time out of the center. We asked our counselor if we could visit a sober living house. The counselors at Michael's House contacted George, the owner of New Step Sober Living. He a-greed to come by and pick up Luke and I from the treatment center and provide us with a tour of his facility. We liked what we saw and were very pleased that the house was primarily for LGBT residents to live after having completed treatment. It was truly a new step in sobriety. Luke and I talked about it in treatment and decided we wanted to get out again and asked George to meet us for coffee in the courtyard to discuss the financial issues and rules of his house. After this meeting Luke and I were very excited about the place and decided we should consider staying in Palm Springs a little while longer after we completed our treatment. That way, we thought, we could sort of ease back into the swing of things and live at the sober living facility and room together. A few days later we filled out the paperwork and pledged that we would live there after treatment. However, before I could move in, I needed to get back to Richmond and take care of some business and see my doctor. In the meantime, Allison and I were getting to know each other a little better, so to speak, and my final days of treatment were fast approaching.

I had not had a dream or at least one that I could remember, in many years but on my 90th day of sobriety, I woke up in shock, anguish, and fear! The dream was very real as if it had actually taken place. I had gone out and drank at a bar in Palm Springs and had lost my 90-day milestone in the program and because of that I could not have surgery. The dream was completely believable and it took me about 30 minutes to realize it was just that, a dream. The odd thing is I was unable to remember any other time, other than when I was a child, of a dream that was so real. I later learned that many people who are going through rehab and have maintained sobriety will either dream or actually go out at the three month point. I am so grateful mine was only a dream and it was a very valuable lesson indeed. Later that day, I went to a 12-step meeting and received my 90-day chip for staying clean and sober. I felt it was my own miracle. The dream that I had as a kid was very vivid. I had fallen off a cliff and I woke up in the middle of the night terrified and did not know where I had landed. It was so ironic that 40 years later I woke up from falling off a spiritual cliff and ended up in a treatment facility with 90-days of sobriety. My spirit I had felt so devoid of over three months ago was slowly returning within me now, 90 days later and that in itself was gratifying.

Chapter 22 – Return to Richmond

I was released from Michael's House on November 7, 2008. A Resident Counselor dropped me off at Palm Springs International Airport at 8:30 a.m. and I boarded my flight to Phoenix, Philadelphia, and Richmond. Once again through TSA with a female name on my driver's license and an "M" for sex. The flight to Phoenix was effortless and I waited in Sky Harbor for about two hours before I boarded US Air to Philadelphia. My flight turned out to be about five and a half hours, and it was basically uneventful.

The weather was a bit rough in Philadelphia with heavy rain which caused our plane to circle the city for about 45 minutes before we could land. I was near the back of the plane and hurried off and found my way to the shuttle for my next fight. Unfortunately all the rain delays caused me to miss my flight because once I finally arrived at the gate the plane had just taken off. I stood in line and explained to a customer service representative the events that had taken place and I was told they could not help me. I was flabbergasted and I was finally given a ticket for the next morning. I requested a place to stay and they would not accommodate me, so I walked out of the airport to smoke a cigarette and came back in but they would not allow me entrance because the ticket I had was for the following day. I was fit to be tied!

I was livid! And to add insult to injury I only had $100 with me and spoke with three different car rental companies and all explained that I did not have enough money with me to rent a car. I was forced to return to the terminal and had to sleep by the ticket counter next to the street with a TSA agent watching me from afar. I wrapped my purse around my shoulders and held on to my phone, it was horrible. I had a huge resentment with US Air because of the nasty treatment. This was the second time in two years this had happened, and I was shocked that it had happened again almost as though it was their policy to mistreat their customers! It's interesting my bags always made it on time and I went straight to the gate but the plane left without me. It's ridiculous to race from one plane and watch the plane you are supposed to be on leave me behind. This happened two different times.

My brother David picked me up the next morning from the Richmond airport and took me home. He had been keeping my car for me after it came out of the shop after I had hit the telephone pole at the baseball field. It was taken back to the shop for a brake job and an inspection so I could drive it back across country to Palm Springs. Ann and David agreed with my decision to return to California because of the events that lead to my seeking treatment. I went back into my home and it seemed shallow and cold as if there was no spirit in there. It was as if it were just a house. Nevertheless, I stayed there all day and night, went to a 12-step meeting, called Ann, and went to bed. It was a very uneventful first day back. I was anxious about the next day because I was going to get my car back and most of all, I would reunite with my beloved best friend, my dog Zeb.

It had been three months since I had been in my house and I was very scared. I had this awful feeling of dread that the boys from the neighborhood were looking for me and I did not want them to find out that I was back at home. Before I left for Palm Springs, I had put word out on the streets that my family had sent me away to a mental hospital and I would probably not return to Richmond. Since I was gone for three months I had hoped my story seemed believable and real to these guys, especially if they rode by the house a few times and saw for themselves I definitely hadn't been around for three months. Nevertheless, I slept with one eye open and I constantly watched my back. My home had been up for sale the day after I went to West Virginia in August. My mortgage was current before I traveled to Palm Springs for treatment, but at the advice of my agent I had not made a payment since it was put up for sale. Her recommendation was to live in California for a while and let her worry about getting the house sold.

I made it through the night and had to wait for my brother to get off work so that I could get my car and of course, my beloved best friend, Zeb. I spent my time cleaning up around the house and going through everything. I packed the things I wanted to keep and put things in drawers that were to be shipped at a later date. Although I hired a professional cleaning company to clean my home while I was in rehab, I still found a crack pipe in one of the drawers in the parlor. I started to freak out and immediately called my sponsor and hysterically told her about my situation. Once she talked me through it, I went out back in the alley, broke the pipe, and threw it in a trash can. All the memories of the past year came flooding back to me and made my stay on Park Avenue more fearful for me. I had my bags packed with all the things I needed for my immediate use, including a few collectables, and placed them at my front door so I could put them in the car for my cross country trip. My first stop was to Philadelphia in order to see Dr. McGinn and discuss my surgery date in January 2009.

My brother David left work a little early and picked me up at 4:00 p.m. We went over to the car shop so I could retrieve my Camry. This was the first time I had seen my car since the first week in August, so I was very excited to have a bit of independence back. My car had been inspected, the brakes repaired, and after I had paid for the repairs, I headed out to find Zeb.

I called Kyle, told him I was on the way, and then called Ann who provided with directions to Kyle's home. After a long anxious drive, I pulled into his driveway and the first thing I saw was his collie. Then I saw Zeb as he looked out the bottom glass of the front storm door. Kyle saw me and opened the door and Zeb just about broke the door down and came racing to me. When he got to me, he immediately lay on his back at my feet with all four legs up in the air and moved crazily in great excitement. Kyle followed within a few minutes after Zeb, just as Zeb had jumped into the driver's seat of my car and on into the back seat and lay down. Poor Kyle, Zeb did not even use the good manners I had taught him to say good-bye! He was just so ecstatic and overcome with emotion that I had returned for him, just as I had promised. I was overjoyed and tears came to my eyes to see Zeb so happy and to finally have him back with me, exactly where he belonged. I paid Kyle what little money I had and thanked him profusely for taking such great care of my boy. In my absence, Zeb had been running two miles daily with Kyle and even had lost weight; he looked really good. Kyle had spent a lot of time with him and I was so very appreciative. It was the best reunion ever for me.

Zeb spent his last night in our house as we started our old routine for the last time. I packed the car with as many of our belongings as possible that morning, and left the back seat empty for him. I wanted Zeb to be as comfortable as possible for this big life changing trip for him too.

Chapter 23 – Our Road Trip Back to California

We departed Richmond at 11:00 a.m. and headed for Doylestown, PA to see Dr. McGinn; I had an appointment with her at 5:00 p.m. I was very excited that I could see my gender reassignment surgery was to happen in the near future. I was finally clean, sober and living one day at a time by staying in the moment. I drove north on I-95 through, Virginia, DC, Maryland, and Delaware. We took I-495 into Philadelphia and arrived in Doylestown at 3:00 p.m. I went directly to Dr. McGinn's office and hoped I could see her early. While admittedly I was over two hours early for my scheduled appointment, I explained to Carol, the receptionist, how helpful it would be if there was any way possible Dr. McGinn could see me because I was headed back out to California. Carol explained that the doctor was in her office doing research and she would be happy to inquire if she would be able to accommodate me early. Thankfully the temperature outside was in the 40's, so I had no problem with Zeb waiting in the car and resting, but I still did not want to leave him there very long.

Dr. McGinn put her research on hold and agreed to see me early, and I spent about 50 minutes with her while she reviewed the procedure and the Harry Benjamin code of ethics for surgery. She told me she wanted me to work with Dr. Michelle Angelo because she would not accept Dr. Bears letter and while she elaborated very little about her reasons, she did explain that she felt he was **not** qualified in this field. I believed there had been some communication with her while I was in rehab. She accepted Dr. Betina's letter, the Clinical Director at Michael's House. Dr. Bears had been contacted by several members of my family and I think he felt threatened that if he recommended surgery for me, my family would sue him. Dr. Bears had told me about this several times during my three years of therapy with him which I found very troubling. Nevertheless, Dr. McGinn felt that once she received the letter from Dr. Angelo my surgery date would be set. We also discussed the fact that having surgery would be helpful in maintaining my sobriety and she wanted to move my date up to December 9, 2008. How coincidental that the new earlier date Dr. McGinn suggested was my mother's birthday; anyway, I agreed that the sooner my outside matched who I truly was on the inside, the better for me all the way around and it certainly would be helpful in maintaining my sobriety and it would certainly stabilize my mental health. I worked with Dr. Angelo over the next three weeks and she was totally convinced of my "Gender Dysphoria", as the DSM-IV described my issue, and that I was in fact female. She immediately wrote the letter to Dr. McGinn.

After I saw Dr. McGinn, Zeb and I loaded up and made our way in the dark to Harrisburg, PA where we stayed the night in a Motel 6 because pets are allowed at the motel. It was again a fearful experience because my driver's license still had an "M" in the sex column and I was kind of in the middle of nowhere in unfamiliar territory. I decided it would be a good idea for me to encounter as few people as possible during my drive across country. It has remained a fear of mine that I would get stopped by a police officer in a small rural area, away from civilization and I would be beaten or killed for being transgendered. I believed that fear was real and had heard stories of transgendered people being physically harmed because of who they were and there was be no sympathy whatsoever.

Zeb and I woke up excited, although a bit cautious and hit the road at 6:00 a.m. We stopped at McDonald's in Wheeling, WV for a bathroom break, a walk, and I ordered food from the drive-thru window. The next stop on our journey was for gas and a walk in Indianapolis near the Lucas Oil Stadium. I purchased gas with cash and had no interaction with anyone else other than the cashier, although I was conscious of the men there checking me out. We made our way through Indiana, Illinois, across the Mississippi River and just south of St. Louis and stopped at another Motel 6 for the night. It was 7:00 p.m. central time and I was completely exhausted. I put Zeb in the room after

260

our walk and ventured across the street for a sandwich and to gas up. I was back in a dash and we walked the grounds and went straight to bed. Zeb and I had a great day with no interruptions or issues.

We were up at dawn and on our way through southwest Missouri and into Oklahoma. I just wanted to get this day behind us because this was an area of the country where I felt the most apprehensive. I prayed that my car would remain sound and I would not have any issues because I just could not shake the feeling that this part of the country simply would not understand or tolerate a male to female transgendered person. I felt very overwhelmed, nervous in fact, and made sure not to speed, used my turn signals when changing lanes, and made sure I read all the signs. I might have behaved overly cautious, but I even made sure I read the "Buy Your Pigs Next Exit" and "Get Your New Dentures in Two Hours This Exit" for fear I'd miss some subliminal message!

We stopped at a really old McDonald's somewhere north of Tulsa for our break and unfortunately the place was packed. I took care of my business and got back on the Interstate. It was interesting to see that I-44 was a toll road and several hours later we had to stop for gas again. We pulled off at an exit about 60 miles from Oklahoma City and the only thing there was a toll booth and a no name gas station. I filled up the tank, went inside to use the facilities and pay for the gas. When I finished I was shocked to walk out and find an Oklahoma State Trooper with a K-9 checking me and my car out. My heart skipped a beat and I thought, "Ok here we go, Bubba's gonna make me his bitch for sure!" But once he saw me walking towards the car he moved on and that came as a great relief. I was minding my own dadburn business but felt like a fugitive because I thought society was out to get me. It was probably my Virginia license plate that drew his interest in the first place and the fact that I was in such a remote area of the country. In my fearful paranoid state, I imagined that the toll booth attendant probably signaled my arrival somehow and it was the trooper's job to check it out. But it was important for me to be very leery of anyone checking me out late at night, in a remote area, and all alone to boot. Zeb and I took a short walk down a very dusty road for a few quick minutes, just long enough for him to do his business and for both of us to stretch our legs. We were back in the car and on the road and the heck out of that area as fast as we could go … and without breaking the speed limit of course!

Oklahoma City reminded me of Charlotte because of its sprawl, as we headed in a blaze to make it into Amarillo before it got to be too late at night. We picked up I-40 near Oklahoma City and arrived in Amarillo just as the sun had set. I stopped again at a Motel 6 and I checked in before I walked Zeb in the Texas dust. It was very dusty in Amarillo and I found it true to all the television shows I had seen as a kid; it was as dusty as an old cattle town. I did not feel comfortable there so we went into the room, locked the door, and ordered a pizza for delivery. I just wanted to eat, sleep and get the hell out of there as soon as possible. Just like Oklahoma, I had a premonition about the State of Texas. I was just scared because I did not know the locals way of thinking, knowing it was not very open-minded. Again, I had to show my license to get a room and I did not want to be blindsided by some local cowboy.

As I drove west out of Amarillo, where the green rolling hills start to take on a brownish desert like look, I could see the full sun come up over the hill and the full moon setting in the west. It was so beautiful. I could see for miles and miles. I stopped at Love's Truck Stop for gas and our normal routine. I went inside to pay and the cashier, who was a cowboy-type about 50 years old, told me he was getting off at 7:00 a.m. and asked if I would go back to his ranch and watch some television with him. I thought to myself that this cowpoke had no idea what was under my skirt so I sweetly said to him, "No thank you Cowboy, not today but I'm sure it would have been one hot rodeo for both of us!" I gave him the sexiest wink I could muster, wished him a good day, and high tailed it out of there.

Zeb and I continued our journey through New Mexico and into Arizona. I watched the gas gauge slowly head toward empty while the signs read no gas for the next 33 miles. I pulled off at a gas station in the middle of the desert and paid a very hefty premium for gas. Zeb and I decided to make the best of our situation so we took a much needed break and went for a nice walk to stretch our bodies.

As I approached the Petrified Forest in Arizona on I-40, I had set the cruise control on 83 mph even though the posted speed limit clearly read 75 mph. My rationale was that each state would give a driver eight miles per hour over the speed limit and although I was speeding, I was still traveling at a safe speed. As I came up over a hill, I noticed an Arizona State Trooper tucked away in a little valley. I looked down, checked my speed, and slowed down just a bit. I thought I was fine until I saw him make tremendous progress towards me with his blue lights flashing and siren blaring; I just pulled over before he got behind me. Fear and panic suddenly consumed me; this was my worst nightmare and the event for which I was most afraid! He walked over to my passenger's side window and Zeb was barking as if to attack him.

He said, "Mama, I need to see your license and registration please".

As my hands shook uncontrollably as I produced my documents. He went back to his patrol car for a few minutes and then approached me again.

The trooper asked me "to step out of the car."
We walked over to the passenger's side of his patrol car. He then asked, "do you I knew why he stopped you?"

I just blurted out, "Yes Sir, I was driving 83 miles per hour in a 75 mile per hour zone and I thought I'd be fine since I set my speed on cruise control and I was almost the only one out on the road."

He was quick to respond and explained that "things are not done that way in Arizona." As he wrote my ticket, he explained "speed limits are in place for the safety and for all citizens to follow."

"So you need to slow down and mind the speed limit. Then he handed me my ticket.

"Here you go SIR!"

I very politely thanked him and got back into my vehicle and calmed Zeb who had been barking hysterically while I was outside the vehicle. Next I settled myself behind the wheel and called that rat bastard every name imaginable. What a damn prick!

I decided after this experience that Zeb and I were going to drive straight through to Palm Springs today. I did not know what to expect when I approached the border patrol checkpoint going into California, nor did I care. I thought, not again as he asked me if I had any plants, vegetables, or fruits with me. I briefly thought I'd try a little humor and say something cute like oh, "I'm the only fruit in this vehicle, do you like bananas Honey?!" But somehow I just don't think Mr. Border Patrol would appreciate my humor so Zeb and I both kept our traps shut tight as a drum and he waved us through and we both were able to breathe again. We picked up Route 95 in Needles, California, and again this time the sun was low and fiery in the sky as the full moon was coming up east of the Colorado River. It was beautiful as I had seen the opposite early that same morning. It was like a gift from the heavens. Obliviously, the full moon had disappeared behind the clouds and it was a very dark ride over to I-10 and Blythe. It was dark the entire way until I finally entered the Coachella Valley where it was magnificent coming down off the mountain and seeing the valley all lit up. A sigh of relief came over me as Zeb moaned himself. It seemed like it was eternity getting though the east side of the valley over to west side or Palm Springs. I pulled into New Step Sober Living and was very happy I finally made it to my new home.

Chapter 24 – Sober Surgery

Luke was scheduled to join me as my roommate in about a week on the day he was released from Michael's House. Allison was using her town time on Saturday and Sunday to spend with me. We shopped on Palm Canyon Drive and visited Starbucks as part of our routine. I had been smoking since I was 21 years old and decided to quit by smoking just one cigarette in the morning for a few days and then eliminating it all together a little over four weeks before my surgery. One of Dr. McGinn's instructions was that I must stop smoking a month before my surgery date or she would not perform my gender reassignment surgery. I quit just shy of a month but the important thing was that I stopped. I had come too far in my journey with the family, job, treatment, and everything else to allow one issue to ruin my lifelong reality of becoming physically female.

Luke completed his treatment and made his way to the house. It was a wonderful reunion to see him out of treatment and doing well. Zeb enjoyed the house and the beautiful back-yard and pool. Allison, Luke, and I pretty much hung out together but it was becoming more of Allison and me. My surgery was only a couple of weeks away and I was preparing for the trip. I had to pay cash in advance which all doctors who per-formed gender reassignment surgery required. Luke agreed to take care of Zeb while I was away and look out for my interests in the house. I had purchased my round-trip airline ticket from Palm Springs to Philadelphia, booked my hotel room through December 21st, made arrangements for my friend Teresa from Richmond to drive up and stay with me the entire two weeks. Dr. McGinn required someone to be with you the entire time through surgery plus an additional week once released from the hospital. I did not have any family member, nor would I ask, who was willing to help me and I was very thankful to have my friend Teresa. I listed my sister Ann as the family contact, and knew if necessary, she would be the one to figure out what to do with me. Ann was my only family member who knew I was having surgery; she just didn't know the official date. In fact, no one in my family knew when my surgery was going to take place, and quite frankly I preferred it that way.

The Surgery

On December 7, 2008, I boarded yet another US Air flight out of Palm Springs to Phoenix, waited again in Sky Harbor for the flight to Philadelphia. I called Teresa from Sky Harbor and reminded her to pick me up at the airport in Philadelphia but she had her dates mixed up and would not arrive in Philadelphia until the next day which meant I did not have a ride to Ben Salem, PA, the location for my surgery. When I arrived it was late in the evening on the east coast. I retrieved my luggage and loaded up in the first available taxi. I knew it would be an expensive ride as I watched the meter fly past $50 on the way to the northeast side of town, just on the outskirts of Philadelphia. I talked to the driver the entire time about me being in Palm Springs, CA, my flight and the fact that I was here to have gender reassignment surgery. I think he enjoyed the conversation, but in all actuality what he really enjoyed was $85 fare he was being paid to get me from the airport to the hotel in Ben Salem after a very long day. After all, it wasn't every day you he got a very talkative transsexual riding in his taxi. I was happy and felt very good about the trip and the events that were about to take place. I walked over to Carrabba's restaurant and had an Italian dinner. It had been a very long journey and the most important event of my life was about to come to fruition.

I settled in for the night and watched a little television and slept like a baby and got up at 5:30 a.m. I walked across the field to DSI hospital and right into admitting to have my blood work drawn. The groups of nurses were expecting me and it was actually a relief to understand that I was expected. Dr. McGinn's had moved her office to the upstairs on the second floor of the hospital in the administration area and I asked the nurses to please let her know that I had arrived. They assured me they would let her know and they had drawn five vials of blood. I read all the pre-op instructions and a nervous excitement settled in my body, mind and soul.

Teresa arrived late in the afternoon and it was a very welcoming reunion. I had not seen her since I was in treatment and it was like I had never been away. We caught up on all the happenings with JRTS and our personal lives. Teresa was my angel for agreeing to come and help me through the surgery; I felt I owed her a great deal of gratitude. She was very inspirational especially since she was Dr. McGinn's first surgery patient in July 2007. She was an excellent reference because of her 16 months of experience. I was excited with anticipation that night and went to bed early. I slept like a child going to bed on Christmas Eve who couldn't wait for the morning to wake and find all the presents under the tree ... only for me, this gift promised to be the most special gift I could ever give myself. The gift of wholeness, the gift of finally being me.

On December 9, 2008, I had been clean and sober for four months and three days. A lifetime of confusion and rejection would soon be behind me. I knew from a very early age that I was female and in the physical body of a male and today I was going to have my body aligned with my mind, soul, and spirit. I felt an inner peace within me when I woke the morning of my surgery. We drove around the field that I had previously walked through the day before, and into the admissions office. I knew without a doubt that this surgery was absolutely necessary for my life's survival, beyond a shadow of a doubt. I was taken in immediately, given a hospital gown, and told to lie down on a gurney after I had changed. I was scheduled for surgery at 7:00 a.m. and Dr. McGinn appeared at 6:45 a.m. with a tremendous smile on her face. With a voice full of love and kindness, she asked me if I was ready, if I had any concerns, and if I was absolutely sure this is what I wanted. I told her without any reservations whatsoever that I was completely ready; this is exactly what I wanted and needed. With my response, the doctor squeezed my hand, gave the order for the anesthesia, and the last thing I remember was seeing the absolutely "loving and benign" look she had on her face.

My eyes opened at 4:12 p.m. and I saw the ceiling of the recovery room. However, the thing that impressed me most was the extraordinary feeling of peace and serenity. It was absolute like none I had ever experienced in my life. I realized I had made it through surgery and an all consuming feeling of self-love and acceptance came over me. For the first time in my life I felt whole and I loved myself. This confirmed that I was truly in the right place, and had done the right thing, no matter what anyone else might think. It was as if all the guilt, shame, anxiety, and all the negative thoughts were instantaneously removed from me. I was now properly aligned physically, mentally, emotionally, and spiritually for the first time in 53 years. It was this spiritual peace that I had longed for and I realized at that moment, I was finally free.

As I languished in my newfound serenity, my room suddenly filled with activity! I was startled into reality and found nurses checking this IV, and that machine, and Dr. McGinn had even slipped in unnoticed amongst all the activity. She checked all my stats, approached my bed, and told me that everything had gone very well during surgery. She told me my interior body was configured so well that it was an easy surgery for her. The surgery took just under six hours and Dr. McGinn allowed me to briefly explore the surgical area with my hand after she examined the area herself. Although I had a catheter in place, the surgery was completely finished and the Dr. McGinn was very pleased with the outcome. It was a feeling of unimaginable peace as they rolled me to my room. Teresa was calling all of our friends and in a celebratory way told them, "It's a girl, it's a girl!" It was truly a life saving miracle!

At the time I didn't know, but it was the beginning of many more miracles that were to come for me and they were to come from within. I was starting the physical healing process which over time, brought to me mental and spiritual healing as well.

268

My thoughts had always been clouded with trying to reach this point of alignment that many of my thoughts and actions were done without the total concentration that was required for sustainable success in this world. My surgery was the beginning of all three phases of wholeness; my physical, mental, and spiritual aspects of who I was as a human being, finally being able to unite in synergism with me had now begun to work together. It gave me the opportunity to pay attention to the lessons that would ultimately change the way I thought so that life could become effortless and enjoyable without living the lie I had become accustomed to living but fought vehemently against.

I was in DSI hospital for five days. My room was spacious and thankfully private and had plenty of room for Teresa, who agreed to stay on the sofa bed in the room. There was a beautiful flat screen television on the wall which remained off most of the time since I spent my time sleeping and recovering. The chef at DSI made three meals for me each day as instructed by Dr. McGinn and it just did not seem like a hospital, these were absolutely great meals; certainly not "hospital food". I had three nurses assigned to me for 24 hours who were absolutely wonderful. They treated me with respect and dignity and their attitude and professionalism was beyond reproach at all times. I joked with them and talked to them on nearly every topic and they seemed to enjoy our jovial conversations. They came in every three hours and changed the ice pack that was placed over the surgical area. The only discomfort that I had was to lie on my back four days. I would move around somewhat, but as the days increased the discomfort increased. Dr. McGinn came every day to check on me and she was absolutely wonderful and very pleased with my healing progress. At 5:00 p.m. on the fourth day of post-op, the nurses came in and told me it was time to stand up. I held out my right arm, they pulled me up, and I stood, but not before yelling out "FUCK" so loud my friends back in California could have heard me! The nurse said, "Now that's fine Kaitlin, don't worry, that's a perfectly good word to use right about now!" Oh yes, I flung the f-word loud and proud and I had to admit I couldn't recall feeling any sort of pain that bad in a long time. Anyway, I took a couple of steps and the nurses put me back in the bed. Later that evening, with the nurse's assistance, I was able to get up and take a quick shower. It felt wonderful, a little wobbly and shaky, but wonderful nonetheless.

The next morning I was up and I actually walked down the hall to the entrance to change my perspective of the outside world. I had a window in my room and I could see the frost on the windows and grounds each morning but on this day I could see frost on the cars. I walked around two more times that day before I was released at 5:00 p.m. to go to the hotel I had selected in the area. I still had the catheter in place and was required to stay nearby for the next eight days. I amused myself by seeing how full I could get the catheter by running liquids through my body. I had to document the quantity and time each day and report the results to Dr. McGinn.

Teresa stayed with me at the local hotel which was about a half mile from the hospital. I was able to walk the parking lot the first couple of days, then I graduated to around the building the next, and then twice around the building later in the week, and I did this about three times a day. Every morning Teresa would go out and pick up a newspaper and bring back breakfast and dinner for us. Normally she would go over to the diner in town. The only problem that I had with the food was she that went to a fast food restaurant one night and I threw it all up. I called Dr. McGinn and told her I was feeling bad and could not hold my dinner down. She asked what I had eaten and I told her she immediately reminded me that fast food was not on the recommended food list. She was right, when I reviewed the list; obviously it was my food selections and nothing else making me ill, and I was very relieved.

Teresa took me over to Dr. McGinn's office nine days after my surgery and the doctor removed my catheter, which was a great relief. She examined her work and thought my progress was good. I asked if I could go home on Sunday and denied my request because she wanted to wait until my next visit on Saturday to ensure everything was fine. I was a little worried because I had a plane ticket for Palm Springs reserved for December 21st, so I hope everything would be fine. That night and into the next morning it snowed and it was a beautiful sight. I have always loved watching it snow and it was the kind that accumulated a little on the ground and more on elevated surfaces as the temperature was just above freezing. Nevertheless, I felt it was gift to me.

My last day in Ben Salem was Saturday, December 20th as I had my last examination with Dr. McGinn. She instructed me on proper dilation and the importance of following the schedule over time. She explained that my vagina was an open wound and I needed to be very careful, especially over the next six weeks. As a matter of fact I could not sit down without the use of an inflatable tire-like device, a "donut", for the next two months because it was painful and quite uncomfortable without it. I had to dilate my vagina six times a day for the first two months and then it decreased to four, then two, and one and then just twice a week. It is twice a week for the rest of my life after the first year. The purpose is to keep the surgical depth and everything open.

That afternoon Teresa took me over to Applebee's for an early dinner and we went to Macy's and shopped briefly for Christmas. Dr. McGinn had told me I could fly home to Palm Springs the next day and we went back early as I was exhausted and went to bed because 4:30 a.m. would come really early. Teresa was going to take me to the airport and we needed to leave by no later than 6:00 a.m.

On Sunday morning, December 21, 2008, we woke up early to a very cold rain falling outside which turned into freezing rain by the time we loaded up the car and started our journey toward downtown Philadelphia. It was very difficult for me to ride in the car and I had to inflate and use my donut to subside the pain from surgery. I-95 from Ben Salem was a sheet of ice as it had now turned from freezing rain to sleet. There were not many of us on the road as we slowly progressed towards the airport. As we entered the airport entrance, I could see the Airport Hilton where I had meet Dr. McGinn about a year and a half earlier. It was a beautiful feeling to have come full circle from that particular point.

The roads were so icy that Teresa had to drop me off in front of the US Air terminal and I rolled my bag and carried a huge shopping bag to the counter. I checked in and told the ticket agent that I had reserved a wheel chair since I just had surgery. She pointed me over to the gentlemen standing across the corridor with wheel chairs and I approached them with my wheel chair pass and boarding ticket. He was not very friendly as I sat in the chair and he wheeled me toward the elevator and up to the second floor through wheel chair access security. I asked him to stop at an ATM which he did and I withdrew some money and gave him a ten dollar tip and he was instantly very friendly. He asked me if I needed to stop for anything and I requested he stop so I could get a cup of coffee and a newspaper. This time I did not have to get up from the wheel chair, he actually went and made the purchases and brought them back to me. He was really sweet and took me to my gate and helped me out of the chair and into a seat. I giggled as I thought to myself, "money talks and bullshit walks."

The flight was scheduled to leave at 9:45 a.m. and we boarded on time and as I looked out the window of the plane it was snowing and the ground was covered. We eventually rolled out from the terminal and waited in line to de-ice twice. I was getting miserable and wondered if we were going anywhere today as it was uncomfortable for me to just sit, but I made the best of the situation. We finally took off two and a half hours later and although I have always been afraid of flying, I was extremely happy to be in the air and on our way. I understood at this point that I would miss my connection in Phoenix that would take me on to Palm Springs but at this point I was happy just to get to Phoenix. I made use of my time by sleeping when possible and reading the paper. Finally we landed in Phoenix and was finally able to move comfortably around and stand up.

We had arrived two and have hours late, therefore just about everyone on my flight which was and airbus full of people, had missed their connection in Phoenix. I had been seated near the back of the plane so a long line had formed to deplane. After what seemed like an eternity I was able to gather my things, deplane, I walked into the terminal and headed straight for US Air customer service desk. I was waiting in line for another eternity, feeling horribly woozy, and all of a sudden my huge shopping bag split wide open from top to bottom and all of my Kotex pads (after surgery I had to use pads for about four months because I'd have discharge) scattered all over the floor along with my dilator, which happened to look like a small, battery powered dildo! Mother of God, noooooo!!!! I was mortified beyond words to say the least. Two women from California dashed over and rendered aid. One of the women gave me a recyclable cloth bag and the other quickly helped me stuff my items back into the bag. It was crazy and I was so embarrassed, maxi-pads, mini-pads, and my damn dildo-looking dilator all over the floor in the most crowded area of the airport. Oh I was a sight all right, gingerly kneeling down to pick each pad up and the worst part was that one of the "eco-friendly" California girls reached my dilator first and was soooo happy to "save" my little "friend" for me. She gave me a very "knowing" smile and squeezed my hand, I thought a bit too friendly, as she placed it in my hand. When she winked, I thought I'd die and wanted to climb into that freakin' cloth bag, Lord have mercy please!!!

With all my things picked up and put away, the crowd dispersed and I was finally back in line. I made it to the counter, the agent placed me on the next flight to Palm Springs which was in about an hour and called for a wheel chair to take me from one section over to the next section and gate. He was very nice, treated me well, and thankfully, did not strew my Kotex all over the airport, so I gave him a $10 tip for his help. My fear of getting to Palm Springs was dissipating as I watched the gate area fill with people. Finally it was time to board and I was assisted onto the plane. The airline kindly gave me a seat in the front where I could stretch out and put my feet in the aisle, and I had no one sitting beside me. I had to sit on my donut the entire trip; as I did for the next several months.

Palm Springs

It was warm in Palm Springs and the sun was bright just getting ready to set as I filed off the plane and into the terminal. The airport in Palm Springs was beautiful and I could walk right outside from the gate into the desert air before entering the main terminal. It was the total opposite of the ice and snow in Philadelphia and it felt very gratifying to be back. Luke and Allison greeted me with hugs and kisses as I walked into the main terminal. It had been a very long day that actually started at 1:30 a.m. California time. I called Teresa to let her know I made it to Palm Springs and she told me it took her all day to drive from Philadelphia to Richmond because of the snow and ice. She had just made it home herself and due to the icy conditions, slipping and sliding, the drive had taken eleven hours. I apologized profusely and thanked her again for all she had done for me and for being such a great friend to me. I never could have survived all of this without her and told her I loved her very much. I really meant it too. Teresa had always been a good friend to me, through thick and thin.

I was back in the sober living house in Palm Springs and the guys in the house were very helpful to me. My roommate Luke had taken care of Zeb for me while I was in Philadelphia and I was very appreciative everything he had done for me. I had to dilate my vagina six times a day, so I needed to stay close to home especially for the next six weeks. Allison came over and we hung out at home and went to Starbucks frequently during this time.

Also during this time I stated catching up on my debts and had several conversations with the Human Resource department with Philip Morris. Gail had been transferred to another area and the one she replaced was back in his former position. My medical leave was due to expire on January 21, 2009 and I would have to go back to Richmond and return to work if I wanted to keep my job. I realized I was not ready to return to work at that time and opted to take a package deal to resign, which would get me close to my early retirement date. I accepted the package deal and they called me and told me my rating for the past year was an "ME" meaning "More Expected". A rating like that meant I would NOT get my profit sharing or raise. I was very surprised to receive news like this because I had always been a top performer with the company. I had always expected more from myself and pushed myself to excel above the rest and in all the 23 years I had been with Phillip Morris, I had NEVER received such a negative review, NEVER! This was blatant retaliation for the fact that I came out as transgendered on the job and I rubbed people the wrong way. I know that normally when a negative review happens the employer must communicate this with the employee throughout the year. Then the employee has the opportunity to make adjustments during that time so that it is not a surprise; but that never took place for me. I knew it meant that if I ever wanted to go back to work at Phillip Morris it would be impossible because of that rating, so in effect they got rid of me on the sly. My intuition told me that basically, they got rid of me because I am transgendered and they could not handle it! That was the sole reason for this event. Regretfully and with a mountain of resentment, I took the package. But let me say it loud and proud: I am grateful to Phillip Morris for all my years of service and I hope that I have taught the people to have some compassion and tolerance for others. Today, I would go back to work there if I could.

Chapter 25 – Palm Springs Life and the Incident on 52nd Street

Now that I had aligned my physical self with my mind, little did I realize that the real work was to come! The real work was to align myself physically, mentally, emotionally and spiritually by tying the four together to make myself whole. In order to do this I had to search for my absolute truth and start not only the physical healing but the spiritual healing that only came from within. I took this road by working the 12-steps, but I also took many exits off the main highway that ended up becoming lessons and wonderful gifts. The gifts were not of a material nature but gifts assisting me with understanding myself. At this point I was five months clean and sober and had gender reassignment surgery. I worked on losing the compulsion to drink and use and having the surgery was just touching the tip of the iceberg to allow different thoughts to enter into myself.

I realized how unmanageable my life had become and the consequences of my drinking and drugging. Although I was successful in my work it all came to a sudden end by falling off the cliff in a very short period of time. I had known for a very long time that I was female but the method of correcting this issue with drugs and alcohol only led to incomprehensible demoralization. I realized that I did this because of the confusion and rejection in my life. Suicide was an option until it was taken off the table. I was made to face the world with my truth and that was not an easy task. I did understand why someone would choose suicide. Family and social pressures were huge and always in the forefront of my mind. Nevertheless, masking my pain with a substance only made matters worse but in the mist of it all it seemed like the right thing to do at the time. Maybe it saved my life, until it almost killed me.

Early in recovery, I was able to look at my 53 years of life experience and with a clear mind, define my own Higher Power.

My definition came from my interactions with people places, things, my own spiritual experiences and the loss of my spirit. My Catholic upbringing was also a part of my definition of my beliefs, but not the way I was taught and not the way I was told I had to believe. I understood that my Higher Power was all loving and that the fear-based God of my childhood religion was not necessarily true. I was not created to live in fear, but to be of service to all. I tried to create everything in my youth but finally learned that I did not have that power. I learned that I had to strive every day to develop the spirit in my body to become a spirit with a body. It did not matter if someone was male or female, what really mattered was that our purpose on this earth was to help one another. I realized that my being transgendered was really a non-issue in the grand scheme of the Universe. It was my acceptance that a power greater than myself could restore me to sanity and help me to find my humility and absolute truth. I made a decision to turn over my will and my life to the care of my Higher Power. I had done this many times before and found help with Sister in 2005. I had turned my will over at that time but only over my transgender issue. Now I had decided to turn over my will and life concerning every aspect of my life, not just being transgendered; no, it was my total life and all my battles with addiction, character defects, and the paths that I had followed. I completely turned over my life and was ready to become a new woman. A completely whole, new me!

So I took my will back, stage right, exit left and off on a side street, I found myself in a relationship with Allison. A female to female relationship, which we both had no experience with lesbian sex, but we figured it out. Many people have asked, "If the physical sexual feeling is still there after surgery?" My response is, "It is much the same, if not a little better." We rented a house in La Quinta on 52nd Street in February 2009. Palm Springs is in the western portion of the Coachella Valley and La Quinta is on the eastern side up against the San Jacinto Mountains. We were a rock's throw from PGA West, the site of the Bob Hope Desert Classic and the golf tournament had just starting the same time we moved. We were isolated by 25 miles from my support system in Palm Springs but I was able to find several 12-step meetings to attend in Palm Desert. A little voice deep down inside me told me this was a mistake, but I didn't listen, so I knew the minute we moved in it wasn't going to work out. Even my sponsor told me if I survived this then I would share my story from the podium one day. Marcie, my sponsor, warned me that starting a relationship so early in sobriety caused many people to relapse and counseled that I needed time to work on myself before attempting to work on a relationship. I explained that I was different and that everything would be fine. However, I was being stubborn and should have listened to both her and that gnawing voice inside myself ... they were both right on target. A relationship was the last thing I needed!

We had a beautiful house with a huge grapefruit tree in the backyard. Our neighbors had lemon, lime, and orange trees full of fruit growing around us as well. We had an enclosed patio where we grew our own vegetables and four glass doors that looked out onto the front yard. We had a very large, L-shaped living room and the dining room was tucked off in its own area of the room. We spent our days going to the gym, shopping, eating out, and attending meetings. Zeb had the run of the house but loved the front lawn and to chase balls and within a month I purchased a black lab puppy for Allison birthday, and she named her Madeline.

The next three months were pretty much the same but I had grown increasingly discontent with driving to Palm Springs every day for my meetings. Palm Springs was where my sponsor and support system was located. Although in the beginning I had looked elsewhere, for my own sake I wanted to be there. I attended the women's meeting and was at first very apprehensive about going because I still had the fear of rejection going on within me. I remained very quiet in the beginning but the women embraced me and help me open up. I think it really started to happen for me when this older lady shared with the group that all she wanted in her life was to be a tall, pretty, blonde and I followed her lead with all I wanted to be was a tall, pretty, and blonde which created a great deal of laughter. My share that night helped me build some self-esteem knowing that the women accepted me. Today they are all my best friends.

I was working on myself and trying to repair my resentments but soon realized I was trying to "fix" Allison as well. This was not a good situation for me because I had started to spend more time working through her issues, and less time on my own. This was exactly what Marcie had warned me about and I had finally understood her admonitions. I was growing further apart from Allison and the way I decided to deal with it was to fly to Richmond and check on my house and visit with Dr. McGinn in Philadelphia.

I flew out of Palm Springs in early April 2009 while apprehensively leaving Zeb with Allison in La Quinta. I made it back to Richmond, rented a car and went to my house in the Fan District. It was now in a short sale and the bank had already declined two offers. I went through my belongings and my oldest of two sisters was kind enough to allow me to store some of my belonging in her basement. I previously made arrangements with Teresa who was more than happy to accompany me, so she and I drove to New Hope, PA., where Dr. McGinn had relocated her office. I had a checkup with Dr. McGinn and she reported that everything was going very well. We talked about the dilations and the importance of its maintenance which I had been doing and am still doing today. The doctor was very pleases with her work and I was too. I thanked her for everything and Teresa and I headed back to Richmond.

While in Richmond, I went over to the Department of Human Service and submitted my application to change my birth certificate. The application was to change my name and my gender. I had to see the Supervisor of the Department because of the nature of this change and I supplied her with the certificate that Dr. McGinn had notarized and issued to me. The last paragraph of this certificate states, "As a result of this process (Gender Reassignment Surgery), Miss Riordan is unable to reproduce as a male and has fully transitioned to a female identity including legal name, phenotype and hormonal axis. From a medical standpoint, Kaitlin Riordan is fully female.

The Supervisor collected my fee and asked how many copies I needed. Then she told me that she did not know how long it would take because she had a couple of others in her office and they had been there a while. I asked her why this was so and she said the Attorney General had to sign these requests and they were very low priority and they would probably be a while. My mind went to the idea that the State of Virginia considered us second class citizens which I believed was true.

When I returned eight days later to Palm Springs and La Quinta I was so very happy to see Zeb. I detected that things were not right with me and Allison as people, places, and things just did not add up. I became very suspicious and knew that if I was going to be any good to myself or anyone else that I had to get out of there and start the emotional healing required from the surgery and my addictions. I understood that in order to be of service to anyone else I first had to work on my resentments and non-sobering behavior and thoughts. So, I told Allison that I was moving back to Palm Springs and I moved back to the sober living house in May.

A few days later, after I moved my belongings from her house, I was informed to check the special announcement section on Craig's List. I was horrified to see a message from Allison. She disclosed my full name, my full former male name, and stated I owed her a great deal of money, and then added the very filthy and cryptic: "never trust a man with a hole". She went straight for the jugular and I was really upset for about a day, but did not allow her venomous words to disrupt the progress I had made on myself. Actually, letting this go was great progress for me.

For me the real lesson of placing principals before personalities struck me like a ton of bricks. I did not respond to her at all and simply and quietly forgave her during my personal meditation. This was huge for me because just six months earlier it

280

would have been unfathomable to know how I would have retaliated! I do know I would have struck back twice as hard and she would have regretted her actions with all her heart and soul, if she would have lived! This was a real lesson for me in humility. Yes, my sponsor was right; I shared the reason why we do not get into a relationship early in sobriety and after having gender reassignment surgery. It was imperative to work on ourselves. Being placed in a male role for the majority of my life, I had to learn how to be my female self and to understand the underlying idiosyncrasies of being female with my girlfriends. I was the only transgendered women in the group of at least 50 women and I absolutely loved everything that I learned. My feelings and emotions were right on with theirs and they thought, knew, and treated me as if I was born genetically female which in reality I felt I was, but for a transgendered person thoughts are from one end of the spectrum to the other because I was trying to figure out what others were thinking of me. It was back to that rejection thing again but I was feeling the acceptance and that was huge.

Chapter 26 – Healing from Within

When I moved back to the sober living house in Palm Springs, I increased my connection with my support system from the women in the meetings, to my sponsor, and to my good friend Luke. Being in La Quinta made me feel very isolated; focus there was always on my past or on some issue with Allison. All I could think about was getting back to my group. I knew the moment I moved out and back, I was in the environment that was right for me to personally grow and continue bettering myself.

Over the course of the next four months I worked on my 12-steps of the program and it was exactly the right thing to do. Since I had my surgery, it was the beginning of being physically aligned with my mind but it was becoming increasingly important for me to heal from within. It was a great time to apply my focus and concentration on positive thoughts and actions and to begin to re-create myself to be my own person and to look for my truth and to analyze the real me. In my 12-step work, I had to take a look at my past and face the truth about the way I treated people and the way I allowed people to treat me. This allowed me to identify wrongful actions and resentments that I had been carrying with me.

I concentrated and looked for the truth deep within myself. I looked back on my life, picked up a pen, and wrote it all out on paper about the people, places, and things that moved me, good and bad in my life. If it bothered me, I wrote about it. If it did not feel right, I wrote it down and held nothing back. I wrote about my family and the fact that they did not want me or love me. I wrote about my own bad behavior, and included the people I had harmed in my life with my actions and words. I had to look at the unhappiness I caused others and myself. I wrote about my married life and the realization that I was not a very good parent. I even analyzed my "justification" for my past behavior and wrote down how I felt about it. Finally, as part of this step, I wrote and thought about my part in all of my actions and resentments. I had never looked at my part in all these interactions with others and it was a totally different perspective. I realized the things that happened in my life were events and things that I often just allowed to happen or I did things because I wanted people to like me, which meant I was not being honest with myself. It was very interesting and revealing, I realized I had been playing the role of the "victim". I wanted people to feel sorry for me because my life was so very hard as a transgendered person.

I came to a hard realization: I had more to do with my resentments than anyone else. I had been depending on the outside world to control the way I felt. I had been living the life of the victim and it was "poor me" as I drank and used drugs and wallowed in self-pity. It was all about me and blaming everyone for making me feel so depressed and feeling the need to escape in such a negative way. I found that looking at only my side of everything was extremely eye opening and revealing. For the first time in my life I had looked at my feelings and the real truth. I knew that I was a female trapped in a male body which really was a huge issue, but a major issue for me was living dishonestly and in fear of persecution for revealing my truth. This was what I called my bondage of self. I did not feel love because I did not love myself. I was a victim of a mental health condition known as Gender Dysphoria which I self-medicated with drugs and alcohol. It came in the form of talking down about other people so I could feel good about myself and through the need to control everyone and everything. I think the only way I was so successful with my job was that it was an escape for me to focus on work and not on my issues. Although, I thought about it every day at work, I had to set it aside because of the demands of production and the everyday immediate changes that had to take place.

After I completed an inventory of myself and the unhappiness I caused others and myself, I had to discuss each issue with Marcie, my sponsor, and in doing so I learned about how big of an ego I had and how low my self-esteem had gotten. I had always thought I had a great deal of self-esteem because of all the successes in my life but learned that it was a huge ego. It had always been all about me and what I wanted. I had always forced my way or the highway. In our discussions there were tremendous pride issues where I would push my will around as if to ask, "Don't you know who I am and look at me, I'm all that", because everything had to appear great on the outside. It was all about appearance which is something I learned from early childhood, it was passed down from generation to generation of dysfunction.

I learned that I had been living a great deal of my life in fear. Fear of losing my family, friends, house, job, and car because I was transgendered. I masked this fear by abusing drugs and alcohol because it numbed my pain and since I had issues with feeling this way, made it easier to deal with all I was feeling. It just did not feel good but with drugs and alcohol the bad feelings would be postponed for a while. It was very difficult and my mind took me to social acceptability and feeling from the family of only conditional love. If I remained male then they would love me but since I was actually female born into a male body then I was not loved.

Also borne out of my alcoholic pride and fear were my biggest spiritual blockers: greed, anger, envy, lust, gluttony and procrastination. I had to take a hard look at each and every one of these issues within me. I felt I needed to determine what it was that caused me to have such character defects. I learned that ego and self will, if unchecked, will and often did in my case run rampant and wild. I had prayed to my Higher Power for everything that I wanted and almost never consciously asked that His will be done. For me there was a lot to be said for people, places, and things that come to me effortlessly. I had always forced my will on everyone and everything, in fact it was a constant battle not to do so. I had to try to understand how to stop fighting everything and everyone in my mind.

In doing this inventory, I answered questions about my various selfish pursuits in sexual relations, defects relative to financial insecurity, and symptoms of emotional insecurity like worry, anger, depression, and self-pity. I had to come to an understanding on my role in each and every one of my defects in character. A revelation where trends of my behavior were identified, lifelong adjustments were found, and I began working on the root causes of each of these issues. I had to take a look at all my personal relationships and search for my truth and I had to discuss all of this with my sponsor.

I had never discussed all my secrets to another human being, so being able to bounce all this off my sponsor was a great relief. The revelation of these secrets allowed me to personally grow and continue to work on myself. It helped me to understand that drugs and alcohol were not the answer to the struggles we all go through in life. It helped me to work on accepting myself for who I was and to accept the things that I could not change in others. It was a cleansing of the heart and a start to repairing the damage I had inflicted upon others. It was imperative that I clean up the mess I had made with my relationships with other people in my life. I knew that going forward I had to keep my own side of the street clean. I had to work on the ever present resentments I felt and the secrets I had so that I could make room for my spirit to grow.

After I had admitted to my Higher Power, myself, and another human being the exact nature of my wrongs, through my inventory, I took the remainder of the next day to let it all wash over me. I became ready to have my Higher Power remove all my defects of character. This was the best way to ask for a new beginning. The removal of my defects only came from maintaining a close spiritual contact with my Higher Power. When I lose the connection by taking my will back, my character defects become more pervasive in my life. Therefore I had to find those character defects and eliminate them in my mind which takes time to do, little by slow. Then I could reconnect with my spirit which reduced the strength, occurrence, and ugliness of the defects. It was a constant battle but one that got better and better, one day at a time, through practice.

The important thing for me was to identify these defects because understanding what they were was half the battle. Now I had something to be aware of and something I could begin to work on. I couldn't begin work on anything that I did not understand and the "how" part had to come from working with my Higher Power. As much as I wanted to make these defects go away on my own I found that it would not work unless I worked in harmony with my Higher Power. Therefore I had to humbly ask my Higher Power to remove my shortcomings. Despite the way I was raised as a child, self-reliance was not enough to revive these shortcomings. I had to ask and work with my Higher Power to help me turn my weaknesses into strengths. I had to yield not to my will, but to the will of the creator. I tried listen to my Higher Power and observed the way down my path to see if doors would open for me and if my path was as effortless and progressive as the grass that grows in my back yard. Just like the grass it had to be trimmed so it would not take over the flowers and would stay right sized and beautiful. This could only be done by constantly maintaining and enriching my connection with my Higher Power. I had to work very hard on my doubt and despair and pray for faith and hope.

I made a list of people that I had harmed and became willing to make amends to each and every one on the list. This list came from looking at my resentments and those listed in my personal inventory. If there was a negative feeling that I had towards people, places, and things then I needed to list it. My list included everyone I needed to forgive or make an amends. This list would be the start of cleaning up the wreckage of my past and sweeping my side of the street clean. It was very important to my recovery to make things right with others. In some cases people carried resentment against me after my amends however, I had to let go and accept the things I could not change just like the Serenity Prayer states. I was very sincere in my desire to

286

right my wrongs. I felt a great relief when I completed this task because a great weight of anxiety was lifted off my shoulders.

I wrote to my mother and father and told them that I had spent 90 days in rehabilitation for drugs and alcohol. I told them that I knew they did not agree with me being female and it was alright if they did not love me, but it did not change the fact that I still loved them very much. I felt as if I had to make it good so they could release me without guilt or fear so I could accept the rejection. Not from a victims view but from the view point that I respect what you believe and I accept you and will love you unconditionally.

My father wrote back and told me it was good that I was straightening myself up but did not agree that I was living under an assumed name. I did not tell him I had gender reassignment surgery because that would have brought him pain and harm. He told me he loved me because the priest said he had too. You know, I took that and I have held on to that love, whatever it is and it took me almost three years through deep prayer and meditation to finally be able to feel the love from my father and my family. Even though there had not been any other contact with them for nearly four years, I finally felt the love I had yearned for all my life. I have learned that love comes from within me and I am the only one that can feel and radiate that feeling therefore, I was learning to love myself and in return, I felt the love of my family.

I felt a huge sense of accomplishment when I made amends to my father. It was such a gigantic relief, like a huge burden was lifted not just from my shoulders, but my heart as well. I had always been obsessed with this issue. I did not want to feel the pain associated with that particular obsession, so I used drugs and drank alcohol until I lost myself and eventually my spirit over it. I always wanted his love and needed him to understand that I would have done anything possible to help them both. My transgendered issue just did not fit within the parameters of their belief system. While I lost my parents, I regained my self-esteem. It was sad that I had to pay such a terrific price to live my truth and found it very difficult to come to the feeling of love, gratitude and acceptance. I had to give acceptance in the hopes of one day gaining acceptance. I also had to accept the fact that alcoholism is a disease and that although my life trauma contributed to my pain and discontent, because it is a disease, then I would have become an alcoholic anyway. This was a hard pill for me to swallow but it is the truth.

I did get something from my relationship with my dad, and that was the strength and courage to be the person I am today, and for that I will always be very grateful. So maybe there were no mistakes in my Higher Power's world; I believed this to be true. The strict and narrow road of my childhood probably saved my life, until it almost killed me just like my drug and alcohol abuse almost did. Searching for the right balance was imperative and would only come through working with my Higher Power to find the livable balance of life, love, healthy living, respect for others, and respect for myself as well.

Each morning after I awoke, I prayed and mediated for a few minutes and my connection with my Higher Power grew. This connection did not grow very fast in the beginning but as time progressed, my connection progressed steadily. After six months of living at the sober living house the second time, I was ready to leave. I had completed the 12-steps of the program and knew that working on myself would continue to be a work in progress. I made a tremendous amount of friends and even went to a women's retreat in Malibu. The retreat was on top of a hill overlooking the Malibu beach; it was a wonderful sight and an even better feeling. It was comforting to be in a weekend retreat with women because I could relate so very much. I knew I was in the right place and it confirmed my womanhood. I had so many good girlfriends and these women helped me with my femininity; it was all so very amazing.

Prayer and meditation became a very important part of my day. I had developed a routine of reading the paper, playing with and feeding Zeb, and then mediating. It was very important for me to do this each and every day before anything else. It was a way for me to seek my truth deep within me. I was not talking about my transgendered truth; I was talking about my spiritual truth. I thought about things like humility, love, gratitude, tolerance, acceptance, and willingness. I actively worked on my emotional instabilities. Knowing that I had a very addictive personality and excess compulsions, I had to think about the things that caused me to get the results that I was getting. If I continued to think positively I would eliminate negativity. I had to learn to think positively and the only way for me to do that was to practice positive thinking and to recognize when negative thoughts crept in and practice changing my thoughts. My morning meditation helped me do this and eventually I started off each day on a positive note.

In August 2009, I had celebrated one year of sobriety and the women in recovery were very kind to me. They gave me gifts and cards with words of great encouragement and allowed me to share my stories of growth. They sang "Happy Birthday" to me for being "1" year old and admittedly, it felt awesome. I felt truly bonded; one woman with a group of women in the fellowship was formed. Later that month, I stood before a group of 40 people and told my story about my transgendered life and my issues with drugs and alcohol. I discussed my solution for this first year, which had been to work with a sponsor, attend meetings, being of service in the fellowship, working the steps and being honest with myself. It was a wonderful experience and it helped tremendously to be able to share my story which allowed the fellowship to get to know me better as I listened to their experiences, strength, and hope in return. I discussed my gender reassignment surgery and discussed how it was a healing process for me. I still had a tremendous amount to learn about living a clean and sober life as a female.

In October, I drove from Palm Springs to Tucson, Arizona, to see Sister and participate in a retreat and learn more about humility. I also wanted to see her again because I had surgery scheduled in November with Dr. McGinn for breast augmentation. She had helped me out so much spiritually dating back to June of 2005. I felt I needed to stay in touch as it helped me to understand that my Higher Power loved me for me. She had followed me from the beginning of my transition, through gender reassignment surgery, and treatment. I wanted to go and pray with her in the church and her chapel before undergoing this surgery. I was able to spend three days with her in prayer and meditation with my Higher Power and discuss humility.

Sister took me to the San Xavier Franciscan Monastery just south of Tucson and I could have sworn that I had been there before in 1970 when I took a cross country trip when I was 15 years old with two Catholic Priests and another guy who was 17 years old, who later became a priest. It felt like it and looked like it, but I was really unsure. I just remember there were two Franciscan monks in a room just like this place, who were drinking beer and watching baseball on a very hot Saturday afternoon. We did not stay very long and I knew we were not too far from Tombstone and Tucson because we had just been there the day before.

We visited the grounds and the church that was built in the 1700's and found it very beautiful. The property had a sereneness that could not have been manmade; it actually felt sacred and there was a sense of peace which encompassed it all. Inside the church was adorned with very old wooden pews and paintings; I could feel the spirituality engulf the entire place. Later we went back to Sister's home in Tucson where I visited the chapel and afterwards we discussed what I learned from working a 12-step program which was really based on a belief in a Higher Power, love, being of service and having a spiritual connection. A spiritual connection between me and God.

The next morning we packed a lunch and headed west on Arizona Route 86 towards Sells. She took me out on the Tohono O'Odham Indian Reservation to show me the face of humility. We visited three settlements between Tucson and Sells and it was amazing to see the Catholic Churches that were built literally out of the land. There was no running water or electricity.

290

Everything was hand-made by the Indians in the tribe which consisted of only seven houses in the village. I heard the children crying as their clothes flapped in the wind on a rope-line to dry. I thought to myself that this was unbelievable in 2009 to still find this type of destitution in the United States. I thought about this as I used the outhouse next to the Church, which was really merely a shack with just a hole in the ground and a couple of two by fours to rest your butt on, and certainly no "out house paper". It was very humbling to say the least. The Indians lived amongst the cactus and tumbleweeds, and I know life for me would have been far more difficult had this been my childhood home. I would think their outlook was probably different than mine since it was a far simpler way of life.

I thought about my house in Virginia which was in foreclosure. It helped me put things in perspective and challenged me to appreciate the things that I had in my life today. I had a very nice place to live in Palm Springs with electricity, water, internet, cable, and trash collection, street cleaning, not to mention my education, friends, bank account and car. Although I did not realize it at the time, it was the beginning of me finding gratitude. We went to the Tohono O'Odham Museum which was south of Sells, out in the desert. When we arrived there was literally nothing around and we were the only visitors in the museum. Not only was it a museum it also doubled as a learning center for the Indians. We sat down outside in a shelter at a picnic table and ate our lunch. Part of the museum was closed for renovations, but we were able to read about and view pictures of the history. The desert was beautiful with saguaro cactus, "people" cactus as I call them because of their long necks and arms. They were really beautiful, about thirty feet tall, and indigenous to southwest Arizona.

We stayed for about 90 minutes and headed back north. We stopped at an old abandoned church and school that was once run by the Franciscan. It was just a plot of cleared desert with these buildings, along with quarters for the priests and nuns. While we were there a school bus pulled up and created a windstorm of dust. The bus dropped off a child, which seemed very odd and out of place since there was no place she could have lived in that old ghost town. We had no idea where she was going or even where she lived and thankfully an old raggedy vehicle drove up who we assumed was her mom, stopped, the girl hopped in and away they went. It was like, wow?! We could almost hear the "Twilight Zone" music playing. Then we proceeded into Sells and stopped by the gift shop which was in a four store shopping center. That was basically it for the booming metropolis of Sells. A grocery store, drug store, and gift shop; mighty "high fuhlutin'"! The houses were built many years earlier and were in great need of repair. We went by the Catholic Church in Sells near the railroad tracks where Sister had spent some time on retreat earlier in her life. It was very quiet there as if it was abandoned. She told me a priest would come out once in a while and say Mass. She explained that the churches off the main drag in the little villages we visited might only get a priest to come and celebrate Mass with the villagers once every two months. I really do not like to refer to these beautiful people as villagers but in retrospect, I think it was true, like nothing else I had ever seen in this country. It made me think that in a world of abundance what was really going in this country of such great wealth that we could allow this to go on without providing opportunities for all people to grow.

We headed back east on Route 86 towards Tucson, past the Observatory, and through the Border Patrol. I was taking in all the beauty of the desert and the saguaros. It was one of my most favorite places in the desert. When we arrived back in Tucson and exited at Starr Pass towards her home we drove up the mountain with the big "A" painted on the side and looked down at the city of Tucson. I could see the University of Arizona and all of downtown with the mountains surrounding the entire city. This was quite a contrast of my experience earlier in the day.

We had dinner and discussed humility. Sister taught me the definition of humility and explained that it meant that I should know myself as well as my Higher Power knew me. It meant

292

that it was more important to forgive than to be forgiven. It was more important for me to give love rather than be loved. I should strive to bring peace to those who are suffering and joy where I found sadness. I should remember that it wasn't about me, but about me maintaining a spiritual connection with the Universal Spirit so that I could be of service to others. It wasn't about what I received; it was about what I could give and in order to give I had to have something to give. She taught me that when I gave, I would receive which is, by virtue, the law of the universe. This rationale was a bit hard for me because I never gave for my own benefit, I always gave so that I could grow and be helpful. I spent the remainder of the evening reading, journaling about humility and I visited with my Higher Power in prayer and meditation.

I woke up early and enjoyed breakfast with Sister before I left to return to Palm Springs. It was close to a six hour drive and as I drove, took in all the gorgeous scenery and absorbed the past three days that I had with Sister, I felt the time passed very quickly. It has always been a wonderful experience when I visited with her and retreated and surrendered to my Higher Power. Her guidance, peace, love, and joy had been instrumental to my growth and development. It helped me align my physical, mental, and spiritual world. It is a part of my becoming whole.

Chapter 27 – Gratitude and Breast Augmentation

When I returned home from Tucson, I telephoned the Virginia Department of Human Services for the second time since I made my application for a revised birth certificate. I repeated this fruitless call in June and again was told nothing had been done at this point. When I called this third time, a rather indigent clerk explained to me that VDHS needed a letter from Dr. McGinn and her personal notes from the surgery before they would change my birth certificate. Now I found this quite ridiculous since they had been provided with a notarized certificate, but I decided not to rock the boat and worked through Dr. McGinn's office and obtained the required information and sent it immediately. Finally in December after numerous calls, my sister Ann the lawyer intervened. She went over and requested that the delays end immediately or legal action would ensue. One week later my sister picked up my new and improved birth certificate and mailed it to me. I swear, it was the best Christmas present a girl could ever receive!

I spent the remainder of October 2009 at New Step Sober Living in Palm Springs and moved up the hill to Desert Hot Springs in November. November was a very busy month as I had surgery scheduled in Levittown, PA at Lower Bucks Hospital just before Thanksgiving. Zeb and I were moving to a nice place about 12 miles north of Palm Springs.

One of the women in my 12-step program group had become one of my go-to people and best of all, my friend. Her name was Beverly and she was a short, pretty, dark haired Italian-Irish woman. One could easily guess with those characteristics she spoke her mind and there was no second guessing what she thought, ever! I had always enjoyed being around people who "told it like it is" and she was no exception. She was never mean but did speak the truth and sometimes the truth could hurt. However, when it was the truth then I absorbed it for about a week or more and then I grew. Her truth to me enabled me to further my growth. Beverly had asked me to move in with her in Desert Hot Springs in order for us to help each other out and to break away from sober living. In my growth of being 14 months clean and sober it was time for me to move forward. Beverly had a black board in her kitchen and she would write words like gratitude, love, and peace on the board. Every morning when I woke up and went into the kitchen I would see those words. One day the word "gratitude" was the one word always left up on the board, with or without another word. That one word stuck with me and became my mantra.

It then came time to fly to Philadelphia and a friend of mine Chris who was from Philly, flew with me. We took a United Airlines flight into Denver and after landing we were invited to the United suite by a gentleman Chris had talked with the entire flight from Palm Springs. I tagged along since it seemed as good as any way to spend my layover time. Finally after two hours we boarded our connector flight to Philadelphia. Chris then talked the entire time about the Phillies and the Eagles with another man; he never talked to me at all. When we landed, we walked to the baggage area, picked up our bags and walked outside. He got into a dark BMW with "Cheech and Chong" looking dudes and off they drove. They managed to wave to me with their stoned red eyes, as smoke billowed out of the car which enabled everyone on the sidewalk to get a good contact buzz. I stood there dumbfounded and thought, "You have got to be kidding me!"

My friend Teresa had driven up from Richmond, picked me up at the airport and then we drove up to New Hope, PA. We arrived at the Nevermore Hotel in town about 9:00 p.m. We both found it kind of comical that male to female transgendered patients of Dr. McGinn who had the gender reassignment surgery had to then spend a week near her office at the "Nevermore". I thought it was very appropriate. I enjoyed the big oak trees and pines that lined the street and the fields near the hotel. It was a large hotel but not much traffic during this time of year. New Hope, PA is a very short distance from where Washington crossed the Delaware River and the area was full of history. The people in the area maintained the old buildings and it was a great pleasure to see and feel all that the town had to offer.

The next morning we went to breakfast at the diner down the street and then off to see Dr. McGinn. I had previously requested that I would like my breast size to be proportionate to my body, not too big or too small. We confirmed that morning that the size of the implants were "500cc med plus" and filled with gel. My breasts had grown with the assistance of estrogen over the course of the past three years and they were a B cup but not fully round by this time. The help with the 500cc breast implants would take my size to a D cup, they would have the roundness I wanted and would be proportioned to my frame. The surgery would be done from underneath the breast and the implant would be inserted into the muscle. Also, I decided to have a brow lift done, which helped open my eyes and brought my hair line down just a touch and got rid of the wrinkles in my forehead. I was having two surgeries done at the same time. I was very excited.

Teresa and I spent the remainder of the day walking around New Hope. We had a late lunch in an outdoor café. It was overcast and chilly and the café had heaters on stands burning off the cold. A group came in right behind us and sat across the patio from where we were seated. They were drinking and the more they drank the louder they became and the conversation started heading south by the minute. I shamefully thought to myself that is how I acted a year and a half ago. It was a good reminder for me to see the change in behavior that excessive drink will bring upon and individual. I too was loud and obnoxious and thought the world revolved around me.

The next morning we were up at 5:00 a.m. and on our way to Lower Bucks Hospital so I could check-in at 6:00 a.m. for surgery at 7:00 a.m. Dr. McGinn was always prompt and per her usual, was at my bed side a minute before 7:00 a.m. and we went over the procedure before I fell into a drug induced sleep. The last thing I remembered was her nod to the anesthesiologist.

I woke up around 3:30 p.m. with a huge ace bandage around my chest and one around the top of my forehead. I felt very calm and collected and it was joyous to wake up with the understanding that I had completed yet another step in my journey. I felt my chest and was elated to find my new breasts there! From what I could tell through the bandages, they seemed to be well proportioned and formed perfectly. Dr. McGinn came in with her customary smile and told me the surgery went very well and she also explained that she had taken out about an inch and a half of "worry" from my brow. I could not see her results because it was all covered, and she further explained that it needed to remain that way for the time being. She gave me a prescription for pain and an antibiotic and made sure I had B-6 vitamins along with Aragonite Montana. I rested in the hospital for a couple of hours and Teresa took me back to the Nevermore Hotel. Dr. McGinn's advice was to stay in the area for a week; she certainly got no argument from me!

I stayed at the Nevermore Hotel in my room and walked the property for three days before I ventured out with Teresa in New Hope. I was very sore and surprised about the pain from the breast augmentation. I realized that when a muscle is cut into the healing process would be painful, I just didn't realize how painful. I had to make sure I slept on my back in an upright position which was difficult for me because I am a stomach sleeper. Somehow I did manage to sleep on my back while I stayed elevate, and I was careful to only use the pain medication as prescribed. All of these measures helped a great deal, and of course having Teresa by my side was a godsend.

On the fourth day Teresa and I went into town for a couple of hours. The Christmas lights were up an in all their glory; it was really a beautiful place. We went shopping and had dinner at a restaurant on the Delaware River. It was the middle of November and quite cold that night. Regardless of the chill, Teresa and I enjoyed our night out together then returned to the hotel. The next day we went back into town so I could walk and get some good fresh air. We walked across the bridge into Lambertville, NJ and looked through the antique shops and art galleries. It was a very pleasant afternoon as we paused to take in the north and south banks of the river. It was so beautiful there, and I thought it was a place that I would possibly consider living later in my life. As I continued to look out at the river, I noticed there was still some orange left on the trees that reflected off the river. I breathed in a nice long deep breath and slowly exhaled a very cleansing breath and thought that, yes, I could definitely live in a beautiful place like this, white picket fence at all …

My last day in New Hope was to meet Dr. McGinn in her office so she could unwrap the ace bandage from my breasts to examine her work. We were both very pleased with the two surgeries. Both the augmentation and the brow lift looked fantastic. Everything was healing properly and she gave me the thumbs up to return home to California. Teresa and I went shopping at a natural food store, had lunch at the diner, and over to the small indoor shopping mall on Main Street and did a bit of shopping. When we retired for the evening, I thanked Teresa for helping me as we prepared to depart the next morning. I was off to the airport and back on United Airlines back into Denver and then on to Palm Springs. The weather was nice this time, the snow was pushed off the runway in Denver, and the sun was bright and 80 degrees in Palm Springs when I arrived. Beverly picked me up from the airport and we were both happy to see one another and to share the story of the surgery and the trip. It had been just fabulous and I was very pleased and happy. Zeb was anxiously awaiting my arrival and he immediately came running towards me when I opened the front door. I walked into the kitchen to get a drink of water and there was the word gratitude written out on the blackboard. Yes, I was indeed very, very thankful.

I rested and immediately got back into my routine. I added wrapping, unwrapping and moving my breasts around as instructed so they would not get hard and cleaned by patting the area around the brow until the new skin grew in. My breasts were sore and it took about a month for the soreness to finally disappear. A week after getting back to Beverly's house we drove over to Cabazon to the outlet stores and had the lady in the Hanes store measure my breasts so I could purchase two sports bras. I was required to wear sports bras for the next couple of months to decrease any movement during the healing process. I was measured to be a 40 C/D, however, because I was still developing due to the hormones, I grew to a full D cup within the next year.

Every morning in Desert Hot Springs, I got up and followed my lifelong routine of reading the paper, drinking coffee, and playing with Zeb. My focus on the newspaper was always focused on reading about the problems and the issues the police were having in the area. I started to focus on the unusual street activity that had taken place to the point that I was talking about it more and more. I would read and go after another cup of coffee and past the board that said gratitude which had been there for at least a month and did not change. I figured Beverly was reminding herself to be grateful. I was growing a little restless, irritable, and discontent about this time near Christmas and really did not understand it only that the neighborhood was bothering me and that I was about 14 miles away from my meetings. I was feeling a kind of a spiritual disconnect.

Every morning for the past six months after playing with Zeb, I would set aside time for meditation and prayer. One day I received a call from my son John who asked me for help with his drug and alcohol problem. I told him that I would call Michael's House and try to get him into treatment. Fortunately there was room for him in the facility and John took the next flight out of Raleigh, NC on the day before Thanksgiving and landed here in Palm Springs. I picked him up and immediately took him to Michael's House. John would remain there for the next 45 days, through Thanksgiving, Christmas, and the New Year.

Also, a few weeks later during meditation and prayer, I came to the realization that I had not been grateful for anything. It hit me like a ton of bricks out of nowhere and I cried and cried. I had been consumed with the things I wanted versus just being grateful for the people, places, and things that I did have. Beverly was with me when this revelation came over me and she said, finally, why do you think that word has been on the blackboard for the past six weeks. I thought, wow, the gifts of the program do grow with time. This was a wonderful gift to realize that it was not all about me and to live in love and gratitude, one day at a time, and it made life not seem as hard. I do not think that I will ever forget that moment because it was so profound, striking, and ominous.

My house in Virginia was still in foreclosure. The bank would not accept two short sale offers and decided to sell it for less than my offers once they took possession. My job at Philip Morris was gone. My family was pretty much non-existent and I was not welcome back as part of the family. However, I was still very grateful for who I was and accepted the fact that I was in the right place. I also accepted the fact that there were no mistakes in my Higher Power's world. It was wonderful to have had the gender reassignment surgery and to be clean and sober. Today a life of clarity and purpose and I still had a great deal more work to be done on myself. With the acceptance I found, I realized that I could not change others, but I could change myself and my attitude, and change it for the better. I found that I was perfectly peaceful with my decision to change.

In mid-December, Beverly took a flight to Fayetteville, NC to see her son and grandchildren for Christmas. Zeb and I stayed in Desert Hot Springs for the next couple of weeks and through Christmas. I ventured out to a 12-step meeting most days in Palm Springs and return to DHS. Zeb and I walked around the neighborhood and battled the wind gusts and took in the beautiful view of the San Bernardino Mountains with their snow covered tops from the floor of the desert. Jackrabbits jumped out from behind the tumbleweeds and aroused Zeb and he would chase them to the maximum of the 25 feet lead and then drag me another 10 feet. It was nice and I admittedly isolated a bit and stayed home with him for Christmas and was lonely. I realized that I was lonely because I wanted to be in that self-pity. Just because I was working on a program of self esteem did not mean that I could not slip back into the "poor me" feeling. I knew where this would lead and I had to change my attitude quickly. Self-pity for me is only self serving and it did not help another person but only transmitted negative feelings to others. I was not about that anymore as I was learning gratitude by getting rid of the ego and doing esteem able things. Actually, I was working on loving myself but I was not there yet.

When Beverly returned we had a little Christmas together and she talked me into going to a New Years Eve Party. I was very reluctant but at the last minute decided to go and I wore a beautiful Victoria Secret pink sweater dress that showed off my new found breasts. I had a lot of sober fun at the party. I saw people, danced and ate some really fine food. It was my second New Year's Eve party without a drink and it was more fun than ever. No hangover for the New Year and January 1, 2010 was full of laughter and joy.

Chapter 28 – Back Down Indian Canyon and to Richmond

The first week in January I made the decision to return to Palm Springs. The 14 mile commute each day to attend my meetings and see my friends had begun to take a toll on me. Additionally, the activity on the streets in Desert Hot Springs was getting very questionable and I did not feel comfortable outside of Beverly's home. Inside it was quiet and serene, it was my sanctuary; but I had begun to isolate inside my home which was not good for me so I moved back to the New Step Sober Living House again for the third time. I moved into a room with my good friend Charlie and spent the next 45 days there.

When I was in New Hope, PA, in November of last year, I had scheduled a facelift with Dr. McGinn for March 2010. At the end of February, Zeb and I packed up for our move back to Richmond and for me to have my final surgery. We set out on I-10 east and stopped in Tucson for about 30 minutes to see Sister, and stopped for the night in Las Cruz, NM and stayed down the street from New Mexico State University. We were up early and made it through El Paso, TX before rush hour, through US Border Patrol Station and then onto I-20 in the middle of the Texas desert, through Midland, Dallas, and on to Longview, Texas late that evening. The hotel in Longview was nothing but parties and police, it was horrific! I slept about five hours and we left on I-20 east and it was dawn as we got into Louisiana.

Zeb and I drove straight through over the Mississippi River and finally stopped in Tuscaloosa, Alabama for gas and a walk. Finally after traveling through Birmingham, Atlanta, Anderson, Greenville, and Gaffney into North Carolina, it was about 11:15 p.m. when we crossed over in the city limits of Charlotte. I called Diane and my daughter Rebecca and told them I was in Charlotte. Diane was expecting me to stay in her home for a couple of days before driving to Richmond.

I was married to Diane for 13 years and she had always been a best friend to me, even in marriage. She helped me with my gender issue and I had always been free to express my feelings to her. She was very open-minded and had a tremendous amount of common sense. She owned a beautiful two story white home in Cabarrus County that looked out over a pond. Her yard was full of beautiful grass and tall oak trees. Behind her house was a field full of cattle and deer ran wild throughout the property.

Diane and I spent two days together and talked about the past, my family, and the dogs. We went into town a couple of times to the huge hardware store, which was her favorite store, and then over to Mr. C's because she always loved his special cheeseburgers with lettuce, tomato, onion, pickles and slaw on top. She was the original "Carolina Burger Girl". We went over to her mother's house, whom I considered to be my Mom. Her mother, Billie, was a wonderful lady and she loved me a great deal and we visited and she asked me about my surgery and was actually very happy for me. I was considered one of the sisters when it comes to the family. Billie, my mother-in-law, was not doing well and was in a hospital bed that was set up in her living room, a central location in the house. Each of the daughters rotated their days and nights to stay with her. I felt very strongly about going to see Billie. It really meant a lot to me.

It was so wonderful to see my daughter, Rebecca, and we had lunch in the old "Surprise Store" which was now converted over to a restaurant. The Surprise Store was an Exxon gas station with an old country type store that sold a few groceries, ice cream, candy, and beer. As a child, Rebecca would ride there with me to get our goodies. I love her so much and really missed her. I hoped our connection would grow stronger over time. I hoped she would forgive me for not being a good parent. The same went for my son Mark. I loved him so much but I had not seen him in quite a while. I spoke with him over the phone and also hoped he forgave me for not being a good parent. I believed that I embarrassed him and I had grown to accept that. I vowed to give him time to wrap the transgender concept around his mind. I had to give it to my High Power because I did not wish to bring harm or discomfort to him. I called Mark and told him I was in town, but learned that he was in school at NC State studying for his MBA degree and could not see me due to taking exams and working on a project.

For me I never grew out of wanting my family's love. I had finally realized this and is has taken me this long to understand and to be able to work on it from within myself. I really did not know how to love because I did not feel the love from my childhood, and therefore felt unlovable. Feelings of being disconnected, affected the way I treated other people, which included myself, my children, my friends, and those I had professed to love and care about in my life. It took the alignment of physical, mental, and spiritual conditioning to finally enable me to approach this subject. Love myself and to be grateful for today. I learned that love was a feeling and I was the only one that could radiate that feeling and it had to come from within me. I was truly beginning to understand that I had done to Mark and Rebecca what was done to me: love them very much, but not possess the ability to show it. It was my hope to stop this inability to show affection; a pattern I believed had come from generations, deeply in my Irish heritage. This lack of affection, or the showing of, is a character defect that I have learned is prevalent with many Irish alcoholics.

I was back on the road again and stopped in Raleigh to see John and his girlfriend. The instructions that he gave me lead me to the proper exit but I had to call for him to direct me to his home. Once I arrived, John was busy packing his things and Shannon was in her room with the door locked and would not come out. John had been communicating with some of the girls from treatment and it had caused a jealous rage. Therefore, John was asked to leave her apartment where he lived. I was not expecting this to happen and it totally caught me off guard as I watch him load his car. He announced that he was coming to Virginia with me.

I sincerely wanted to help him out, but had only arranged a room for myself with my friend Bethany and there was no way for him to stay there. I told him that he could not come to Virginia and he was desperately trying to find a place to stay. We talked for about an hour about his current situation and he was able to go to his mother's house in Fuquay-Varian for a short time. This settled it for the day and I had to give it to my Higher Power and promised to keep in touch with him to make sure he was good for the time being. I left and proceeded north on I-85 to Dinwiddie which was about 25 miles south of Richmond. I was staying with Bethany and her mother on seven acres of land out in the country. Bethany was the Secretary of JRTS during the first year of the support group. She had transitioned on the job and was an electrician for a train wheel bearing manufacturing company.

Before having surgery Bethany was going to quit her job because, like most of us, she believed she would not be accepted. However, I spoke with her about this issue and convinced her to go to the highest person in Human Resources and discuss transitioning. I told her it would be very difficult in this area to find a job and she was making good money and needed to hold on to the things she had today. She followed my advice, transitioned, had gender reassignment surgery and today is a very productive leader with the electricians within that organization. I was so happy to see her and Mom again and Zeb had a little playmate in Duke, her Shih Tzu. They welcomed me with open arms and admittedly, it was great! Bethany's home was my home. Spring was just around the corner, the days were getting longer, and the trees were just barely showing signs of new life. I had a very nice bedroom that looked out into the backyard and beyond into the acreage of trees. Everything was just lovely; I couldn't have asked for anything better.

We had a nice dinner and caught up on the things that were going on in our life. Bethany and Mom were doing well. Bethany was doing great with work, riding her motorcycle, and hanging out at Starbucks with her friends. She was still the Secretary at JRTS and filled me in on all the events that were taking place. It was very nice to hear that the organization was still helpful to other transgendered people.

During the week, I contacted Teresa and together we made arrangements for our trip to New Hope, PA. to see Dr. McGinn. I decided to have a facelift performed by Dr. McGinn which I hoped would take away a few years and would also work towards enhancing my facial feminization. Fortunately for me I looked female from all perspectives but I also wanted to look younger. I felt young, but I want my outsides to match the way my insides felt too. I felt certain that the only thing that would give me away as being transgendered female was my voice because it was a little deep. I could choose to have surgery to raise my voice but instead chose to practice the higher pitch sounds through internet vocal programs. Besides, I had spent well over $100,000 on myself and I was perfectly happy with all my surgeries thus far. The vocal cord surgery would mean that I could not speak for two weeks and I decided just to work more on my inner spirit. Perhaps someday I may take the trip to Seattle to have it done, but for now I felt happy with how I turned out so far.

Teresa and I drove to Philadelphia, past Lincoln Field, then just a short distance north to Levittown. We stayed at the Homestead Suite just down the street from Lower Bucks Hospital. We settled into the room for the coming week and went down the street to a diner and had dinner. I was in the bed relatively early, excited about seeing Dr. McGinn and completing pre-op the following morning.

Early the next day we drove up to New Hope, PA and I saw Dr. McGinn. We reviewed the surgery and I told her I was ready and signed all the paperwork. It was a short visit and Teresa and I were off into New Hope for a walk and a little shopping. We returned to Levittown, had dinner at the diner and then retired for the evening. I had to get up at 5:00 a.m. and be at the hospital at 6:00 a.m. I must have slept well because it was morning before I realized it and we were off. I checked into Lower Bucks Hospital and paid the hospital and the anesthesiologists. Most insurance companies will not pay for any or even part of gender reassignment surgery. I had to pay the surgeon, hospital, and anesthesiologist cash in advance before all the surgeries were performed. After I made my payment, I had to go to the lab and then upstairs to the operating room.

Just like the two previous surgeries, Dr. McGinn appeared at my bedside at 6:59 a.m. and was ready to operate. We went over the facelift surgery again and the last thing I remembered was talking with her. The next moment for me was 3:30 p.m. in the afternoon laying on a gurney in the recovery room and the nurse said they wondered if I was ever going to wake up. I had been out like a light for a couple of hours after surgery, but I felt wonderful knowing that facelift was complete. I could not wait to get up and take a look. When I was finally able to get up off the bed, I sat down in the chair and realized I had a booming headache. Teresa was back at the hotel resting so the nurse called her to come over. We were only about five minutes from the hospital so it was not long before she arrived. However, it seemed like eternity to me. It was getting dark out and I had to wait for a while until my headache subsided. Teresa took me to the hotel, put me in the bed, and she went out for some dinner. I did not eat very much that night and had to lay on my back with my head elevated somewhat and fell to sleep.

The next morning I was up early and decided to uncover my face and look to see if the wrinkles were pulled out and if I looked younger. Admittedly I was frustrated because there was still some facial hair if I looked really close, because the electrolysis from previous year had not taken care of them all. So instead of being negative, I was determined to be positive and was thankful to Dr. McGinn. I rested for the next couple of days in the hotel; Teresa would go out and bring me back some food. Zeb was in Virginia with Bethany and I would call each day and speak with both of them. The one thing I had to do each day was to pat the incision area with diluted peroxide and keep it clean. Some of the facial hair around the incision had to grow and I would hide it with my long bleach blonde hair. We stayed a week in Levittown before I had a follow-up visit with Dr. McGinn so that she could examine her work. I pretty much rested, went to the diner each day, and watched March Madness basketball on the television. Dr. McGinn examined my surgical scars and gave me the thumbs up to ride back to Richmond with Teresa. I was healing nicely and Dr. McGinn asked me to send her a photo of the side view of my face in about a week to make sure the scabs were healing correctly. Oh sick me saved the scabs and put them in an envelope because I was so happy with the outcome!

The real joy was in being female. I was working very hard on myself through the program and always started my day with meditation and prayer. The women in California were teaching me how to be a lady. I hung out with the women in the program and we went out to retreats and restaurants; we shopped and talked about medical things pertinent to women and we even talked about men. We sat around and talked about our feelings and truth be told, having the ability to express these feelings was a huge relief and actually being able to cry when I felt sadness was very cleansing. I was taking care of my physical self and was also learning the emotional aspect of being truly female. From a male perspective in that role I would study how women acted and I found the emotional release was the true feminine side which I had always carried inside me but hid for many years.

We had loaded the car prior to the visit in anticipation of going back to Richmond and left New Hope in the early afternoon. We stopped at the Chesapeake House on I-95 for a break and had a late lunch before we preceded into the Washington, DC, Northern Virginia traffic. We cheated and took the car pool lane and made it around without being stopped for not having enough people in the car. We made it to Richmond at dusk and I picked up my car from Teresa's house and drove the extra 25 minutes back to Dinwiddie. When I arrived, Zeb, Duke, Bethany, and Mama Anne were glad to see me; Zeb licked me to death and there were hugs all around. I definitely felt the love. We had a wonderful dinner and the conversation was centered on Dr. McGinn and the surgery and of course I was asked to show it off. Bethany also had her surgeries with Dr. McGinn and was tuned in very closely.

In Dinwiddie with Bethany and Mama Anne, I began to be pulled back to the San Jacinto Mountains and the feeling was becoming more intense as each day passed. I was missing the support that I was given from so many women in the Coachella Valley and I realized it was a very healing place for me. I spent the next several weeks recovering from surgery and Bethany helped me clean the incision with the diluted peroxide each night in the area around my ears. They were difficult to reach and she stood over me with my head bent down and took care of the area in a matter of seconds. I was grateful for everything that Bethany and Mama Anne did for me but I had made my decision to return to California.

I called my sister who had stored some of my belongings in her basement and made arrangements to pick them up. She gave me a one hour window to come by and get my things. My son John agreed to accompany me and to use his car so that we could pick up as many of my belongings as possible. My sister did not spend any time with us other than to show us where my things were stored. After that she went outside and worked in her yard. During this hour I came to the realization that I had to simply accept things the way they were and not worry about other people's prejudices. I further realized this was not a visit; it was a "get your things and go" situation. It took us about 50 minutes to pack the cars with as much as we could pack. As we were leaving I walked up to my sister, gave her a huge hug, and told her I loved her. Now I had more things there, much more, but my time was up so I told her she could just keep what was left in the garage. It was very sad and cold especially since we were once very close. She looked at me and all she could say was she wanted her brother back. I left with love, emptiness and thoughts of I was still the same person but I had to let it go and give her to my Higher Power. I was only responsible for me and I had to always remember to "keep my side of the street clean". There was no resentment on my part, only a prayer for forgiveness.

John decided he was going back to California with me so we scheduled the time to leave in a couple of days; he would follow me from Richmond to Palm Springs in his own car. Just as we settled on this schedule, Diane called with the news that her Mom had passed away peacefully in the hospital. Although it was expected, I was very sad about the news and told Diane I would be in Concord within 48 hours to help her. John went to see his mother in Raleigh and I immediately rushed to Concord to be by Diane's side during her time of loss.

When I arrived Diane and her sisters wanted me to stay at her Mom's house and said I was one of their sisters. I was so grateful and loved them all very much felt like I was truly part of the family. I attended the funeral and all the family activities with Diane before and after the funeral and said my goodbye to one of the most beautiful and accepting ladies in the Universe. It was emotional, devastating, and comforting wrapped into one. After the activities, I went back to her Mom's house for my last night on the east coast for a while. John met me there that night and we went to bed early so we could get an early start on our trip to California.

We left Charlotte, NC at 9:00 a.m. on I-85 and picked up I-20 in Atlanta. We stopped near the Georgia – Alabama border, Tuscaloosa, AL, and again on the west bank of the Mississippi River before we got into Monroe, LA late that night at the only hotel that accepted dogs, the Motel 6. The stops we made were for gas, food, and to walk Zeb. Zeb was making his third cross-country trip and the trip seemed to be becoming routine for him, although we were both anxious to get back to California.

We were up early and had coffee and quickly got across the border into Texas through Tyler, Dallas, Midland-Odessa, and hit the blinding setting sun as we crossed the Continental Divide once we reached I-10. We made it to El Paso around 9:00 p.m. and crossed into New Mexico and stopped in Las Cruz for the night. It was a very long trip but we made it with stops along the way every four hours for Zeb to take his bathroom breaks. I said a quick hello to the Las Cruz Police Officer who was patrolling the parking lot. Zeb and I took a walk and then we went off to bed. I was very cautious when I traveled across the country because of being transgendered. I knew there were people out there that often became very violent towards people like me. November 20th is transgendered remembrance day and prayers are offered to all those transgendered people who have been murdered over the past year. Unfortunately, the list is not short. Since my surgeries and with the change in my appearance, there was little for me to really worry about today; and even less so since my birth certificate, registration, and driver's license all reflect my proper name and gender: "F" for female.

We were off for Palm Springs 6:00 a.m. and made stops in Las Cruz, the west side of Phoenix, Blythe, and finally home in the Coachella Valley by 5:00 p.m. John and I walked into the New Step Sober Living at dusk and we could see the lights from the White Party that was going on in Palm Springs. This was my forth time back here and George laughingly said he had put a boomerang up my butt! Nevertheless, John and I stayed in Charlie's room for the next three weeks before we rented a condo near the Indian Canyons.

Chapter 29 – Make Up Your Mind

I rented a very nice condo on La Verne in Palm Springs that was furnished. We had a beautiful up- close view of the San Jacinto Mountains, a nice green backyard, and a swimming pool about 30 yards away from the back patio. There were palm trees all around, a private front patio, a large living and dining area, two bedrooms and baths, and a very quaint kitchen. It was absolutely perfect. My sponsor's father helped me locate the condo, and John, Zeb and I moved in on the first of May.

John and I were both in the 12-step program and we talked about how the program might help him with his schizophrenia. He went to meetings everyday and made many new clean and sober friends. He visited his psychiatrist in Rancho Mirage and became compliant with his medications. The combination of the two was very helpful for him and on good days he would maintain a good balance. However, there were days when he was really down and out and a meeting or talking about himself would help. For the past 10 years, John had been talking to me about his feelings and about the fact that he had been hearing voices. Many years ago we had often stayed up until 5:00 a.m. and discussed the same issues repetitively until he felt more comfortable and had calmed down. This was a time I had seen the greatest growth in him and now he utilized both a 12-step program and his psych medications.

I continued to work on myself and started to outline a consulting firm for transgendered people, to be used by businesses. It was an aspiration of mine to finish its development soon so that I could conduct seminars across the country. This would be for educational purposes for those businesses that have a person transitioning on the job. I also started outlining my own story. I wrote the beginning of this book during this period and had a few friends read it and their encouragement was outstanding. However, money was getting tight because I had been using my savings to live on so I decided with two years of sobriety under my belt, to go to work for the treatment center that had help me in the beginning. After I had worked for Michael's House for two weeks, I realized this was not a part of my Higher Power's plan. I did not know what the plan was but only that I was working the grave yard shift and the condo next door had begun renovations on my first day on the job. Jack hammers, nail guns, and foul mouthed men from the moment I walked into my home in the morning and it went on all day long when I was attempting to sleep. This obnoxious noise continued well beyond the two weeks I was employed at Michael's House. During my meditation it came to me from my Higher Power that this was not the right place for me and deep inside, I felt the same way. My Higher Power and I were definitely on the same sheet of music on this one! Although I supported and enjoyed helping others in treatment and was very grateful for the opportunity, it simply was not my purpose.

Luke and I spent time together a couple of days each week, mostly enjoying a meal, shopping, or discussing our recovery. I went to at least one meeting everyday and spent a lot of my time with the people in the program.

In late August, I received a phone call from one of my high school friends named Tom. Tom was the manager of the baseball and football teams that I played on in high school and he always took great care of me and my possessions. He had been talking with my sisters and found out that I was in California and wanted to come visit me. He also had two daughters, one in Los Angeles and the other in San Diego. Since Palm Springs is about 100 miles from both cities he could see us all. Tom came out to Palm Springs for about three days and I introduced him to my friends and showed him around. It was good for me to start reconnecting with people from my youth. Of course there were lots of questions about me being transgendered and I patiently answered as many questions as I felt comfortable doing. With everyone I explained that I knew when I was very young that I was female. I also discussed the denial I felt for so many years and the feelings of guilt, shame, and anxiety that accompanied those feelings and was ever present until I finally gathered the strength and courage from within to do something about it.

In September, I found myself missing Virginia again and decided to pack up John, Zeb and myself and head back across country to Bethany's house, while John arranged to stay with a friend in Richmond. It was my dream to be close to my family so that hopefully a little at a time, we could reunite. I thought that being in California was too far away to keep in touch. If I were closer to them, I thought that perhaps one day they might want to see me and I could just ride right over and all would be well. I wanted to at least let my family know that I was there for them if they ever needed me. My parents were getting older and their health was slowly deteriorating. I wanted to be available to help and in retrospect this was probably my own "self-will" running wild and me retuning back to that ugly place of "why can't you just love me?" I had been in acceptance of the things the way they were supposed to be but I thought it was possible to try and force some kind of solution. I was taking back my will and acceptance.

On September 27, 2010, John, Zeb, and I headed back east. We returned the same way we had driven earlier in the year. This trip was a little bit different because it involved the "Las Cruz hotel incident". What happened, a bothersome white dude came out of his room while I was loading my car to leave and followed me, apparently trying to ascertain which room was mine. He pretended to walk over to the trash bin but I kept him in the corner of my eye because I immediately noticed he was watching me. After all, no one has THAT much dreaded trash in their hotel room and if they did, they would most likely wait for maid service! He got a big surprise when Zeb and John came out with me! He immediately backed off and we got back on our way. Then the morning after we stayed in Shreveport, LA, again I was packing up the car and this black dude stopped his car, struck up a conversation with me; supposedly he was just being a gentleman and wanted to know if I needed any help. Oddly enough, he sped off like a bat out of hell as soon as he saw John and Zeb exit our room. I was very grateful for Zeb and John during moments like these when anything could have happened.

We made it to Charlotte in three days, record time for us! Once again I stayed with Diane before I went on to Richmond. I called Mark and Rebecca and told them I was on the east coast and wanted to see them. Rebecca and I decided to eat lunch again at the surprise store and she was as beautiful as ever. She had a wonderful job with Price-Waterhouse and had a Master's degree in Accounting and a BA degree in Mathematics from the University of North Carolina. She was always a very bright and talented young lady and full of life and ambition. Mark was still studying at NC State and working to finish the semester in his MBA program. Mark had a Master's and Bachelor's degree in Sports Management from the University of South Carolina so this would be his third degree. I used to visit with him and go to William Bryce Stadium to watch the Gamecocks play football before he understood that I was transitioning. I did not sit down with them to explain what was going on with me because I was assumed I would be rejected. I was just allowing time to heal which I now believe was the wrong thing to do.

John went to see his mother in Fuquay-Varina and then met me at Bethany's house to drop off a carload of my belongings. Zeb knew exactly where he was and although Duke, Bethany's dog, was not all that excited, he eventually warmed up to Zeb over time. The leaves were still on the trees in Dinwiddie and they had just begun to shed their green for their autumn colors. I had always loved the fall in Virginia because the colors were so beautiful and vibrant with the oranges, yellows, and deep reds flying through the air.

I settled in and made myself at home with Bethany and Mama Anne; I had to admit, it felt very nice. I had put aside my work on consulting and writing and worked on my resume and began applying for jobs in the area. I thought that if I could find a good job and house in the area, and then reunite with my family, I truly believed all would be right in my world.

While in Virginia I interviewed with four companies. Twice with two of the company's and especially one in particular, at the end of the second interview the interviewer had the gall to say: "Look there's no doubting your skill set, but really man, what's your deal? I mean c'mon, what's up with you?!"

I looked at him in stony silence, actually quite stunned, and said nothing for a few seconds. We sat just listening to the clock tick and I finally said, "What exactly are you referring to, the fact that I'm slightly taller than the average woman? Or is it that you haven't seen 'California bleach blond' hair on a woman in this part of the country? Or is it that you aren't accustomed to meeting a woman with such high educational credentials with an impeccable work history to boot?!"

The interviewer sort of laughed in my face and said, "Look you KNOW what I'm talking about dude. I don't care what's on your resume, it's YOU! You waltz in here dressed like a woman and I want to know what's up!"

Again I was shocked that a person in human resources would behave so inappropriately, but I took a deep breath, maintained my composure and matter of factly answered,

"I am a female and have the birth certificate, ID, and whatever else you may think you need to prove it. And before a fly flies straight into your mouth, yes I am a transgendered female which simply means I had gender reassignment surgery, but I am a female nonetheless. I have an MBA geared towards Finance and am fully qualified for this position. The genitals I have between my legs certainly would have no bearing on crunching your numbers, or your ass if need be!"

This was a finance company with the responsibility to meet and present to clients; surprise, surprise, I received a form letter two days later stating I was not qualified. Like anyone else, I'd rather have been told the truth about why I wasn't being hired than be lied to via a form letter. I knew I wasn't being hired because I was transgendered, so just have the balls to come out and be truthful about it. After that fiasco, I decided to just walk into any future interviews and be on the offensive; I told them up front that I was transgendered and explained that if there was a problem with then we should not waste each other's time with going through the motions of a fruitless interview. In retrospect, I think I did this to avoid further embarrassment and pain; I just didn't want to deal with anymore ignorance. Today, I fully understand it was none of their business. After I spent about two months job hunting, attending job fairs, and being treated like crap at interviews, I could see the business environment in Virginia was not a healthy place for me. Although I had transitioned on the job with Philip Morris in Richmond, it was much different when job hunting. I do think it remained important for those who were transitioning to stay with their current employer, transition, continue to work and then if need be, look for a new position while continuing to remain employed. In other words, don't leave a job unless the work environment became completely unbearable. But no one should ever tolerate a hostile work environment; that it was illegal and there were remedies for all employees already in place for that issue. No one had to tolerate bullying on the job ... or anywhere else for that matter.

While in Richmond, I had the opportunity to meet two girls from JRTS that transitioned on the job. They were both fired within two months after they completed their transition. One of the women had worked in a motorcycle repair shop for 30 years, had great performance reviews and after her transition, in her last two months of employment she was suddenly not "performing to expectations". She had done nothing different except transition on the job. The same thing was true for another lady who was an auto mechanic at a local dealership. Two months after her transition, her performance was suddenly so poor she had to be terminated without the benefit of even placing her on a corrective action plan to improve her performance. To top off the madness, Virginia was a right to work state so the law favored the employer and the girls had no recourse except of course to file for unemployment.

I attended the November and December JRTS monthly meetings and was able to discuss the history of the support group. There were two nursing students from the Medical College of Virginia that were interested in understanding us from a viewpoint of our medical needs upon entering a medical facility. I explained to the group that this support group was formed to help each other in transitioning so that we could make informed decisions and support one another. The group was for educational purposes not only for people in transition, but also for those who wanted a greater understanding of the transgendered community. The nursing students were in the right place and it was wonderful to meet those who wanted to participate from outside the transgendered community. JRTS was also for the families of those in transition to enable them to understand more about their friends, siblings or children. The December meeting was a Christmas party and it was wonderful to see everyone again. We took a picture of the original founding members of the JRTS group and those who were carrying the group forward. It was a very nice Christmas party.

Thanksgiving Dinner with My Sister

My sister Ann invited me over for Thanksgiving dinner. This was the first time in five years I had been invited to a formal dinner in their home or with anyone in my immediate family for that matter. It was very nice to sit down with Ann and her children, Cub, Warren, Erin, and Colleen. We all had a very good time and it was a great opportunity to see my nieces and nephews, talk and catch up with their lives and activities. Ann made dressing and rolls from the recipe that my mother used all her life. The recipe came from my grandmother and it was a wonderful taste of home. It was a bit of a madhouse but everyone got along well and it was almost a shame that 24 hours of cooking was devoured in 45 minutes! It was a heart filled loving day for me and I was beginning to feel love from my family once again. Love, gratitude, acceptance, and open-mindedness were wonderful feelings that could only be radiated from within me.

John was living in the Byrd Park district of Richmond with a friend when he relapsed on drugs. Sadly his one year sobriety date was just around the corner. He called me and told me what had transpired and I told him to get his butt back to California where not only the environment was much safer for him, but he also had a wonderful support system built in to his living arrangement. So he called Roberta, his girlfriend, and she flew to Richmond and they drove back together, the same route that we had driven. They arrived in the Coachella Valley on December 5th and I told John I would most likely be back out there at the end of the year. The support and attitude of the people in general was much more open minded in California than in the Mid-Atlantic and the South. It was unfortunate but that was the reality. John went back to Roberta's house and started from square one with his sobriety. I was very grateful that he had made it back to the meetings because many people have to hit rock bottom and in many cases it took a trip to jail or even prison to bring them back if they did not die first. I have seen four people over the past three years take their own will back, do what they wanted to do, abuse drugs and alcohol and it all ended in death. Such a tragic waste of life ...

I went back to my sister Ann's house on Christmas Eve and had Christmas dinner. I spent the day catching up with her and the children, from lawyer activities to boyfriends! Cub was there from Atlanta, Erin was home from William and Mary College, Warren was off from high school and Colleen from middle school. I talked with the kids about school and their friends. Ann's ex-husband and the father of her kid's, Jacob, came by for a few minutes to visit and join the festivities. It was very pleasant to sit around the table and have a conversation with my sister and my nieces & nephews. Ann gave me a beautiful ceramic plaque for Christmas which read "Sisters Make the Best Friends". This was really special to me because I had fought rejection issues since starting my transition from male to female.

Yes, finally we are sisters and she recognized me as such! Ann understood that I was returning to California after Christmas and we hugged and held each other for a while and said our good-bye's for now.

On Christmas morning I got up around 6:00 a.m. Zeb and I naturally went through our morning routine. Mama Anne, Bethany, and I enjoyed a full breakfast together and then exchanged gifts. I gave them the best coffee Starbucks made because it was their favorite hangout. They gave me a beautiful angel made of silver to protect me in my journey. I enjoyed my time with them so much and was very grateful for them. They provided me with a lovely place to live while I was trying to figure out where I belonged. However I felt pulled back to Palm Springs, and that "pull" was just as great as it had been the last time. I was truly drawn to this area and I decided I needed to stop fighting it and needed to understand that my will was not always the best.

At noon, I left Bethany's house and drove to South Richmond to Stephanie and Brandon's home. Diane and Alisha were there and it was planned that we would celebrate Christmas together. This was just like the Christmas's past except Stephanie and Brandon came over to Diane and my house in Goochland for Christmas each year from 2000 - 2006. I had not seen Stephanie and Brandon or their son Wyatt for several years. My transition and the toll of substance abuse had kept us all apart. It was a wonderful and glorious feeling to be accepted back into the fold after I completed my transition and successfully recovered from my problems. We all had a wonderful Christmas dinner which featured ham with all the trimmings and afterwards we exchanged gifts. Diane gave me a handmade purse with a matching hat that she designed and made herself. It was exquisite! Stephanie gave me some very nice makeup and a necklace with a matching earring set. The kindness they showed towards me was refreshing and my physical change was becoming more acceptable with my stepchildren. Only 11 years ago, I had walked Stephanie down the aisle to take Brandon's hand in marriage. Life felt wonderful and it took on many different facets but the

320

only way to live, regardless of who we were, was to live each day in love, gratitude, and acceptance. I firmly believed that on this day, we were all in that exact place, and in that exact frame of mind.

Just after I arrived at Stephanie's house the sky, which was very cloudy, began to release a few snow flurries and then an hour later it was heavy snow. We were being blessed with a white Christmas! This happens only occasionally in Richmond on Christmas Day and it was absolutely wonderful and felt so peaceful as if the heavens were in harmony. By 5:00 p.m. the snow had begun to pile up and it was time for me to say my goodbye's to Diane and the family before I had to head back to Dinwiddie. Diane told me I should move back to North Carolina because she knew that I had been happiest in this part of the country. I did love her, the sisters and loved the Charlotte area. Its beauty alone was one reason for me to give it full consideration if I were ever led back to the area ... The roads were slick as I made my way down Chippenham Parkway to I-95. Eventually I made it back to Bethany's house and found that three inches of snow had fallen on the ground and it was continuing to come down in full force. Bethany, her mom and Melissa, who preceded me as president of JRTS, had Christmas dinner at their home during the afternoon and were still there when I finally made it. We chatted, had coffee and cake for a short while and then went off to our rooms to settle in for the night.

The next day I focused entirely on my return back to California. I picked up my u-haul trailer for my car and began loading it with the things I planned to take back with me. I felt sad because I wanted to be close and available to my family but after three months in the Richmond area, I only saw my sister Ann and my brother David. John was back out in California struggling with his recovery. Mark and Rebecca were in Charlotte. Diane, the sisters, and my step children where in Virginia or North Carolina, but I was deeply drawn back to San Jacinto Mountains in Palm Springs.

I planned to hit the road for California the following day, but before I did I thanked Bethany for everything she has done for me. I was very grateful she allowed me to come into her life, home and to be a member of her family. I was always welcomed there and this was truly a gift that she shared not only with me but with others. It was the ultimate humility to give so lovingly of herself and her home to others that were in need. I cherished her and Mama Anne in my heart.

The next morning Bethany left for work around 5:00 a.m., well before I had woken up. I sat with Mama Anne and she truly wanted me to stay but I had already committed to returning to California because of the pull from my Higher Power. So with a heart filled with love and gratitude I kissed her goodbye and got on my way. Zeb jumped in the back seat and we headed to Fayetteville, NC to pick up Beverly, a good friend from Palm Springs who was there visiting her grandchildren. She had agreed to ride back with me to California. When I left the house I almost could not get out of the driveway or the long narrow dirt road that led out to the state maintained road because of the snow and the freezing temperature. None of the snow had melted since Christmas Day, which made the road particularly tricky. It was very cold outside, especially for a converted desert rat like me!

It was noon when I pulled up in front of Beverly's son's home at Fort Bragg, NC. Beverly had been visiting her daughter-in-law and grandchildren since the middle of October. Her son was in US Army and deployed to Afghanistan. Now it was time for her to return to her home in Palm Springs. We loaded her suitcases and belongings into my u-haul trailer and off we went through the back roads of North Carolina through Albemarle, Concord, and then onto I-85 just north of Charlotte. It was significant that we went right through Albemarle because on this day, it was Zeb's birthday and he was born here exactly nine years ago. Zeb was the alpha male from the litter of seven.

Luke was home for Christmas and invited us to stop by his parent's house in Dawsonville, GA. It was very dark and the sky was filled with beautiful bright stars as we made our way through the foothills of the Appalachian Mountains and into the city. Luke's house was very lovely and styled like a lodge that one would see in a badlands state like Montana. Luke's father was from Montana and it was reflected in the architecture of his home. The invitation was extended for us to stay the night and he gave us a tour of his parent's home. It was a festive time, very comfortable and relaxing as we caught each other up on the past several months of our activities. The last time I had seen Luke was in September, just before I had left for Virginia, so it was really wonderful to see him again.

The Journey Home

The following morning we had a big breakfast before we started our cross-country journey once again. Prior to my arrival, Beverly had not been feeling well and her illness was beginning to get a little bit worse. However we decided to continue our trek; we made our way to Monroe, LA by the evening and settled in at the Motel 6. We exchanged Christmas gifts at this time and she gave me a book that set a new course and awareness in my life. The book was titled, *The Secret*, by Rhonda Byrne. This book further awakened my spirit and helped me to realize my priorities and to regain my courage to become creative, to live my dream and to bring it into reality. It was a boost to the things I already knew and practiced but brought into consciousness. It gave me that push and inspiration to work hard and press forward by making progress each and every day. It provided me with knowledge and understanding that dreams can come true.

The next day we made it to Midland, Texas but not without some communication mishaps. I was pressing on to get back to California as soon as possible and was not quite listening or understanding Beverly. She was getting sicker and I needed to stop more than I had been doing. It made for a long ride that day which ended with a bit of resentment between us. I had been a people pleaser most of my life and was not trying to antagonize her, but apparently I had done a really good job in doing just that and she became quite angry with me. I had to use my program to listen and try to understand her issues to get us through the day of driving. Thankfully the resentments passed after a short period of time and we made our way back to Palm Springs the next night, on New Year's Eve.

After I dropped Beverly off at her home, I arrived at the New Step Sober Living house for my fifth time at 11:00 p.m. on New Year's Eve. George came over at 11:45 p.m. and all four residents (me included in that number) sat on the back patio and held a meeting in the cold blowing wind. We each listed the things we wanted to let go of from the past year on a piece of paper and at midnight, burned them in a small fire bowl. I wrote that I needed to stop moving from one coast to the other and that I needed to stay in one place and establish roots in order to further develop and grow. I pledged to myself to stay in this spot for at least a year. Now it was 2011, a new year and a new beginning. At the age of 56, I decided to reinvent myself. I had learned to walk through my fears and live on life's terms. I had learned to accept myself for me and to be loving and kind to others and live life with gratitude.

I still had a fear of financial insecurity so I continued looking for a job just like I was doing in Virginia. I made it my job during the month of January to look for work at least six hours a day. I discounted the notion that unemployment in the Inland Empire was 12 – 14 % by wrapping my mind around the fact that 88% of the population in the state was employed and that I was just like that percentage. I was educated, clean and sober and had worked very hard on myself each and every day for the past two and half years through utilizing the 12-step program. Although my character defects were not gone, they were improving, I was more aware of them, and was making progress one day at a time. I believed that if I was in harmony with the universe, I would accomplish my goals.

Five weeks had passed since I had decided to make my job to find a job. I applied for and was interviewed for a job as Supervisor / Manager in Production for a bottling company in San Bernardino. After a couple of day's salary negotiations, I accepted the job I was offered. The job was 53 miles from the house and I commuted back and forth from work each day. I worked six days a week, approximately ten hours a day. I got up each morning at 3:15 a.m., dressed, went outside to meditate and gave thanks to my Higher Power. I would read portions of The Secret and said a prayer before I left for work at 4:25 a.m. I had a very positive outlook on my life and carried that into the Plant each and every day. I found that my positive outlook seemed to increase my group's production over a short period of time.

The hours were long, the trip was long, but the money was good. Empowering the workforce was a constant battle; helping them understand that they needed to change the way they were thinking and that it was team effort. To believe that we could reach higher levels of efficiency and over time we would produce at least 98% efficiency levels on some days would take some work, but I felt was doable. I could take this example and recognize their ability with a tangible event as proof. This was very rewarding to be able to accomplish. My boss wanted to move me up in the organization and had asked the Operations Manager who was in Texas to speak with me but even after he said that he wanted to, the conversation never materialized. We met for a brief period of time several times on the production floor. My thought was that he knew that I was transgendered and I know how the majority of people in the South feel about that issue. They are very closed minded, possibly due to their lack of education on the issue. It created a tremendous amount of fear, prejudice and hostility within them. It seemed to be the nature of the beast and still in 2011, the sign of the times in which we lived. It was still unacceptable regardless.

After four months of working it occurred to me that I was not really contributing a lot to society or myself. I was attending less 12-step meetings because of being so exhausted after I got home from work each day between 4:30 – 5:30 p.m. I felt that I could do so much better and it would be very meaningful to share my life with the world in the hopes that I could help another person walk through their fears. Maybe I could help families understand some of the trials and tribulations of a transgendered woman and the deep rooted philosophies of society that must be overcome by the transgendered individual and those they affect. Therefore, from a deeper spiritual place through meditation and prayer I was led back to writing. I notified the company that I was going to leave in two weeks because I was going to finish writing my book. I think too that I had been in operations management for 27 years and felt it was time for me to move forward and share my experience, strength, and hope. It seemed far more important to me. I had to trust my Higher Power that it was the right move for me and that financial insecurity would not creep back into my life. I made a decision to turn my will and life over to my Higher Power and to write one paragraph at a time and ask for the words each and every day.

I worked my first week of the notice and my boss picked my brain about continuous improvements and how to make the facility better. He wanted to know how they could keep me and I gave him a high figure; his response was to explain that there was no possible way the company could give me the raise I requested to keep me. I was finally off on Saturday, walked out the door Friday and told everyone I would see them on Monday for my final week. I made it back to Palm Springs feeling really good that I was off for two days and went to my 12-step meeting and then returned home and went straight to bed.

Chapter 30 - Tragedy Strikes Our Family

On Saturday, June 11, 2011, at 7:00 a.m. my cell phone rang and woke me up but I could not get to it in time to answer it so I rolled back over and slept another 30 minutes. When I got up, I walked over to the kitchen area of my studio apartment and picked up the phone and listened to the voice mail. It was my brother David and his message was "please call me as soon as you get this message". Naturally my first thoughts were that something had happened to my mother. I took a few deep breaths, meditated for a few minutes to prepare myself for the worst, and steeled myself for the return call.

I called him back and said David, "this cannot be good." He said that "it was not good." It was bad news about Ann's son, Robert Warren. "He had fatally shot himself in the head with a shotgun early this morning." I was stunned! He was only 17 years old! I did not know what to say, what to think, what to do; I just burst into tears. I told him I would contact Ann as soon as possible. I called her after I finished crying so that I could at least be coherent. It was hard to believe because I just had Thanksgiving and Christmas dinner with him and he was so alive and full of life. We joked about the moose that I told him lived in my backyard when he visited as a little fellow. It was unimaginable. I called Ann and she asked me to come to Richmond to be with her. I told her I would be there. I immediately called Beverly and she came over and helped me by finding me a flight and going with me to find a couple of appropriate black dresses that I could wear to the funeral.

Beverly dropped me off at the Palm Springs International Airport at 6:30 a.m. on Sunday morning and I was on an American Airlines flight to Dallas before I caught a connecting flight to Richmond. I landed in Richmond, Virginia at 5:30 p.m. eastern time and my brother David met me once I exited the plane. We discussed the events that had taken place the day before and the condition of our sister. David took me to his house and I saw my nephews Hunter and Patrick and my niece Julia for the first time in six years. Prior to my arrival David and his wife Melanie had explained to their children that their Uncle John was coming for the funeral but that Uncle John was now a female and was now named Aunt Kaitlin. I did not know the particulars of the conversation only that this was a giant leap for David and Melanie. They were accepting to a certain degree, but they had not discussed this issue with the children until now. The children were wonderful and anxious to meet me. Julia was so cute and in the third grade, Patrick was older and in elementary school and Hunter was in the Governor's High School. The plan was for me to stay at their house for the week. Shortly thereafter, David took me over to Ann's house and she was so very happy to see me. I told Ann that I was only there to help her and although the majority of my family did not want to have anything to do with me, I was there for her and would help her in any way. She told me she loved me and thanked me for coming and asked me if I would stay with her this week and I agreed.

The crowd of people in Ann's house slowly disappeared as the evening progressed. I sat on the front steps of her house with Colleen, the youngest of the four children and listened to her. She was very close to her brother and said that they had just recently formed a pact to be friends forever. During the day she had walked down to Warren's favorite place in the woods near their house where he would fish and she was looking for a "sign" with the hopes of understanding that he was fine. Then suddenly a bolt of lightning clashed and she wanted to know if that meant he was fine. I reassured her that Warren was speaking to her and was in a good place. It was about 11:00 p.m. before Ann and I could really talk privately and she explained the details of her son's suicide. That he had just finished taking his SAT's for college admissions, had taken something to stay up and study, just broke up with his girlfriend, and had gotten into some medication that was in his Dad's house. He was in the basement of the house, lying on the floor under a blanket when the shotgun he was holding went off. We discussed that we both believed that

328

in our understanding of our Higher Power, there were no mistakes, and all we could do from this point forward was to cherish and celebrate his life. We discussed the need to be in acceptance and live for today in love and gratitude for the things that the universe has given us. Ann had been awake for the last 36 hours and needed to sleep so I encouraged her to lie down and try to get some rest.

On Monday morning, the neighbors and friends started dropping by at 11:00 a.m. to check on Ann and the children. Some brought food, some flowers, and some simply brought their condolences. There was a huge amount of food from the day before, enough to fill two refrigerators. Needless to say no one went hungry with all the rolls, hams, and casseroles people had brought. We ate anytime we needed to throughout the day. The priest came by and discussed the funeral with Ann, Jacob, and the children. The children selected the reading and songs for the mass which was being held at the Cathedral of the Sacred Heart in downtown Richmond.

Ann asked me to go with her to Joseph Bliley Funeral Home with the family around 5:00 p.m. because Warren would be available for a viewing for the immediate family only. We piled into three cars and went off to the funeral home. We were greeted at the door of the funeral home and escorted to the area where Warren was at rest. We sat outside the chambers as the funeral director told us that his head was covered and they had done the best they could to put his face back together. John Richard (Cub), the eldest of the children, spoke up and told his mom and dad that he would go in and look at his face and would recommend the removal of the blinder. John Richard came back out and said no, it really does not look like him. So the blinders stayed on and we filed into the chamber and we all cried, held hands, prayed, and asked for God's mercy on his innocent soul. It was a very sad occasion. It took me to a place of deep sorrow for Warren, his brothers and sister, Ann and Jacob. It made me so very grateful that I had spared my own life when I had reached the point of "to be or not to be" because of my own transgendered issues. I understood that place where you fear society, work, and your own family because you are different and you lose hope that anyone else will ever understand. It's a very lonely place to be and try to live from, but it happens every day with our prejudices towards others. I have always thought that we were supposed to love one another as our Higher Power has loved us. The infliction of fear to change behavior is absolutely unconscionable but it is used as a driving force.

I was there to help my sister and the family and that is exactly what I did. Later that night, I discussed with Ann the way I felt when I had that 9mm stuck to my head in a drunken state and how easy it is to go there when one feels destined for hell. Fortunately for me I needed to live my life as me. Those of us in the transgendered community did not understand why we were this way, but we all felt that we were born this way. It is truly a bondage of self that will only allow for life to be meaningful when we stop living a lie and become our true self. It was imperative to fix ourselves and to truly be able to love ourselves so that we may one day radiate that love to others. I think that for much of my life, I did not love myself therefore it was very difficult and probably impossible to show love to another human being. Although I thought that I was doing just that, it was not the deep radiation from within. I had treated my spouses and children with love that I did not know existed until the past couple of years I had found for me. It was the breaking of the chain of being inside the box in my thoughts from the core of my family unit.

Ann and I discussed unconditional love and how we both understood that love and gratitude were two of the secrets of a harmonious life. I accepted the fact that I could not visit with them and that I had to respect their request, especially since I had asked for acceptance, I had to give acceptance as well.

We discussed the priest who told my dad that he had to love me. I explained to Ann that today, I embrace that love and hold on to it inside me because I can build from that point. I could feel the love that I have always wanted from my dad. I reasoned

330

that a parent must love their child regardless of who they are and rather than sit in self-pity and ask incessantly, "why don't you love me?" I had to flip it in my mind. It all came from the way I thought and no one could change my thinking but me. It had been so helpful to look at the positive side of life rather than the negative all the time. When I thought good and positive thoughts, there was no room for the bad or the negative ones. I could only think one thought at a time and millions in a day but I tried very hard to make them all positive through vigilant practice. I could stop the negative simply by realizing that my thoughts were negative and to take measures to turn them around immediately. This only came from constant work, practice, focus, and concentration. Even in this tragedy I told Ann we had to live our life with love and gratitude. We had to seek out the positive things in ourselves and try to understand that there are no mistakes in God's world. We had to be grateful for the time that we all had with Warren and remember all the great qualities he possessed. His life may have been taken so that he could somehow save the lives of others. We had to believe that this was the truth; it somehow helped give meaning to his death. We sat quietly together for a while, both lost in our thoughts of Warren and the day's events. We finally got up both with tear filled eyes, and wordlessly hugged each other and went to our rooms for a very sleepless night.

Diane had come to Richmond Monday evening and was staying with Brandon and Stephanie. She called early Tuesday morning and asked if she could help out in anyway. I told her the time of the viewing and the service so she could attend with our family. She took the information but called back an hour later and asked if they could come over and help out around the house. Diane and Stephanie came by and offered to clean the house for Ann, which I thought was so very kind.

I wore a conservative black dress with black stockings and heels. Jocob, Ann, and the children were all ready at 3:30 p.m. and we drove over in three cars. I felt a bit of anxiety because I knew my parents and siblings would be there however, Ann, David and I had discussed this previously and I told them I was there to help and support my sister and her children. When we arrived I sat in the second row on the side of the room where the family was greetings other family and friends. The casket was off to my left and directly in front of me was a television screen with pictures of Warren showing him in various places and in different phases of his life.

My Mother and Father came into the room and they seated themselves on the other side of the chapel but in direct view of me. I saw the glare in my Father's eyes as he looked directly at me; the tension felt as if it could be cut with a chainsaw! This was the first time I had seen my Mother and Father since the day they told me to never come back on January 6, 2006. It had been five and half years; two and half of those years had been total hell for me. I do not think they will ever realize the pain I went through when I was thrown out of the family and the total abandonment I felt. However on the flip side, I understood that I too had caused them great pain. But for me it was a life or death matter. My brothers with their wives sat next to my parents as did my older of the two sisters. David, Melanie, and the children were in their own group between us.

It was interesting that I was at peace and I think it had come from the way I thought and the experiences of working on myself for three years. I had come to terms with everything and accepted everything and finally was able to love myself. The fear, guilt, shame, and anxiety that I had felt from years before were no longer present. I sat quietly and patiently and got up once an hour to walk outside to smoke a cigarette with one of Ann's really good friends. Outside with Claudia we discussed the laws of the universe, light, darkness, love, service and the things that I had learned in my program and studies. The thing about her was that she knew these principals and had been practicing them all her life and she was very successful in her ventures. It was amazing to me.

As I sat, my friend Paul and his sister Sue came up and sat down with me. I had not seen him in over 30 years. We quietly talked about our times as children and he complimented me on my appearance. He wanted to keep in touch so we exchanged our information. My Aunt's Rosemary and Margaret Ann sat with me separately for a while and asked me about California and if I was happy. I told them about Palm Springs and admitted to be very happy now that I was living a truthful life. They told me about their lives over the past five years and it was heart-warming to be able to talk with them again. My cousin Kathy sat down and told me everything that was going on with her and her mother Maryanne. My mother's best friend and her husband spoke and asked if I was happy with my new life and when I said I was they smiled warmly and wished me well. Their two daughters, Michelle and Joan, also spoke to me with great kindness.

There were so many people at the viewing that the greeting line to speak with Ann and her family continued until 9:00 p.m. During the entire three hours my father walked around and stood in front of where I was seated and looked at Warren's pictures on the television with the grandchildren. He never once acknowledged my presence or even said one word to me. My mother, other brothers and sister, their spouses and children did not acknowledge my presences either; they walked around as if I did not exist. I had flown here from California to support my sister and family. I had no expectations whatsoever of being reunited with my family. I did hope that an amends could be made but that never happened, not on this day. That night as I laid my head on the pillow, I was ever so grateful to have seen my parents and siblings once again, even under such horrible circumstances. This was as good as it was going to get and I was very grateful and I held on to it. I thought how sad of a situation that Ann has lost her son and that was what it took to bring us all together. I decided to look at it as a step toward progress instead of one of negativity. The last time we were all together was Christmas Day 2005. I had made a formal amends to my family in 2008 and I wanted to be sure that I kept my side of the street clean.

My daughter Rebecca drove up from Charlotte, NC on Wednesday morning and arrived at Ann's house just before noon. The funeral was scheduled for 3:00 p.m. and we had plenty of time to talk. I had not seen Rebecca in about eight months and I was happy that she could make the time to attend. Rebecca drove me downtown to attend the funeral and as we walked the three blocks from the parking deck and met Diane, Stephanie, Brandon, and Wyatt at the entrance to the church. We found David and Melanie with Ann in the back of the church as we waited for the funeral to begin. My Mother and Father came in and stood about 25 feet in front of us with their back turned toward me. The pall bearers brought in the casket and we followed them in to the front of the church and took our seats; I sat with Rebecca and Diane and my brothers and sister were in the pew right behind me.

The Funeral Mass was beautiful and Warren's three siblings participated in the service by reading scriptures from the podium. The priest had kind words about Warren and talked not knowing why a young man was taken so soon but explained that it was all part of God's plan. Jacob spoke to the attendees and there was great pain coming from his heart about how much he loved Warren and how much it hurt him so deeply that he was gone.

Ann then approached the podium and spoke these words: "My friends who know me well, knew I would have to get up and speak today. We now know that Warren took a drug for which he did not have a prescription. And the result of taking that drug was a chemical imbalance that stripped away his inner strength, his resilience. No one is to blame. No one in this room is to blame. So if you are sitting there thinking that you said something, or didn't say something, or did something or didn't do something that caused him to do this, you are wrong. No one is to blame. I've forgiven him for what he did and you need to also."

"Many of you have asked me how I have been able to hold up and get through this. Well, I'll tell you. Very early on, I chose to focus on what I had been given by God and not what I lost. I am focusing on the 17 wonderful years I had with that sweet boy. I have to focus with gratitude on what I had, not what I lost. It is the only decent way to live."

"Many, most of you, have come to me and asked what you can do and how you can help. And you have told me that you would do anything, anything I asked. Well, I have a job for each and every one of you."

"I want you to think about the worst relationship you have in your life. The person you just cannot accept for some reason. The person you cannot accept because they are different from you, or they do not dress the way you think they should or they don't think the way you think or believe something you don't agree with. The person you just cannot accept. Or that person who has hurt you so badly, even if they have hurt you so much that you are justified at being angry at them. I want you to contact them and repair the relationship, forgive them and accept them."

One of my favorite quotes is:

> *When the time*
> *Of our particular sunset comes*
> *Our things, our accomplishments*
> *Won't really matter a great deal*
> *But the clarity and care*
> *With which we have loved others*
> *Will speak with vitality*
> *Of the great gift of life*
> *We have been to each other.*

After her eloquent poem, she finished:

Now you don't have to tell me when you do this; but if you want to tell me about it, then that would be fine too. And I know you will do it, because, you see, you've told me you would. You already told me you would do anything for me. And this is what I'm asking you to do. Do it for me. Do it for Warren, that sweet, kind, gentle, compassionate soul. Love each other with clarity and care so that it will speak with vitality for the great gift of life we have been for each other.

Ann was looking directly at my parents, brothers, and sister when she was talking from the podium.

At the end of the Mass we all followed the casket out the doors of the church and I stood on the steps and looked at all the people. Rebecca walked over to her Grandfather and Grandmother and spoke with them for a while. This is the first time they had seen each other in 15 years. I stood alone on the steps and watched and walked out to the sidewalk and waited for Rebecca. We were all going back to Ann's house to take part in a reception.

At the reception Rebecca was getting reacquainted with her cousins. Diane, Stephanie, and I fixed a plate of food and sat down at the table in the kitchen. My mother and father were on the other side of the kitchen and my dad fixed a plate and went outside on the front steps. My mother went into the dining room with my brother and sister. Diane finished, walked out front and sat down with my Dad and had a conversation I was not privy too. Once I was finished eating I parked myself in a chair on the screened in porch. I sat there for an hour and a half. My two Aunt's, Rosemary and Margaret Ann sat and talked about their lives. Margaret Ann had lost her son about 10 years ago and was discussing it. My sister came out to the porch for a couple of minutes and sat down and asked me how I was doing and told me about her knee surgery and left. My brother came out to say good bye to Rosemary and as he turned to leave, asked how I was doing and I said I was doing really well. Then everyone was gone except the abundance of food.

I visited with Rebecca and rode up Three Chop Road to the gas station and we filled her car. Rebecca was getting ready to drive back to Charlotte that evening because she had to be back to work the next day. I told her how beautiful she looked and how grateful I was that she had come. I asked her to call me when she arrived back home and then I told her that she had a wonderful future ahead of her. I told her that she could be anything she wanted to be, she just needed to do the footwork.

We cleaned the kitchen, stored the food in a cooler and the refrigerator. I made two plates for my mother and father but they had already left so I stored it in the refrigerator in case they came back the next day. I talked with Diane on the phone that night and I told her I had made plates for mom and dad and considered taking it to them, to their home. Diane was honest with me and told me that would not be a good idea. I remembered that she had had a conversation with my father, so I took her advice and did not take the plates. I explained to Diane that I had made the plates because she told me earlier that my father was not eating very well because my mother was forgetting to make meals. My mother was diagnosed with dementia and had always had the fear of Alzheimer's ever since I can remember. My grandmother had Alzheimer's and for some reason my mom thought it was a genetic conclusion that she would inherit it.

On Thursday I began the arduous task of cleaning the house, consolidating the food into larger containers, and making space for the new food by giving away and eating the old food. The worst of the day was that Warren's body was being cremated. Ann and Jacob were at the funeral home and afterwards, came home and collapsed. I went off to see my endocrinologist that I loved so dearly; this wasn't unusual as I typically made an appointment with him every time I came back to Richmond. I needed to get out of the house and feel just a bit of "normalcy" if that were possible, so I called that morning and he had a cancellation. Afterwards Ann and I spent the remainder of the afternoon and evening in the kitchen or on the porch together. Her good friend from work and in the neighborhood stopped by and the door was constantly revolving until midnight.

On Friday I stayed around Ann's house all day. I cleaned the house and then prepared myself for the trip back to California on Saturday morning. Ann, Jacob, and the children went to St. Paul's Catholic Church at 10:00 a.m. Warren's urn was being placed in the wall of the church at 11:00a.m. Ann just wanted her immediate family present, but my mother and father showed up anyway. During the burial a cat came and lay down beside the urn and Warren loved cats. Ann was especially moved by this and came home to tell me all about it.

Ann told me she wanted me to know Mom and Dad were invited to come by after the service. I told her that was great and asked if they knew I was still in town and she said she did not know. I was sitting on the back porch when my parents came into the kitchen. My father took one look at me and sat down with his back right shoulder facing me. My mom sat down across from him and looked out the picture window glass onto the porch right at me. Ann told me that she my mother and father had this conversation:

"Well I believe that's John sitting out there", my mother excitedly exclaimed.

My father haphazardly glanced over his shoulder, barely looking in the vicinity my mother indicated and sort of gruffed in response, "Hrrumph, where I don't see him".

"Yes, yes I do believe it IS John" my mother said adamantly.

My father, very agitated, got up from the table and said, "It's time to go, get your things, we're leaving, end of discussion".

Without a word, Ann handed father the two plates of food I had made for them and he took them from her hand. My mother got up from the chair, hesitated one final moment, and looked right at me as though she wanted to say something, thought better of it, and headed out the same door they had entered. The last thing I saw was the back of their heads as they disappeared from the kitchen. My father never once even glanced my way...

I went with Ann's family to Colleen's middle school graduation and afterward's we all went to a very fine Italian restaurant. It was very nice and when we came home Ann went out to buy some apple cider and her friend Claudia came over and they drank into the morning. I went upstairs and packed my bags because David was picking me up at 8:30 a.m. to take me to the airport for my return trip to Palm Springs.

Final Return Home: A Time for Healing

It was 101 degrees at my layover in Dallas. I walked outside the terminal to have a smoke and spoke with a young soldier on his way back to Afghanistan. He was 27 years old and serving his third tour of duty overseas. I thanked him for his service and listened to his stories of home and the horrors of war. When I arrived in Palm Springs, it was 110 degrees and I thought I was going to melt! Beverly picked me up from the airport and I was ever so grateful for her air conditioned car! It had been a rough week, but I felt progress had been made between me and my family. Sadly the progress came on the heels of a very devastating loss for my sister and us all.

That night in my studio apartment room at the sober living house, I thanked my Higher Power for allowing me to see my family for the first time in five and half years. It did not matter if they spoke to me or not, it was still very gratifying. For my amends to my family, I told them that I loved them very much and I just sincerely wished they could realize how very much! I poured my unconditional love out to them all in Richmond and I was so grateful to have been of service.

Working in harmony with my Higher Power, my love, gratitude, acceptance and truth, all started with me and it was a feeling that can only come from within. This has truly been a release from the bondage of self.

Chapter 31 - Healing in North Carolina

I made an amends to Kathleen in April 2012 by writing her a letter to let her know that I thought she was a wonderful mother to our children and that she was right in so many respects during the time we were married. I told her she could see the dysfunction of my family long before I even realized it and that I was truly sorry for the pain that I had caused her. I never received a response but hoped that my amends could bring about some healing some 21 years after our divorce. It was long overdue but needed to be stated as my character defect of procrastination had taken hold for many years.

My son Mark, who I had not seen since his Master's graduation from the University of South Carolina in May 2007, called me a month previous and told me that he was going to marry Jessica on August 11, 2012. Since Mark had been too busy to see me the last three times I was in North Carolina I had an understanding that he was very embarrassed about me, his father, now having gender reassignment surgery and living as a female. I asked Mark, "Do you want me to attend your wedding"? Then the most precious words came over the cell phone, "Yes". I told him, "I will be there"! He told me about his new job as a District Manager for a food chain and that he was going to relocate from Charlotte to Raleigh so he could work his district. It was a very pleasant conversation and I was very grateful and happy to be included in this event.

As the month of August was rapidly approaching, I was editing this book and felt as if something was missing from my story and realized that this upcoming event could be the final chapter for now. I have learned by working my program with prayer and meditation I need not be in fear but to walk through it with courage and dignity. However, some fear began to creep into my life as the calendar changed to July. That fear was that I was going back to North Carolina where the environment may not be friendly toward me. A transgendered woman, seeing Kathleen and many former neighbors, including Mark's in laws all of which I knew but they had not meet Kaitlin. I had fear of rejection but I also knew that I wanted to be a part of my children's life and make a living amends to them. I had to go through this for my own sake and walk through this wonderful opportunity. I had fear of leaving Zeb because he was having some difficulty in walking but made arrangements for a friend to stay with him in my condominium while I was gone. Although these thoughts were present in my mind it was not like the fear from the past, it was one of great anticipation of righting a wrong of not being there for Mark and Rebecca when they were teenagers.

Kathleen called John while he was at my house in July and she was making arrangements for him to get to Banner Elk, NC for the wedding. I asked to speak to her and we talked about having John fly with me on the flights that I had already booked. She asked me, "when are you coming" and I told her "Wednesday, August 8th". I gave her the flight numbers and she stated she "would try to book that for John".

I asked Kathleen, because I was unsure, "Can I come to the rehearsal dinner"?

"When are you coming to Banner Elk"?

"Friday morning".

"Well, you can come to the rehearsal dinner but it's probably would not be a good idea. Mark and Rebecca have not told their friends about you and this wedding is about Mark and Jessica and it is not about you. So you should only come to the wedding and you must keep a low profile because the focus needs to be on them".

Crying, I realized that my children were still embarrassed about me. I said, "I agree".

Then she talked with John about picking him up Thursday in Charlotte and asked if he could stay with me Wednesday night. I told John that he could stay with me at Diane's house in Concord.

I needed to be careful with my money because it had been a while since I had earned any money because I needed time to write. I had not made arrangements to get from Charlotte to Banner Elk and was thinking that I could use my 1995 Ford F 150 that I had given Diane to make the two and a half hour trip. But the next morning in quiet mediation, I realized that this trip was not about money rather one of healing and love. I reserved a rental car and called the Mountain Lodge in Banner Elk and made reservations.

I called Kathleen and told her, "I can bring John to Banner Elk on Friday and that he can stay in the hotel room with me so you do not have to pick him up or find him a room".

"Ok, that will be fine".

She stated, "You can come to the rehearsal dinner but you will have to maintain a low profile with the children".

"I want to come to the rehearsal dinner and I am not about the grandiosity so we can play it by ear when I get there".

"Fine".

"Ok, have a great day". "Bye".

I thought to myself, this is a huge lesson for me because it truly is about love. It's about gratitude for being included and it's about what I can give, not what I can receive. For me I can take my place and radiate the joy, happiness, and love from within and hopefully it will be felt so that all will share in the peace.

I had my long halfway down my back platinum blond hair toned down with the assistance of my hairstylist Jamie who applied Carmel lowlights. On August 3rd, I took a shopping trip to the Outlet Mall in Cabazon. I asked my friend Beverly to accompany me on this shopping trip as she once owned a Wedding Service in El Segundo, CA. At Coldwater Creek, I purchase two beautiful earth tone outfits perfect for the North Carolina Mountains. Then, I went over to the shoe store for beige two inch wedged heeled Taos. They were beautiful. I was going to wear the linen outfit to the rehearsal dinner and the wide legs pants suit to the wedding.

Beverly's son, Donovan, came over the night before the trip because I wanted to instruct him on how to look after Zeb. I showed him the method of preparing his food and the administering of his glucosamine and medications. Also, on the fact that it was forecasted to be 114 degree in Palm Springs during the week and Zeb could only go out multiple time during the day for only a couple of minutes. When the sun went behind the Mountain in the evening then he could stay out longer.

My son John and his girlfriend Roberta picked me up at my house in Palm Springs at 730 a.m. and she dropped us off at the airport. Luke and Gabe, two of my friends were on the same flight to Phoenix. They were flying to Atlanta and we were on our way to Charlotte. The four of us had lunch together in Sky Harbor before heading to the gate. The flight was uneventful and I landed in Charlotte at 715pm. Once in a rent a car we drove up I-85 over to Concord to Diane's house.

Once we passed the Fire House on Gold Hill Road and made a left onto gravel and tar road and while avoiding the pot holes. We approached the pond where the road circles around it. We took it right, around the pond and at the opposite end of entry was Diane's beautiful white two story wood frame house. With the spot light on it looked the same as it did two years ago, only that the Leyland cypress trees that I had planted had grown several more feet. Alisha, my step-daughter was sitting in the dark in a Cracker Barrel rocker with a cushion on the front porch behind the white wooden rails and we did not know she was there until she said, "hello". Diane walked out the front storm door and I gave her a kiss and a huge and did the same to MJ and Oddie. Alisha walked over and hugged us both. They were very happy to see us. We sat, talked, and caught up with each other until 1am and then we all went to bed.

Thursday, John took the rental over to South Park Mall and met his mother and Rebecca for lunch. They shopped for about two hours and John came back to Diane's house about 5pm with several bags of pants, shorts, underwear, and a belt. Meanwhile, Diane and I ventured out to the bank, drive thru cigarette shop, Tractor Supply, Aldi, a food store, and over to Mr. C's to get the famous Carolina Burger. Alisha was working and we were all back together by 6pm and we cooked pork chops and sausage on the grill and Diane made her famous stewed potatoes and Alisha her zucchini.

The next morning John and I were up at 8am and we drank two pots of coffee between us and loaded up the Grey Ford Fusion rental with our suitcases and computer and started our journey to Banner Elk, NC. We drove over to Huntersville to pick up I-77 and headed north, stopping in Statesville, and over to Boone where Appalachian State University is located. We stopped at the Hess gas station in Boone and I gingerly went into the ladies restroom after giving John some money to buy us a soft drink. The car now filled with gas we went up two stoplights and turned left and we were 12 miles from Banner Elk. Boone and Banner Elk are west of the Blue Ridge Parkway. Banner Elk is in Avery County which is the last county in North Carolina before crossing over to Tennessee and I refer to this area as moonshine country. I was a little cautious but went about my business as usual while being aware of the environment and not looking for the good ole boys. Finally, up the Tynecastle Highway and drove about 2 miles passed Sugar Mountain, a ski resort, to the Evergreen's Mountain Lodge in Banner Elk. On Sugar Mountain there was a tall skyscraper towering high above the mountain and below it built into the side of the mountain was a beautiful large looking estate that must have been the resort. A golf course was nestled down in a valley below the resort.

The clerk at the front desk gave us a paper bag which had a handle and a gold "R" embossed on the side that contained one beer from Blowing Rock Brewery, a Sun Drop soda, two Moon pies, and two packs of Lance peanut butter crackers which was a gift from the bride and groom. Our room was on the second floor and we parked the car in front of the room, unloaded the trunk, and proceeded up the steps to the room. Using the electronic card John swiped the door unlocked and we found our place of rest for the next two nights. There were two queen sized beds that the mattresses were puffed up in the middle and John said, "There is a hill in my bed", and we laughed. The carpet was a deep burgundy color and the furniture was typical Southern hardwood, North Carolina style. I put the beer and soda in the refrigerator.

I hung up my clothes, showed John the outfit I was wearing tonight for the dinner and then opened my suitcase and walked out the door and stood on the balcony looking at the mountains. Unknown to me at the time, I was facing Beech Mountain which was about a mile away. It was beautiful, green, and full of trees and at the top it came to a point and stood high and mighty. Three-fourths of the way up Beech Mountain I could see the face of beautiful homes or estates that were lined up straight across. I pulled out my cell phone while admiring the beauty and texted my son Mark and told him I was in Banner Elk and gave him my room number. The Mountain Lodge is where the invited guest was staying and the wedding planners had worked out a special price for us all.

I walked back into the room and John was calling his mother to see what his instructions were for the remainder of the day. I could hear her through the cell phone as he told her the room number that he was in.

Kathleen told John, "You are the Best Man and need to come down to my room and get your clothes. We are leaving for the Rehearsal at 430 pm so you need to be dressed and we will drive you over".

"Ok, I will come down in a little while. How about Dad, what time and where should he show up"?

Through the phone came, "He said he was not coming until Saturday and we do not have him on the list to attend".

I thought to myself and did not say anything "he", so that's the way it is going to be.

John hung up the phone and said, "She said you are not on the list and cannot come. "That is bullshit, you came all the way from California and you have to sit in your room! I really feel bad for you."

"It's ok son, you go and have a good time, and I'll find something to do."

It did hurt but when I left California I knew that I could not have any expectations and needed to be grateful that at least I was invited to the wedding on Saturday and the Farewell Brunch on Sunday. It was a great lesson to have learned, especially from my trip to Richmond a year ago, that if I stopped fighting everything and everyone that things have a way of working themselves out. Although, very disappointing, I remained calm and accepted things for the way they are.

John went down to his mother's room, picked up his clothes and came back within thirty minutes. We stood on the balcony look out toward the mountains and it vast array of green. My room was five rooms from the staircase that led down to the parking lot and I heard someone coming up the steps and I turned and it was Mark, who is now 29 years old. He walked a little side to side in his 5'7" stocky frame, almost square like, short light brown hair, blue eyes, in his beige pants and blue with white striped collared golf shirt and smiled. Immediately, I walked fast towards him and gave him a hug that lasted for about a minute. This was huge for me because Mark had not seen me since the transition, just after his graduation from college.

"I am so happy to see you! "It has been a long time. "How are you doing Mark?"

"I am doing great and just finished playing golf over at Sugar Mountain. I got your text and wanted to come by and say hello."

The words were unbelievable to me and touched my heart deeply and I felt the emotion being forgiven and love at that time.

Mark walked into the room with John and I and opened up the refrigerator and I told him he could have that beer but he said, "I have already had six on the golf course and I have to get ready for the rehearsal soon."

He sat down on the bed and I in the chair and told him that "it had been way to long for me to see him."

"That's ok."

"No it is not ok, I am just so grateful to see you now."

He told me that he shot, "three over par and missed three putts that he should have made" and then discussed me playing golf with him one day.

"You will have to tee them up from the blue and hit them straight down the middle if you are going to play with us."

"I can play with the best of you."

He looked at his watch and said, "I have to go and get ready now."

"You know that I am not going to able to come to the Rehearsal dinner tonight. I just want you to know that I would really like to be there but as long as you know that I am willing then it will be alright."

"Yea, ok, I am going to have to go. I wanted to come by and say hello".

"Ok, see you soon."

Mark left and John started to get ready for the rehearsal. All the groomsmen wore khaki pants, white shirts, orange ties, and brown Docksider's, slip on shoes. I thought that it was interesting because my outfit was the same colors. I was very grateful that Mark had come by and I know that it took a lot of courage on his part because of the years of separation and then finally meeting his father as a female. It restored my hope for the weekend, make it a little easier to swallow the initial pill of rejection, a chance to reconnect and he added to the joy that was in my heart.

After John dressed and was ready to go we stepped out on the balcony to enjoy the cool weather, he was getting ready to walk over to his mother's room. Mark was three doors from my room and I heard him as he stepped out on the balcony in a beige suit that matched the groomsmen. He walked over to me and I pulled out my cell phone which had a camera and took a picture of him. He was having a great time, joking with his friends, and drinking a Coors's Light. He was extremely happy and it just flowed out of him. I watched Mark and his groomsmen walk down the steps, heading for the Rehearsal. John too, had walked down the balcony and out of sight. As I pondered on the balcony, I saw Kathleen and her boyfriend drive by and she was looking right at me and I waved but there was no wave back. As the car passed I spotted John sitting in the back seat as they rounded the corner of the building.

I thought to myself and hoped that they would all have a good time. I reminded myself that I need not have any expectations and to just be grateful for being there. I said the serenity prayer and went inside and sat disappointed for a while but not one of self-pity which I used to do all the time. It was more of a feeling of just being with me and I turned on the television and watched the Atlanta Braves play baseball. I pulled out a resume that a friend asked me to edit and worked on it for a while. Eventually, I opened the refrigerator and opened the Sun Drop soda, ate the pack of peanut butter crackers, and the Moon Pie. This would be my rehearsal dinner as I did not feel like venturing out alone nor did I feel it to be wise. The baseball game had just ended when John came back to the room and we walked out on the balcony again and I asked him about the Rehearsal.

"I am the Best Man and we had dinner at some winery and they severed chicken."

"Did you have a nice time?"

"Yes, but I am ready to go back to Charlotte."

"Really"

"Yes, I just feel more comfortable there and beside it bullshit that you could not come to the dinner."

"John, please do not worry about me it is fine."

About thirty minutes later Mark appeared again at my door and said, "Come on down to the party at the bar, that is where everyone will be."

"Well, maybe so..." it was thumbs up and he was off. By this time it was raining outside and I stepped out again with John and he said, "Come on let's to the party."

"I don't know John, if I should, I am not dressed."

"Mark invited you."

"Well, let me get dressed and I will go down there but you have to come with me."

It was rainy and cold outside so I put on a nice pair of jeans, long sleeve black top, and wore a jacket as John and I walked down the steps to the lobby which had a brick floor a couple of sofas and a counter where the clerk stood waiting for guests. Through the lobby was French doors that led to a restaurant and bar area with tables, chairs, and booths beyond the dining area behind a glass wall was the bar and there were about 30 people in this area celebrating with the soon to be newlywed couple. Beside the glass wall was a table set up with stainless steel pans that were covered and a burner was turned on underneath to keep it contents warm. Kathleen was standing there to the entrance of the bar next to the table and I saw my daughter Rebecca through the glass before saying to Kathleen, "hello, how are doing?"

"I am doing fine, how are you."

"I am well."

"You should not be here. Mark and Rebecca have not told their friends about you and this is not the time or place for you to show up. Rebecca is here with her future in-laws and does not want to have to explain to them who you are. I think that you need to go."

Understanding that I do not want to fight anyone or anything I simply said, "Thank You". I turned around and walked back to my room the same way that I came. John, who was close by turned with me as I walked out.

"What happened?"

"Your mom said that I should not be there". Hey, this is her party. John, I have stopped going to places that I am not welcomed. Son, you have to go where the love is and this is not it. I have to live with love and tolerance and respect personal boundaries and that is what I need to do".

He followed me up to the room and said, "That is bullshit, what are you going to do stay in the room the whole time. All the way from California and you have to stay in the room that's bullshit…" Then John went back downstairs to the party.

I lay on the bed and turned on the television and flipped through the channels and found a station on cable broadcasting the news from Charlotte. A station that I would always watched when I lived there. The door to the balcony was cracked opened as I could hear their partying going on outside. Mark knocked on the door and opened it and sat down on the bed across from me while drinking a beer from a large glass.

"I went downstairs to the party but your Mom told me that you were embarrassed for me to be there. So, I left. I am not here to embarrass you, I am here for you."

"I am not embarrassed and I do not care if you are gay or transgendered. This wedding is for Jessica and I do not want to have to spend my time explaining to everyone who you are. I respect Mom but she does not speak for me. You are an invited guest, I invited you".

Mark's phone rang and he told the person who called, "I'll be back down in 5 minutes, just give me 5 minutes". Mark stayed for an hour and fifteen minutes and we talked and his phone kept ringing and he kept telling each person, "I'll be back in 5 minutes".

He said, "Let's get it straight, Mom was there for me and you were not. I wanted a home with a Mother and a Father but it did not happen. I respect Mom and I listen to her".

"So, what can I do now?"

"What do you mean?"

"As a parent? Offer advise?"

"As a parent? You were not there for me so I am not there for you. As far as offering advice, I have Mom and I talk with her about things, and I have my friends as you can see so if I need advice or to talk I will talk to mom then my friends, and then maybe you."

"What can I do to somehow restore our relationship?"

"I do not talk with Mom or my friends everyday. I talk with them a couple of times a month and I make my own decisions so if you think you need to talk with me all the time I don't do that. I have my work and I'm getting married."

"So, what can I do to help you?"

"I invited you and everyone else here to celebrate with me and to have fun. That is what you can do, celebrate with me and have fun."

"I have to protect Mom and Rebecca and that is my role. I will not let anyone hurt Mom or Rebecca."

The phone interrupted him.

"When did you know that you were a female?"

"I knew from a very early age that I was different but I did not want to be this way and I fought these feeling for many years not believing it was true. I was very confused and finally reached a point where I did not want to live any longer." Mark gave me a very puzzling look like that is crazy.

"Why did you have three children then if you knew you were female?"

"I am very grateful for my three children and to why am I transgendered I cannot answer why, all I know is that is true."
The phone rang again and Mark said," I am in room 209, come on up."

John and Rebecca were there in 2 minutes and came into the room. All three of them were sitting on the bed next to each other. I picked up my phone and took a picture of my three children together and it was a wonderful feeling for me to see them together. After about a few minutes and another phone call I told Mark, "You should go back to your party everyone is looking for you". Rebecca chimed in and said "we should go back."

I thought that it was good for Mark to begin to get his feelings out and hoped that it was a little way toward healing. I encouraged him to say what he needed because I know that the only way to build back my connection with my son would be for him to tell the truth about his feelings. He was right with everything that he said and I told him. It was very healing for me because I wanted to face the wreckage of my past with him so that in hopes of a better future. I told him that it takes a man to have the hard conversation and discuss one's feelings regardless of the unpleasantness and in revealing the truth progress may be restored. I hope that Mark can forgive me and that he finds his peace. I have to surrender my will to my Higher Power.

I went to bed with the feeling that a great deal had been accomplished. I was very grateful that on this day I had finally seen my son and that my children where with me in one place at the same time. How powerful this was in my healing and the love, gratitude, and peace that came over me as I fell asleep. At 3:15 am, I was awaken by laugher and loud talking and as I tuned in I heard that it was Mark and all his buddies having a great time going back to their room. Mark had stayed with his friends at the lodge overnight and they were enjoying every moment.

John and I both woke up at 9am and I told him that we should get out of the room for a while and find something for breakfast. Instead of driving around somewhere, we went downstairs to the restaurant and had the breakfast buffet and John his normal French toast. We were on our final cup of coffee when standing outside the restaurant door was Mark and I heard him tell the waitress that they need a table for 11. They were all talking over one another and finally came in and sat two booths away from us. John went over and spoke to his brother and when he came back we paid the bill and left.

I asked John to ride with me and show me where the wedding was going to take place, since he had been there the night before, so we drove about 5 miles down NC- 184 and 105 to Camp Yonahnoka at the Eseeola Lodge. Through the tall old trees and the curved paved road we drove. There were folding chairs set up out from a large oak tree, a pond, golf course, and Grandfather Mountain in the background. I drove past the lodge and it was opened and I could see that the bar was set up. It was a beautiful sight as the sunlight was weakened by the clouds and the green of the surrounding mountains reigned in their glory. In five hours the wedding was to take place.

Once back in our room John had to prepare for the wedding as Best Man. He was to meet his Mother at 2:30 and ride with her over to the wedding site because a half hour later pictures were going to be taken so the wedding party had to leave early. Mark came into my room and I was lying on the bed with the television on watching the Olympics.

"I want to apologize for being such a dick last night."

"You do not need to apologize because you told the truth and that makes you a man." I appreciate the fact that you could get it off your chest."

He walked out onto the balcony where John was smoking and came back into the room about 3 minutes later with two of his groomsmen. "I want you to meet Phil and Zack; they are two of my friends from college. You remember Phil; he went to the football game with us."

"Yes, I remember Phil and Zack it is nice to meet you."
We exchanged some pleasantries and the three of them left proclaiming to get ready for the wedding three rooms over from mine. After about 45 minutes, Mark came out of the room while I was standing outside in his beige suit, white shirt, and orange tie. He was drinking a Coors Light and I took a picture of him and he looked so very handsome. He was laughing, joking, and cutting up with his buddies.

At 2:30pm, I watched the procession leave the Mountain Lodge. There was a procession of 10 cars and a truck. I looked over at the beauty of Beech Mountain and thought about the wedding. I knew that the people in attendance would be former neighbors, friends, and Kathleen's family. Some apprehension started to resonate with me but I have done this before at the Funeral in Richmond with my "family". I just knew to go with love and gratitude in my heart and just mind my own business. I took my time and very slowly started to prepare myself for the wedding. I wore wide legged beige pants, brown tank top and cardigan, and a matching vest with earth-tone colors embroidered into the fabric. It was time for me to drive to the wedding so that I would be there 20 minutes before it started. As I left the room, I had that nervous feeling from many years ago of going out as a female for the first time. It lasted only a couple of minutes and I knew who I was and living my true self. I think this came to mind because I was coming out to a group of people who had not seen Kaitlin ever and I knew someone would ask "who invited her." I proceeded with the knowledge that it was not about me nor should it be. I was going to the wedding to only celebrate with my son and that is all that mattered.

I slow drove through Linville, NC and stopped at the speed bumps and pedestrian crossing on my way to Camp Yonahnoka. The sun was now bright and the sky had the color of Carolina blue with a few cumulus clouds scattered throughout. It was a beautiful afternoon and I was glad that I wore a cardigan because it was a little cool. When I arrived there were about 60 people waiting for the wedding to start. My son John meet me in the parking lot and I asked him if "he was ready?" We walked into the open air lodge and I told John that "I am going to sit down at the table and stay in the background." After about 5 minutes of sitting and checking my email on my phone, Debbie, a former neighbor and friend walked up to me and sat down. We exchanged greetings and a hug as it had been at least 15 years since I had seen her. It was very pleasant and I did not expect this from her. I told her "that my name was Kaitlin" and she said "I know that" and asked me "are you happy?" "Yes," I told her that "I had gender reassignment surgery in December 2008" and it seemed that it did not bother her. Her husband John, who I had worked with at Philip Morris in Concord walked over and asked me "how are you doing" and told me that "you looked good." I exchanged the pleasantry with him as he looked good himself. Then the two of them went back to where their children were standing between the lodge on top of the knoll in the grass overlooking the big oak tree and folding chairs. Grandfather Mountain loomed in the background and was named this because it shapes gave it the appearance of an old man. It seems serene at this moment.

The crowd of about a hundred and twenty began to meander down the hill and I blended myself in with this group staying to the outside and found a place on the forth row to the right on the end. I sat alone and listened to the classical music and I noticed those who stuck their nose up in the air at me. It was fine because I was staying with my purpose and I know it was not my problem. The groomsmen and Mark took their place followed by the bridesmaids and I looked at my three children standing there and I could feel the joy in my heart. Suddenly the classical music changed to a Credence Clearwater Revival song and down the grassy aisle came the bride all dressed in a beautiful flowing white wedding gown.

When the magistrate asked "if anyone knew why these two should not marry to speak now or forever hold your peace". Mark turned around to his groomsmen and opened up his arms with his palms up and looked at them all with a smirk and a joyous smile. Those in attendance laughed and with no objections Mark said his vows. Then it was Jessica's turn and the magistrate asked her to repeat do you take Mark in sickness and health, Mark chimed in and said, "You better think about it" and the group laughed again. Jessica said her vows and the two were pronounced husband and wife.

The families of the bride and groom posed for pictures for the next forty five minutes and I pulled out my cell phone camera and took a couple of pictures of the bride and groom with John, Mark, Rebecca, and Kathleen. I stayed in the background and watched my children and as I thought there were no pictures of me with the couple or anyone else it gave me a feeling of rejection as if I was a bad person but I quickly changed my thoughts back to, it is my responsibility to fill myself up with joy and no one could do this for me but me and it was a little sad but I was in acceptance and I tried to remain grateful.

I stood at a round table for about an hour and had a glass of lemonade and talked with those who were catering the party. John and I would walk about the grounds and watch the men play a bean bag toss game. The children were on a swing set and slide away from the lodge and it was nice to feel such happiness. I watch the people during the reception and another former neighbor of mine came over and spoke with me. He was one of Mark's friends that lived down the street when they were young. His conversation prompted his mother to say hello and ask me how things were going and where I was living. I told her about Palm Springs and while doing so her husband who used to hang out with me came over and shook my hand. His daughter followed and wanted to come and visit with me in Palm Springs and I gave her my card and told her she was welcome.

The buffet dinner was served and by this time most had were already eating and I grabbed John and we made a plate of southern fried chicken, macaroni and cheese, and green bean. We found a spot at the table where Jessica's father was sitting and I asked him if it would be ok if I joined him. John and I sat down and I talked with her Dad about California and the University of South Carolina football games that we had attended. I asked if he was still going and he said he has to split his time at other universities where his two other daughters were in attendance. It was a nice conversation and when I finished, Mark spoke and payed tribute to his Yaya that had passed away two years earlier. The reception party with the exception of a few of us danced in a circle to a tribute of a Greek song. It was very nice.

I watch Mark and Jessica dance with each other and then with various people before cutting the cake. I stayed to myself but did talk with a girl who was from Santa Barbara and now living in North Carolina. Finally, Jessica was free and could go and congratulate her and she thanked me for coming. After three and a half hours at the reception, I walked up to Mark on the dance floor and congratulated him and told him I was going back to the lodge. He told me to wait a minute and he finished his dance and told me to follow him.

We walked outside alone and around the corner and he asked me "if I had a good time."

"Yes, it was very nice and I am so proud of you."

356

"How did you like my tribute to Yaya?"

"It was so very wonderful of you."

"So, why are you leaving?"

"It is getting dark and I should get out of your way so that you can party with your friend."

"You do not have to go, you are an invited guest."

"Thank you, but I should be getting along."

He gave me a hug and I told him, "I will see you at the Farewell Brunch."

We both walked up to the entrance of the lodge together and I found John and said "Love you to Mark" and drove back over the speed bumps in Linville over to Banner Elk and climbed the steps to my room.

I told John, "I kind of wish I had stayed a little longer, but for some reason it just seemed like the right thing to do. I did not want to push my luck." It had been a wonderful ceremony and reception and I was very grateful to have been a part of it.

"I am glad we came back because I am tired."

"Yea, I guess so; you have been gone all day."

I settled in for the night and went outside at 11:15pm because I could hear that most were coming back from the reception. John called his mother and she was continuing the party and took John out to a bar and pool hall. I could not sleep; waking up many times, until John finally came back in at 3am.

"I am glad you are here because I cannot sleep with you being out. I thought you were tired?"

"We went down the street and I played pool all night and I did not drink," John replied.

"Great, so how about going to bed" and that was the last of the day for me.

Sunday morning we were up at 8am and John went down to the restaurant and made us a cup of coffee. We packed our bags and placed them in the car. We had some time before going over to the brunch so we hung out in the room and watched a couple of the groomsmen wonder about the location of their car. "I cannot find my car, does anyone know where I had left it". I started to laugh because I remembered those days and now I was watching how I used to act. It was a good reminder to see from where I came. Phil, who was two doors down, knew that he had left his car back Camp Yonahnoka and he asked us for a ride. I told him that I would take him in a few minutes but needed to do a couple of things first. I dressed in my orange top the same color as the groomsmen tie and John walked down to Phil's room about 20 minutes later and he was ready to go. I drove Phil back over to the Camp and told me that he could not attend the brunch because he had to work on Monday and now lived in Baltimore which was a long distance. He talked about his work and remembering me at the South Carolina football game. He was a salesman for an office supply company and I told him I knew his National Sales Director who lived in Palm Springs. He said that he knew his name. It took about a little over ten minutes to get to the camp and I told him "to have a safe trip home". His response was "thank you, sir" and I just had to let it go. I waited to make sure his car started, waved, and drove off shaking my head and just laughing.

Once back in the room, John was dressed and ready to go and I went down to the lobby to turn in our keys. Kathleen was there talking with John and Debbie, former neighbors, as I strolled by to the counter and finished my business. I told John and Debbie "ya'll take care of yourselves" and they each said, "Good bye."

I drove through Banner Elk with my son John past Lees-McCray College and then on the other side of the mountain and came to the center of town which had twenty building on the main street and plenty of signs directing people to the ski slopes and special offer notices for rafting, climbing, and skiing. The hardwood trees were old, big and round at the base, and I noticed they were very hardy, in great shape for the next winter. The oak leaves were the size of my hand, green, shading the gravel road that we turned onto before parking on the side and down below it dropped straight off.

Jessica's grandfathers house was built on the side of the mountain, wood frame, rustic, and looked like a ski lodge. The steps leading up to the house was made of wood and they were new built with a banister. They were built around the big oak and beech trees that had claimed the land long before the owners. A small trolley car sitting on tracks sat at the foot of the steps and I was told by Jessica's cousin it was used to shuttle groceries up to the house. The main deck was up high on the second level and provided a panoramic view of the mountain. I could see a very large estate made of stone off in the distance on the other side of the mountain and a clearing for a couple of power lines that fed electricity to an unseen settlement down below. The remainder of the view was green and I could see the forest for the trees. I thought that this would be a great place to get snowed in with a fire in the large fireplace and write.

John walked into the first level of the house with me and there was a couple of sofas, a bar, and television and I said hello to the men watching the Olympics basketball game. So, I went upstairs to the kitchen and living room and said hello to the ladies and introduced myself to them. Then I sat at the kitchen table and had a cup of coffee. Greg, Jessica father, short black and grey hair, glasses, stocky, came up the steps with food for the brunch. I helped him distribute it around the table and Mark appeared at the top of the steps say, "What's up everybody". I gave him a hug and made myself a plate of food along with the others and went through the living room to the deck overlooking the mountain and sat at a nice picnic table with an umbrella standing in the middle. Jessica's grandmother and Amy, a pretty tall brunette who was Mark's associate at NC State during his MBA work, came and sat with me. Another couple that Mark had attended USC joined us moments later and then Mark came and sat down right next to me. Then another college buddy of his sat on the other side of him.

The discussion and focus was on Mark and he talked about his job, his impending trip to Costa Rica for his honeymoon, and much about Gamecock's football. He told us about his shenanigans with ESPN College Game Day when they were in Columbia and how they asked him to remove his flag behind Lee Corso. He laughed and laughed as they told stories on each other and just laughed. I told a story on him as well when we were at the Alabama- South Carolina football game. Mark and I were sitting in the student section in the end zone and just before the game started he said, "I am going down to get a Coke." So, I gave him $10 and asked him to "bring me one". He was back in a flash and handed me the drink. Then he took out his cell phone and unscrewed the antenna and poured a light brown liquid into his drink. "Here have some", he said to me and I smelled the Jack Daniels and poured me a little. It was funny; I had no idea until then that it was not a cell phone only a flask. As I told the story, Mark spoke up and was laughing and said, "Too bad it was not back in the day with those really big cell phones". He was conjecturing what it would have been like with a cell phone the length of his forearm and it was really funny, he describes it picturesque and I know I could see him doing that. It was very healing for me to be there, as all I ever really wanted was for my family to love and accept me. These past four years have taught me that I cannot will anyone to love me that it must come from within and this has been a beautiful lesson. It's kind of like you cannot be late until you show up.

I was so grateful to spend these three hours with my son. I know that I was not there for him when he was younger and I regret it. I feel as if the door is cracked opened for me to try and build a relationship with him, which is something that is important to me and I understand that it will take time but at least a movement in the proper direction is occurring. These past four years of being clean and sober has provided clarity in my life and I have to turn everything over on a daily basis. But it is those that have come before me in sobriety that have helped me to learn how to love myself, to be grateful for what I do have today, how to seek and find my innermost truth beyond being transgendered, and to live in acceptance as there is no mistakes in my Higher Power's world. I used to think that I was the center of the Universe but have learned that I am only a part of the whole. I think that Sister Teresa wraps it up best with, "I am only a drop of rain in the sea, but without it the sea would be less". Today, I have to do my part and keep my side of the street clean and if someone, something, or some place is bothering me then there is something wrong with me and no one else. I must look inside to find the cause for this restlessness, irritable, and discontent feeling. Find the cause through silent concentration has set me free to practice a positive mental attitude towards life with the understand that I was made this way for a reason and I believe it to be so that I may be of service and help other people. So, I am very grateful to spend this time with Mark.

When the Farewell Brunch was over, I said goodbye and thanked, Jessica's parents, grandparents, and Kathleen for having me. I wished Mark and Jessica a great love and told them I was coming back for a visit. John and I walked down the wooden deck steps to the gravel road and drove down the mountain through the main area of Beech Mountain and into Banner Elk. "I guess we need to go back to Charlotte the same way we came. We can stop once we get into Boone".

"Did you have a good time?"

"Yes, it started out rough but ended very nicely." I had to remember the last time all these people had seen me I was a male, drinking, and full of grandiosity. I do not blame them for being cautious, however, I am very grateful that they all could finally see me as a female, sober, and keeping my side of the road clean".

Unfortunately, I do think that my huge lessons in life have come from being transgendered and an alcoholic because I was masking my pain the wrong way. Once the internal acceptance of being transsexual was realized within me it helped ease the pain, but the rejection over this issue allowed me to create for myself a downward spiral that only recovery could have solved. My recover is contingent on the maintenance of my spiritual health and I have the opportunity to develop a relationship with my God, not the God I was told that I needed to believe in. My

Higher Power today is all loving and does not want me to live in fear and rejection. My High Power fills me up from within and I have to keep a conscious contract with Him through silent concentration and mediation on a daily basis. It's unbelievable what the quiet concentration can reveal which today I understand to place these thoughts into action and assess the result in order to understand if I am in God's will or self-will. It takes willingness and practice to accomplish a reliable intuition along with a clear mind and everyone can achieve it. It was not my plan to be transsexual or alcoholic and I wish it on no one, however, there is a solution to me being made this way. There is a solution of living a full and joyful life without the fear from those in society who choose not to be educated.

My final day in Charlotte was spent with Diane and reworking her resume, sitting on the front porch or back deck, talking about her ventures and plans. She fed the ducks that come over each day from the pond, played with the dogs and just relaxed and hung out. I had scheduled a dinner with my daughter, Rebecca, and a couple of conversation with her before settling in a place in Charlotte for dinner. I did not have much interaction with Rebecca during the wedding as she was very busy with her bridesmaid's activities, boyfriend, and his parents.

Rebecca and I met at 8pm and were immediately shown a table and we simply talked. We did not talk about my transition but had a conversation between a parent and a daughter. We talked about her job and her plans for the future. She asked me about this book and I told her I had to write the final chapter which is of this past week. "I thought I was finished writing all the chapters but this experience must go in the book." She thought that it was great and she wanted me to send her the chapters that I have finalized and I told her "that I would."

After dinner we sat outside on the metal bench in front of the restaurant and I showed her the picture of her and her two brothers. She showed me how to send the picture to her by text message because she really wanted a copy. I probably was the only picture of just the three of them together in such a very long time and I was happy she had it. It was very healing for me to have had this dinner and conversation as it was very pleasant. After almost 2 hours she needed to get home and get ready for bed because work came early the next morning and besides she was still tired from the weekend wedding. She is so beautiful and smart and has some of my facial features and everyone could tell she was mine. I can see my little baby girl being born 27 years ago and so special at Cabarrus Memorial Hospital. I was in gratitude and felt that I need to somehow find a way to be closer to my children, all three. I had placed so much emphasis on my mother, father and siblings love that in my self-centerness not shown my three the love. I want to show my children the love and hope that one day they may feel it. Am I being too hard on myself? No, it is my reality, but I can start the healing. I pray it does not take as long as it did to destroy it.

The next morning, John and I slept late into the morning and split a pot of coffee and loaded the car. We sat on the front porch with Diane and Alisha and talked about our trip back to Palm Springs. Diane and I agreed that it was wonderful to see each other again, as I could tell anything. We discussed that it would be nice that one day, I would return to the Charlotte area. I do have a lot love in North Carolina and it has taken this long journey to realize the depth of this love. I told her that after this book is published then more would be revealed. We gave each other and kiss and a hug and I went inside to say goodbye to the dogs, and Alisha. I felt a little sad as I back out the driveway.

John and I stopped in Harrisburg because I wanted to see the oak, birch, and Leyland cypress that I planted 17 years ago at the house we were living. The trees had grown very tall and John took a picture of the oaks and birch that were in a perfectly straight line down the side of the acre lot. They were beautiful and I told him that I was happy to see them and that they had survived and doing so well.

We stopped for lunch, rental return, shuttle bus, TSA, and on the plane to Phoenix. I was missing Mark and Rebecca already and wished that they could come with me. I missed Diane, my step-daughters, and the sisters. North Carolina, although humid, was very beautiful and my heart was full of gratitude that my life was aligning itself physically, mentally, and spiritually. At the airport in Palm Springs, I felt there was hope for a new beginning at my age of 56. My bondage of self was slowing going away.

When the breath of this body is gone and the heart makes it final tick, the only thing that remains is the spirit, a spirit which does not have a gender, and becomes reunited with the spirit of the Universe.

About the Author

Kaitlin Sine Riordan has an MBA from Pfeiffer University in North Carolina and a Bachelors of Art Degree in Economics from the University of Richmond in Virginia. She worked in Operations Management for 25 years with a large southern tobacco manufacturing company and was promoted through the years to Principal Supervisor of Continuous Improvement, a high profile job within the organization. She transitioned on the job from male to female. Kaitlin organized, named, and founded with others, the James River Transgender Society, a support group in Richmond, Virginia. Her lifetime struggle with Gender Identity, lead to alcohol and drug abuse which took her to Palm Springs, California for rehabilitation before having gender reassignment surgery. Kaitlin is the Father (now Mother) of three beautiful children and two step-children and was married twice. Zebedee a Black Labrador Retriever of 11 years has been by her side through the pain, the healing, and the recovery.

Kaitlin welcomes your comments. To send a message to her and to order her book, email Kaitlin at:

kaitlinsine@gmail.com

Her website is www.kaitlinriordan.com

CPSIA information can be obtained at www.ICGtesting.com
Printed in the USA
BVOW030425020513

319659BV00002B/5/P